THE 1900s LADY

ABOUT THE BOOK

High Society in the Edwardian Era, the greatest luxury period in history — and the last — that brief but glorious age of Edward VII, "Upstairs and Downstairs", Jenny Churchill — sumptuous living and entertaining on a grand scale. Kate Caffrey describes in fascinating detail the intricate arts of being an Edwardian — the Zenith of sophistication in the cult of the lady.

The fabulous marriages, the trans-Atlantic fortunes, Dukes and heiresses, the Gaiety Girls and coronets, Deauville, Monte Carlo and the Riviera, Saturday-to-Monday at country house parties, Fabergé, Worth, silks, satins, tails and white-lace balls, the fabulous hats, the Ascot of *My Fair Lady* — the Edwardian Age, a collector's world.

ABOUT THE AUTHOR

Kate Caffrey was born in England and educated at Exeter University. She first became interested in history when a friend began reminiscing on the fall of Singapore and prisoner-of-war camps in the Second World War. She wrote *Out In the Noonday Sun* about the fall of Singapore. Since then her brilliant historical works, the prizewinning *Mayflower* and *The British To South Africa*, have attracted international acclaim.

THE
1900s LADY

KATE CAFFREY

GORDON & CREMONESI

Designed by Heather Gordon-Cremonesi
Set in 'Monotype' Scotch Roman and printed in Great Britain
by W & J Mackay Limited, Chatham

ISBN 0-86033-014-1

Gordon Cremonesi Ltd
New River House
34 Seymour Road
London N8 0BE

Acknowledgments

I wish to thank the following for permission to use quotations:

from THE YOUNG VISITERS, by Daisy Ashford, to Margaret Steel and Clare Rose, and Messrs Chatto and Windus;

from THE GOLDEN AGE and DREAM DAYS, by Kenneth Grahame, to The Bodley Head;

from KIPPS, by H. G. Wells, to the Estate of H. G. Wells;

from PRESS CUTTINGS, by Bernard Shaw, to The Society of Authors on behalf of the Bernard Shaw Estate.

In the United States, the excerpt from THE YOUNG VISITERS, by Daisy Ashford, copyright 1919 by George H. Doran Company, is used by permission of Doubleday and Company, Incorporated.

I am also much indebted to the following people for information, advice, and appreciative encouragement: C. D. Black-Hawkins, Esq., C. J. Brereton, Esq., Dr Stephen Doree, Dr Michael Martin, Clive Fleay, Esq., W. Mackenzie, Esq., Mrs Ruth F. Butterfield, and, as always, my agents, Elaine Greene and Isla Yardley.

Kate Caffrey
London 1974–1975

Contents

1   Galanty Show   9

2   The Golden Age   32

3   To Market, To Market   56

4   Much Noise on the Stairs   78

5   The Colonel's Lady   103

6   The Wider Stage   130

7   Overture: Beginners   147

   Appendix   167

   Bibliography   169

   Index   171

Until August 1914 a sensible, law-abiding Englishman could pass through life and hardly notice the existence of the state, beyond the post office and the policeman. He could live where he liked and as he liked. He had no official number or identity card. He could travel abroad or leave his country for ever without a passport or any sort of official permission. He could exchange his money for any other currency without restriction or limit. He could buy goods from any country in the world on the same terms as he bought goods at home. For that matter, a foreigner could spend his life in this country without permit and without informing the police.

—A. J. P. Taylor

An Edwardian hostess was expected to provide attractive premises, delicious food and drink, perfect service, and a handsome, well-dressed, agreeable company. . . . [Nowadays] a hostess could give a party in a damp cellar all over beetles and attended by insolent half-wits, and if only the supply of alcohol and tobacco were unlimited, no one would complain.

—Stella Gibbons

CHAPTER ONE

Galanty Show

On history's clock it was sunset, and the sun of the old world was setting in a dying blaze of splendour never to be seen again.
—Barbara W. Tuchman

There she stands in familiar silhouette—upright, rigidly corseted, swathed in rustling silks, the intricately draped skirt and full sleeves balanced by the wide hat on puffed-out hair, gloved hand holding a parasol, face delicately enamelled with cosmetics. In hundreds of photographs and paintings she stares coolly out at us, her thoughts concealed behind that splendidly maintained façade.

Technically the reign of Edward VII opened on 22 January 1901 and closed on 6 May 1910: nine years and fifteen weeks. Normally, however, the term "the Edwardian period" is taken to mean the interval between the death of Queen Victoria and the outbreak of the First World War. Most people looking back appear to see it as a kind of halcyon time separating events each of which ended an era. Few English people in 1901 could remember an England of which Victoria was not queen: and all historians emphasize the irreparable break that the Great War, so called until its second instalment started in 1939, cut in the life of the nation.

What, then, was the Edwardian lady?

She appeared first in black. Few customs have changed more violently in less than a lifetime than has the wearing of mourning. Precisely prescribed, carefully graded degrees of mourning clothes proliferated as the nineteenth century moved, with the life of the little old Queen, towards its close: second wives were expected to signify by their black garb the passing of first wives' parents. How much more, therefore, would the Edwardian lady, hardly yet aware that she was now Edwardian, put on black for the mother of the Empire! She even saw to it that her small daughters' underclothes were threaded with black ribbons.

With somewhat difficult timing, Queen Victoria died on the eve of the annual January White Sales. In the great new department stores of London and the provincial cities hundreds of assistants toiled all night to sweep away every trace of white and colours and veil their halls and display windows in black and purple. Every lady possessed black clothes as a matter of course: maids knew that they must pack at least one black ensemble in the luggage taken on a visit, in case of a sudden bereavement. Not for the Edwardian lady the hurried scramble to the dyer that many poorer women had to make.

But the whole apparatus of official grief extended far beyond the clothes, elaborate though these were in an age when mothers went into black for six weeks for the parents-in-law of their married children. There were innumerable details in addition: black-edged writing paper and envelopes, black wax with which to seal them, black-edged hand-kerchiefs bought by the dozen, cambric for ordinary occasions, finer cambric for the special events. There were the massive funerals: black horses, black plumes, black streamers round black top-hats, mourning-cards, monuments for the tomb. Harrod's 1900 catalogue quoted children's funerals from two pounds ten shillings according to the child's age and the required "appointments". Special shops flourished, as well they might, where one could deal with virtually all these matters under the same roof. Jay's General Mourning Warehouse, Pugh's, and Peter Robinson's nicely named Court and General Mourn-ing House—known to its patrons as Black Peter Robinson's—all pros-pered finely in Regent Street, as did the Argyll General Mourning and Mantle Warehouse, which gave out free copies of a book called *Mourn-ing Etiquette*. It is impossible to visualize the Edwardian lady without some black trappings about her at frequent intervals. When she was widowed, it usually meant, or was expected to mean, black for life. The death-rate, too, was almost three times as great as it is now.

It is equally impossible to visualize the Edwardian lady without horses somewhere in the picture. A person of today magically trans-ported back into England before 1914 would immediately exclaim in astonishment at three things: dark-hued clothes; not a head without a hat; and horses, horses everywhere. The motor car was a new toy: 23,000 of them were registered in 1903, when the speed limit of twenty miles an hour was made law, and in 1907 a prudent purchaser, living in the country, brought along twelve spare tyres with his big new open tourer, which had one burst, four punctures and a flat in a trip of 140 miles. Yet the car caught on fast. In 1901, 15,000 cars were bought at an average price of £390 each, and in 1913 the figure was 338,000, average price £340. Still, the horse remained supreme, and the pace of a horse the only pace for a man in a hurry over most English roads.

In the opening years of this century a "lady" could be identified as such on sight. The word was scrupulously used. Today it is bandied about so freely that it has lost any meaning other than a basic indication of the feminine gender: the charlady, the tea lady, the lady in a shop, the lady doctor and the lady teacher, for example, are all phrases in current use, to the point where any female with genuinely lady-like pretensions is likely to insist that she is a woman. Over-gentility, followed by a growing imprecision in the term, has almost robbed it of all significance.

But before 1914 the word "lady" meant exactly that: not simply the wife of a peer, but a woman in easy circumstances, assured, socially so well placed that everywhere she would be accorded respectful consideration: one who could not possibly accept paid employment, nor would need to: one whose father, brothers, and husband were landowners, perhaps Members of Parliament, or safe in the upper echelons of the Law, the Army, or the Church. Not necessarily did she have a title—some of the greatest ladies were wives or daughters of Mr Something who regarded the Norman Conquest as a parvenu expedition best ignored.

That was a lady then: to some, the embodiment of the graces of civilized living, of social status and charming influence; to others, a parasite battening on the wild inequalities of the system, a beautifully caparisoned toy, a symbol of what was wrong with decadent old Europe; to others again, a stultifying agent determined to keep at bay the forces of progress and of female emancipation. It was a word that could hardly ever be used of an unmarried woman, certainly not of an unmarried *young* woman.

Of course, there were many females then who enjoyed all the social success of the "real lady" and often had, or seemed to have, more money: daughters of wealthy merchants or industrialists who had married into old-established families, fashionable beauties who had contrived to make the leap from the stage to the peerage, spectacular mistresses who set new fashions. But to the great established political and social hostesses these never quite gained acceptance, though some of them won uneasy toleration.

Women in this admired exalted position in the complicated social scale were all the more easy to identify because there were comparatively so few of them. In 1901 there were seven million households in England and Wales. Four hundred thousand people declared their income for tax purposes at over four hundred pounds a year. Income tax started at one hundred and sixty pounds a year and was paid by fewer than a million people. There were four million women in employment, nearly half of them in domestic service: the rest had jobs in factories, post offices, business offices where they were quaintly called "type-writers", shops, or the Board Schools. Drab and under-privileged as these positions seem to modern eyes, they still carried a greater degree of independence than domestic service did, and by the end of the nineteenth century ladies were being warned in highly respectable magazine articles that servants would not consent indefinitely to spending their days in cellars and their nights in attics. That redoubtable social critic Mrs C. S. Peel stated flatly in 1902 that mistresses of households did not always know enough or bother enough to train their daughters in the proper supervision of a house.

Certainly there was plenty to do. Coal fires, oil lamps, stone-floored kitchens, long flights of stairs, polishable surfaces and a thick clutter of furniture and ornaments took hours to manage, and Edwardian meals were heavy and as elaborate as possible. Afternoon calls were frequent and formal, dinner parties hardly less so. Even houses of minimal social pretensions had maids, referred to with wry accuracy as slaveys, employed, as often as not, from the age of twelve as half-timers working not more than twenty-seven and a half hours a week for a weekly wage of half a crown or perhaps three shillings. (There is a slavey helping to serve the post-funeral meal in H. G. Wells's *The History of Mr Polly*.) Complaints about finding and keeping good servants were constant—witness the same author's genteel Folkestone afternoon parties in *Kipps*. It was easier to get girls than men, who were less readily ordered about, had heartier appetites, and cost their employers fifteen shillings for a licence. But there were still twelve menservants to every hundred house-occupiers in Westminster in 1901, eighty maids to every hundred in Hampstead; fewer than half employers of servants had only one, while one-tenth had more than three.

Europe, in this period, dominated the habitable globe. Four-fifths of the world's surface rested under the control of three European powers, Britain, France, and Russia, half the world's trade and industry belonged to Britain, France, and Germany, all articulate peoples modelled themselves on Europe. It was easy to settle or travel all over the Continent: no legal documents of any kind, including a passport, were needed until one reached the frontiers of Russia or the Ottoman Empire, and the standard currency everywhere was, literally, as good as gold.

The march of progress revealed itself by the railways, the civic buildings, the theatres and opera houses. The first Promenade Concert in London took place in 1895, the first film of Derby Day a year later (the winner was Persimmon). In 1897 the Royal Automobile Club was founded, in 1898 the Folk Song Society, in 1900 the famous "Two-penny Tube", the Central London Railway. In 1903 came Letchworth, the first Garden City Limited. The long peace for England in Europe (for, unless one counts the Crimean War, an English army had not fought on European soil since Waterloo) had produced a social system that looked utterly settled, making gradual, gentle progress within its framework towards apparently greater liberality (the Elementary Education Act of 1902, the year in which the Order of Merit was insti-tuted, was considered an important advance towards enlightenment, as in 1904 was the creation of the Workers' Educational Association). There had been many rumours of wars, the great Powers in their diplo-matic quadrille had drifted towards the brink but had retreated in time, and no European war had broken out since 1871.

But the century started in war for all that. Five hundred thousand British soldiers were, unaccountably, unable to bring twenty thousand South African Dutch to a standstill. Despite this, a full-scale European war was believed unlikely, especially by the multitudes who read Nor-man Angell's best-seller *The Grand Illusion*, first published in 1909. In this he demonstrated convincingly that modern war bore as hard on the victor as on the vanquished and thus proved war impossible, or so it seemed.

Only a few hard-headed characters truly saw it coming: Bismarck, who said that some damned foolish thing in the Balkans would set off another conflict and who predicted the Kaiser's fall twenty years in advance; the fiery First Sea Lord, Admiral Sir John Fisher, who picked Jellicoe to be Nelson when Armageddon came; and the massive Lord Kitchener of Khartoum, who foretold a war involving millions and lasting three years to begin with. The Kaiser himself did not, ap-parently, see war coming. When he came to the throne it was like turning a deprived child loose in an enormous toy-shop: all he ever really wanted to do, and he achieved this, was to make Europe hop. For all its hindsight atmosphere of tranquil sunset glory, the Edwardian period was jumpy with rumours of disaster, crackling with new ideas and developments under its enamelled surface.

And a very splendid surface it was. Great new buildings of opulent grandeur rose everywhere: in London alone there were Westminster Cathedral (1895), the National Portrait Gallery (1896), the Tate Gallery (1897), the Victoria and Albert Museum (1899), and the Wallace Collection (1900) ushered in the new reign, during which arose the Old Bailey, the Ritz, Middlesex Guildhall, the Piccadilly Hotel, Hampstead Garden Suburb, and Selfridge's. The first year of George V's reign saw the completion of three notable London landmarks—Admiralty Arch, County Hall, and the Victoria Memorial. The characteristic buildings of the period were massive yet frivolous, solid in stone or brick with stone trimmings, with a kind of contained exuberance in stone swags and carvings, domes and pillars, rows of round windows like portholes, mansard roofs trimmed with decorative ironwork. Two perfect survivals, dating from the same year, 1907, are the Royal Naval College at Dartmouth in Devon and the University College School in Hampstead. The ideal incidental music for photographs, especially of the capital, in the Edwardian period, is of course, the overture *Cockaigne*, composed by Edward Elgar in 1901.

New movements began to show, some disturbing (militant suffragism), some prestigious (the launching of the *Lusitania* and the *Mauretania* in 1906), some simply appealing (the Scout and Guide movements). But what today is called technological change was showing too, though it was still hardly recognized for what it was.

The film and the popular press, twin phenomena of all the winds of change of our turbulent century, actually appeared to the public eye in the closing years of Queen Victoria's reign. In 1896 the first public film performance took place, at the Regent Street Polytechnic; in that same year the Photographer Royal filmed a tree-planting at Windsor by the Tsar and Tsarina of Russia. Also in 1896 Alfred Harmsworth brought out his new daily paper, the *Daily Mail*, price one halfpenny. He referred to it as the busy man's paper, but it included a woman's page, devoted to fashion and domestic topics, and a social column of more or less gossipy comment about the doings of the socially prominent. Four years later, Arthur Pearson started a rival paper, the *Daily Express*.

These two newspapers did much to shatter the image of the papers that existed up to that time. The large sheets of close print unbroken by headlines or pictures, unfolded in leisurely masculine seclusion, usually ironed by a servant before being placed on a lectern in the library of a private house or club, compelled belief. Parliamentary debates were printed in full, more often than not; comment was serious; "it must be true, it was all in the paper" was no joke. Even provincial papers of modest circulation took their task solemnly: the small town of Skibbereen, near Cork, had a paper, the *Skibbereen Eagle*, which opened its editorials superbly with such resounding sentences as: "We have our eye on the Emperor of Russia". But the new style of journalism began inexorably to change all that. In 1903 Harmsworth actually planned a newspaper specifically for women, produced by a staff the majority of whom were women: called the *Daily Mirror*, it was a failure, and an expensive failure, too, losing more than a hundred thousand pounds for its proprietor before he changed it into a tabloid in which no story was more than 250 words long and photographs of engaged girls from high society ornamented its pages. It now did much better, and entered the arena of pin-ups and cheese-cake in 1905 when it followed an Australian swimmer named Miss Kellerman round the English south coast resorts. She was, however, photographed either fully dressed or with only her head showing above the water.

Perhaps this was as well. Swimming costumes were unbecoming, to say the least, incorporating long stockings and a kind of knee-length bloomers under a skirted top garment with sleeves. Weighed down by all this wet bulk it is not surprising that serious female swimmers were few. Mostly, like Ouida's Lady Dolly in *Moths*, they were content to venture into the water to about waist depth, where they bobbed and screamed and splashed coquettishly before retreating to change in the modest shelter of the bathing-machine — a kind of wheeled hut that could be moved to the water's edge, or even beyond it, allowing the lady to enter the water without showing a scandalous glimpse of legs. Sunbathing was unknown: the Edwardian lady on the beach protected herself against the dangerous rays with a shady hat and a parasol, for suntanned skin was a blemish of which to be ashamed, and sea-bathing itself a rather disagreeable health measure for women and children.

Indeed the faces of ladies of fashion were unnaturally pale. It was a great period for cosmetics, as most periods have been, though Mr Terence McLaughlin makes the very interesting point that there have been throughout recorded history two basic styles of make-up. One is the doll face and the other is the chipmunk face. The difference lies in eye emphasis. The doll face, like that of the Japanese geisha, employs little or no eye make-up: the chipmunk face, like that of the Disney animals, emphasizes the eyes. It goes with periods of greater equality between women and men, while the doll face appears in periods of female subjection. The Edwardian lady was emphatically a doll face.

The nineteenth-century rise in industrial productivity led to the manufacture of what might be called chemical cosmetics, in contrast with the herbal ones of the seventeenth and eighteenth centuries. The chemicals were, on the whole, far more harmful, based recklessly on substances only imperfectly understood by the makers. They evolved a white skin paint made of white lead in a cream base, which often ate into the skin so that thicker and thicker layers of the paint had to be applied to conceal the increasingly pitted surface. Yet these paints had charming names like Blanc d'Argent and Blanc de Perles. There was a Crême Admiratrice, recipe unspecified. Some skin lotions were made with terrifying ingredients such as arsenic or prussic acid. One hair-removing cream had slaked lime in it. One skin beautifier was given the rather repellent name of Oil of Ants. Rice powder, dusted over the white paint or fluffed straight on to the skin, swelled in the pores (where it could get at them) and caused them to enlarge.

The white paint, referred to as enamel, was the recognized make-up base, used by Queen Alexandra and, especially in the early years of the period, by every lady of fashion, some more lavishly than others: Mr Cecil Beaton has described his Aunt Jessie as covering not only her face but her neck, arms, and back with enamel, which the family called "whitewash". Then the pearl powder or rice powder was patted on with big swansdown puffs, and rouge blended with greater or lesser skill on the cheeks. Some ladies, mistrusting rouge and wishing to display tinted complexions all the time, had their lips and cheeks tattooed with delicate natural-looking colouring by such famous practitioners as George Burchett, who used harmless vegetable extracts. Aunt Jessie had mauve eyelids, and one beauty book published in the eighteen-nineties gives the old Roman recipe of holding a needle in a candle-flame and using the resultant black as an eye-liner, but in general the ladies left their eyes alone, except for the terribly dangerous practice of brightening their sparkle with drops of belladonna.

Yet some cosmetics were not harmful. The firm of Pond's made Vaseline so popular that most people never realized it was a brand name. Pearl powder was made from bismuth oxychloride. When Miss Helena Rubinstein emigrated from Poland to Australia she took along a dozen pots of her mother's beauty cream, made of herbs and almond essence by Dr Jacob Lykusky. Her own soft clear skin was so much admired by the wind-roughened Australians that she set up in her own business on a borrowed £250, brought Dr Lykusky out to assist her, and by 1908 included in her clientele the great singer Nellie Melba.

She introduced tinted cosmetics, which were far less harmful: simultaneously in London Mr Willie Clarkson was doing the same with his Lillie Powder, tinted with very small quantities of carmine and sienna which he added to talc worked into melted lanolin. The proportions of talc to lanolin determined the degree of "cling" and the finished product was scented with violets. Sarah Rachel Leverson, operating her daringly named beauty salon in Bond Street under the name of Madame Rachel, gave that name to the "rachel" shade of face powder, still in use today. She also sold a scent called Jordan Water at ten guineas a flask. Ladies sprinkled on their handkerchiefs a few drops of Atkinson's lavender or other makers' heliotrope, orris root or roses, but the emotive perfume of the time was violet. One must not forget, however, that a faint smell of sweat, referred to elegantly as "bouquet de corsage", was claimed to be attractive to gentlemen. If true, this was as well since there was a lot of it.

Before making up, the ladies washed with Windsor soap made by the Yardley Company of Thorney Street in Bloomsbury (who moved to

Bond Street in 1910). Other renowned cosmetic names were beginning to show in an unobtrusive way. In South Molton Street Mrs Frances Hemming's salon, supplying creams, lotions and three shades of rouge, received her clients in quiet upstairs rooms guarded by a coloured maid stationed at the curve of the stairs; the ladies came in, heavily veiled, through the back door, approaching along the cobbled mews as though they were going to a scandalous assignation. Mrs Hemming prospered finely and her salon became the distinguished House of Cyclax, helped, no doubt, by Mrs Hemming's skilful yet delicate advertisements for Veloutine Powder, Bâton au Raisin Lip-rouge, and Fard Indien eyebrow colouring.

Most shops concealed cosmetics as if they were objects of sin until Gordon Selfridge opened his dazzling new store in Oxford Street in 1909. There he placed tinted face powders, lip salve and rouge on open display and encouraged customers to select and experiment, though already some young girls were marching boldly up to the counters and asking clearly for powder, rouge, and eyebrow pencils. It did not take long for other great stores to follow Selfridge's lead.

An increasing vogue continued for do-it-yourself make-up: in 1910 the *Daily Mirror Beauty Book* gave recipes for home-made lipstick and eyebrow-darkener, instructed the reader how to curl her eyelashes, and, casting ahead to a practice made popular many years later, suggested elongating the eyes with a pencilled line. One short-lived freakish trend of the late eighteen-nineties died out in the opening Edwardian period: breast piercing, whereby, on a similar principle to that of ear-piercing, the nipples were fixed with tiny gold or jewelled rings. It was said to improve the bust line, making it curvier, and to produce a pleasant sensation as the rings moved against the clothes fabrics, but its disadvantages clearly outweighed these benefits.

Mr Clarkson's Lillie Powder was, of course, named after Lillie Langtry, who from her early teens had aimed, deliberately or not, at becoming a professional beauty — what today would be called a pin-up. When she was only fourteen, local villagers spread rumours that she owed her lovely complexion to rolling in the dew and putting raw minced meat on her face, and it is true that the Pears Soap Company paid her one hundred and fifth pounds for advertising their products in later years. Born Emilie Le Breton, daughter of the Dean of Jersey, she was married from the schoolroom to the widower Edward Langtry. His main interest was yachting: Lillie seems never to have found him very interesting. She was twenty-four when she made her first entry into London society, a pale, shy, violet-eyed young lady, taken into dinner in May 1877 by Lord Randolph Churchill, who wrote in a letter to his wife:

I dined with Lord Wharncliffe last night and took in to dinner a Mrs Langtry, a most beautiful creature quite unknown, very poor, and they say has but one black dress.

The one black dress appeared so often that a Mrs Dudley, inviting Mrs Langtry to a ball, asked her if she could not possibly wear something different. The result was a confection of white velvet which caused such a sensation that the guests stood on chairs to get a better look, and thenceforward her reputation was assured. She was mobbed in the streets, her portrait hung in the Royal Academy, her postcard photographs sold in thousands. Prince Leopold hung a pencil drawing of her above his bed, and his scandalized mother, Queen Victoria, stood on a chair herself to lift it down. By 1882 the Jersey Lily was known everywhere as an aspiring actress and the mistress of the Prince of Wales. No less a person than Bernard Shaw felt it was a bit unfair that one woman should be intelligent, daring and independent as well as beautiful.

Crown Prince Rudolph, Randolph Churchill, Oscar Wilde, James McNeil Whistler, even Gladstone, gasped and commented on her loveliness and charm; when she went to America, millionaires showered jewels and compliments upon her. She had her own yacht, her own racehorse, Merman, which won the Cesarewitch, and a lavish life-style divided between the stage and her house at Ascot, called Regal Lodge.

In her stage dressing-room stood a dressing-table of white enamel ornamented with cupids and butterflies and draped with old rose satin over muslin, its looking-glass lit to her special design that produced pink, blue, and amber colour effects, and its top crammed with brushes, combs, scent bottles and powder boxes of solid gold engraved with her initials. At Regal Lodge her own dressing-table was bare of visible cosmetics, but there stood close by a second, bearing the Prince's brushes and combs. The bed cover was purple and gold with a gold royal crest, and the shower was silver-plated. By 1900 she was described as handsome rather than beautiful, and one New York observer said that the whitewash with which she was covered did not hide the roughnesses, hollows and wrinkles of her skin, but she was forty-seven then and had certainly made her effect. Ellen Terry commented on her performance as Rosalind that the part required an actress rather than a pretty elocutionist, but it is only fair to say that had she stood speechless and motionless on the stage the theatre would still have been packed. The unfortunate Edward Langtry sought consolation in the mists of alchohol to an ever increasing extent, ending up bankrupt and dwindling away in the Chester County Asylum.

The possibilities are always interesting for a girl who has been brought up to think herself plain and then finds that this is not so. Still more interesting is it if she has been sternly repressed as an adolescent and told that showing one's feelings openly is "servants' behaviour". Elinor Glyn was barely out of the schoolroom before she made the exciting discovery that gentlemen flocked to her. Proposals followed, from all sorts of wealthy men including a duke; she accepted Clayton Glun, a landowner in Essex, who started off romantically on their honeymoon in Brighton by hiring the public baths so that she could swim alone, very slowly, wearing nothing but her long auburn hair. After that gesture he seems to have reverted to his somewhat stuffy norm, but plenty of appreciative admirers crowded round to dance with her, read to her, pay her lavish compliments, and attempt to flirt. She preferred to pour her romantic feelings into her books and to cherish her appearance. This later she did with something called "the secret treatment of El Zair", as well as scrubbing her face with a dry nail-brush. She also considered it "pure common sense" to sleep with her feet pointing towards the Magnetic North.

Elegant ladies sometimes sacrificed looks to comfort and the pursuit of beauty at night: Sonia Keppel, when travelling with her mother, remembered hating the sight of Alice Keppel deliberately blotting out her own beauty by piling her hair under a mob cap, putting on a shape-less nightgown, greasing her face, and tying a black silk band across her eyes.

In an age when the powder compact was unknown, ladies with a dislike of shiny noses had recourse to something called Papier Poudré. Astoundingly, it is still possible to find, though not without difficulty. Papier Poudré is exactly that, powdered paper. It comes in small books, two inches by three, and to use it one tears out a leaf and wipes the face with it. It is most effective. Surface grease is absorbed and a smooth light matt appearance restored. The paper is very thin, pale rachel in colour, and has a flowery scent redolent of its prime time.

The Marcel process of hair-waving was established by 1890 and by 1910 had swept the world. Briefly, it produced delicate waves and curls all over the head by using curling-tongs. A rival method was introduced in 1905 by Charles Nessler who dampened the hair with chemical lotions and then put it up in heated curlers, a process modified by Ernest Suter and E. Fredericks whose hot-waving (forerunner of the early permanent wave) persisted for years. The most admired colour of hair was a pale nut brown: blonde hair was considered "unfortunate". This light brown went with coral rather than carmine lips, a peaches-and-cream complexion, and the sweet pea shades of dress — rose, pink, mauve — that absolutely belong to the opening years of the twentieth century.

Night after night in the warm summers the great houses of Mayfair were filled with these lovely creatures in lace, tulle, satin, sparkling with jewels and decked with flowers. Outside the great squares smelt of lime leaves, warm earth and horse manure: the usual sound was horses' hooves and the rumble of carriage-wheels, coming through orange and green sunsets and departing in the pearly dawns when the air was fresh with the street-sweepers' hoses.

Somehow the one cosmetic irrevocably linked with the Edwardian lady was rouge. Possibly this impression is intensified by the influence of Daisy Ashford, who wrote *The Young Visiters* when she was only nine. Her heroine, Ethel Monticue, never stirs a step without her rouge; setting out at the beginning of the story she announces uncompromisingly to Mr Salteena:

> I shall put some red ruge on my face said Ethel because I am very pale owing to the drains in this house.

On her way to London it appears again:

> Ethel had on her blue velvit get up and a sweet new hat and plenty of ruge on her face and looked quite a seemly counterpart for Bernard who was arrayed in a white and shiny mackintosh top boots and a well brushed top hat tied on to him with a bit of black elastick.

And, of course, in London it cannot be neglected:

> Ethel skipped into her bedroom and arrayd herself in a grass green muslin of decent cut a lace scarf long faun colored kid gloves and a muslin hat to correspond. She carried a parasole in one hand also a green silk bag containing a few stray hair pins a clean handkerchief five shillings and a pot of ruge in case.

Least of all can it be omitted for the proposal scene:

> She looked very beautifull with some red roses in her hat and the dainty red ruge in her cheeks looked quite the thing.

Little Miss Ashford included in her masterpiece an appealing portrait of Edward VII while still Prince of Wales. He appears at a levee in "a lovely ermine cloak and a small but costly crown" and slips away for a quiet drink:

> Presently his Highness rose I think I will have a quiet glass of champaigne he said you come too Clincham and bring your friend the Diplomats are arriving and I am not much in the mood for deep talk I have already signed a dozen documents so I have done my duty.
>
> They all went out by a private door and found themselves in a smaller but gorgeous room. The Prince tapped on the table and

instantly two menials in red tunics appeared. Bring three glasses of champaigne commanded the prince and some ices he added majestikally. The goods appeared as if by majic and the prince drew out a cigar case and passed it round.

One grows weary of Court Life he remarked.

Ah yes agreed the earl.

It upsets me said the prince lapping up his strawberry ice all I want is peace and quiut and a little fun and here I am tied down to this life he said taking off his crown being royal has many painful drawbacks.

Being royal certainly had many painful drawbacks for the man who gave his name to the period. Albert Edward's childhood, mapped out for him meticulously by his humourless father who wished his training to produce the perfect man, filled with critical comment from his mother who could not understand why her son was so woundingly different from her husband and did not realize that she would have detested any son who resembled Albert too closely, is so well known that there is no need to dwell on it. He was nearly sixty before he was treated as an adult by his courtiers or allowed to see a state paper. Naturally he revolted into the only interests open to him: those untouched by his mother. He adored clothes, good company, pretty women, gambling, eating, travel and sport. To her this was all insufferably raffish, yet as a wife she had thoroughly enjoyed dancing and parties, riding and reviewing troops, laughter and pretty dresses. Even the effort of the Diamond Jubilee procession had given her genuine pleasure. But her lively youth was lost to her memory during the long years — almost half her life — of the widowhood that today would be described as neurotically exaggerated, and she had forgotten that her first request as queen was to be alone: alone to relish her position, to feel unsupervised, uncriticized, free to breathe. As the years of widowhood stretched out, filling the rest of the century, her life crystallized into a framework ever more narrow and rigid. Inevitably her elder son chafed under restraint, inevitably he eased the conventions that bound him wherever he could.

Perhaps the key to his character lay in the fact that he preferred France to Germany. As a child accompanying his parents on a visit, he had said to Napoleon III: "You have a nice country, I should like to be your son." This remark is most revealing. Napoleon III, accurately summed up by Mr Edmond Taylor as the nearest thing Europe ever produced to a Mississippi river-boat gambler, presiding over what Mr Philip Guedalla called the gaslit tragedy of the Second Empire, was the antithesis of Queen Victoria's German relations: relaxed, soft-spoken, wreathed in cigar smoke, sleepy-eyed, living in the most beautiful of capitals made glorious by Haussmann's new-cut boulevards. Paris, even after the Second Empire had crumbled in ruin and disgrace, retained a champagne atmosphere.

It was full of good company, too, and rapidly growing into the Englishman's legendary vision of the place where one could get away with behaviour that would raise censorious eyebrows at home. By the end of the century this vision seemed reality: the farcical comedies of Feydeau, the music of Offenbach, the burgeoning painters of the Post-Impressionist School, combined with the matchless French cuisine so satisfying to a compulsive eater like Edward VII — no wonder he was drawn to France as he could never be drawn towards the comparatively stuffy, earnest, banal and increasingly Prussianized country next door ruled by his unpredictably volatile army-mad nephew, Wilhelm II, Emperor of Germany.

How much Queen Alexandra's loathing of Germany intensified her husband's feelings is hard to decide. It is likely that her opinion did nothing to make him more favourably disposed towards that country. Her hatred of it sprang most obviously from the Prussian seizure of the Danish provinces of Schleswig and Holstein in the sixties, but she never changed her mind, so that it was natural to her when her son, the future George V, was made honorary colonel of a Prussian regiment in 1890 to write him a letter in which her emotions characteristically exploded:

> And so my Georgie boy has become a real live filthy blue-coated Pickelhaube German soldier!!! Well, I never thought to have lived to see that! But never mind, it was your misfortune and not your fault.

Alexandra of Denmark had married Albert Edward, Prince of Wales, in March 1863. Their lives developed a pattern that looked regular because of their movements through each year from one place to another. By the end of April they were at Marlborough House in The Mall ready for the London Season. In late July the Prince attended the Cowes Regatta, going on from that to a spa in Europe, most often Marienbad or Karlsbad (today Marianske Lazne and Karlovy Vary in western Czechoslovakia), there to repair, or attempt to repair, the ravages of eleven months' overeating. Sometimes he spent part of that time at Biarritz. Then they went to Scotland for the grouse shooting and deer stalking, staying at Abergeldie near Balmoral. By the Prince's birthday, 9 November, they were at Sandringham, where they stayed until the middle of March, when the Prince went to France for six weeks, usually to Biarritz or the Riviera with a few days in Paris at either end.

His two English houses had been his own choice: Marlborough House was done up to his own specifications before his wedding, and he had bought Sandringham because it was the only big country house available at the time. Its owner, the Honourable C. S. Cowper, had been forced by the conventions of the age to retire to the Continent after marrying his mistress, Lady Harriet d'Orsay, and the Prince bought Sandringham for £220,000, spending a further £80,000 on improvements and alterations. It became, and remained, his favourite house, and, curiously enough, it was also the favourite of his second son and grandson, George V and George VI, both personalities entirely unlike him in other ways.

The aristocracy of England in 1901, like its king, saw itself as European. It was not only that many great families included Europeans among their members, not only that Edward VII was described as the uncle of Europe, closely related as he was to almost every royal family on the Continent, and there were many royal families then. But travel abroad was so easy, so simple, for anyone with the price of the fare and the modest hotel bills in his (or her) pocket. Even as early as the eighteen-seventies, Anthony Trollope's Palliser novels show Madame Max Goesler going off almost casually to Warsaw, Prague, and Vienna in a liberated spirit impossible for many English people even yet, and in some ways more freely than it has been possible for anybody since 1914, for she required no passport, no visas, no entry-permits, no hours of badgering (or being badgered by) clerks in offices, no enquiry as to her political or ideological affiliations. All she had to do was buy a ticket and catch a train.

Yet for all their European links and likings, English society before the First World War was firmly rooted in England, and above all in the English countryside. The great houses, built or rebuilt in the finest styles of English architecture, set in parkland well stocked with oak and elm and bounded by walls five or ten miles round, certainly seemed to supply all the essentials of the good life. The scents and sounds of beautifully tended gardens came in at the windows, people rode before breakfast over velvety grass, returning to vast punctual meals perfectly served.

Above all it was agreeable to be the son of such a house, coming home from school or university to find all his old friends waiting for him with treats: the butler, cook, footmen with his favourite dishes, the maids with his freshly prepared room, the head keeper with his new gun ready and his place at the shoot reserved for him, the fishing keeper telling him of a good salmon or trout, the coachman and grooms with his hunter and pony in splendid trim, a cricket week organized, a house party, nanny in the nursery waiting to hear all about him, the ladies of the house making a fuss of him, visits to every corner of the estate culminating in the ritual of stable parade after church on Sunday morning.

In the stable yard the shining well cared-for carriage-horses, hunters, cobs and ponies leaned out of their stalls to eat the newly washed carrots laid on the ledge for them, the straw edges of their litters exquisitely plaited, their coats gleaming, their harness spotless. But it was Heartbreak House for all that.

Even the middle-classes could keep up a style of living that surprises the present-day reader. Senior civil servants had regular dinner parties from early February until late July, dining out at least twice a week in groups of ten or a dozen, with good amateur music after the meal. They went to luncheon parties, tennis parties, garden parties, and, like the aristocracy, subscribed to the elaborate ritual of afternoon tea. It was perhaps the halcyon time of suburbia. Trim villas with evocative names like The Laurels, standing in neat gardens, contained a firm family life, gradually relaxing to permit croquet on Sundays (with an indoor variation on rainy days played on a green baize cloth spread on the dining-table), and church connexions encouraged amateur dramatics, music, tennis and badminton. The little boys went out in the ubiquitous sailor suit, usually blue, sometimes white, and the little girls in bunchy white dresses with floppy hats and black stockings.

Never perhaps in recent times has the surface of life in England presented a more perfect façade to later observers. The Edwardian period does seem, at a hasty glance, like the long garden party on a golden afternoon that so many of its memoirs say it was. But so often these memoirs were written by those who were inside the garden. And even there, all was not quite as fixed or as serene as it appeared.

The period occupies a pivotal position between the nineteenth and twentieth centuries, not really Victorian, though the diehards tried to keep it so and pretended that it was, not truly modern, though many ideas considered post-1918 were already showing. It had been compared with the English Channel, a narrow passage made turbulent by strong opposing tides. It has also been compared with the opening of the seventeenth century. Both began with the death of a celebrated queen regnant after a long prestigious reign with England gaining power, assurance and possessions; both began with anticipation of profound change. On the last day of 1900, Wilfrid Scawen Blunt wrote: "And so, poor wicked nineteenth century, farewell!" and, three weeks later: "The Queen is dead of an apoplectic stroke, and the great Victorian age is at an end. This is notable news. It will mean great changes in the world."

The sense of the end of an epoch pervaded all aspects of life at that moment. Within a month some three thousand elegiac poems on Queen Victoria were published in Britain and the colonies. All were rather dreadful, poetically speaking, but all vibrated with real feeling and the majority referred to her as "mother"; yet in England at the time, especially in the industrial areas, there was a powerful core of republican principle that hoped to see, and see soon, the abolition of the monarchy in favour of an elected president, though whether on the French or the American lines (without or without a Prime Minister) is not clear.

Some observers simply felt a sense of apprehension, of stepping into the unknown. One such was the writer Elinor Glyn, who watched the Queen's funeral procession and thought of it as the funeral procession of England's greatness. Another was Rudyard Kipling who, G. K. Chesterton considered, loved England not because she was England but because she was great, and whose altering views were revealed in two poems: the *Recessional* of 1897, a sober warning to avoid mistaking pomp for responsibility, and *The Islanders* of 1902, in which he rebuked England for fawning on younger nations "for the men who could shoot and ride" and for busying herself with "trinkets", contenting herself with "the flannelled fools at the wicket or the muddied oafs at the goals". The huge correspondence provoked in *The Times* by this poem showed surprisingly, two-thirds agreement with Kipling despite furious protests from sportsmen and headmasters. In January 1902 General Sir Frederick Maurice stated in *The Contemporary Review* that sixty per cent of Englishmen were unfit for military service.

Some observers were more cautious. C. F. G. Masterman wrote in 1905 that the keynotes of the age were expectancy and surprise, as was normal in a time balanced between two periods of great change. On the one hand was still breathing past, on the other the future coming to birth, so that this was a time of waiting. H. G. Wells summed up the first decade of the century as one of "badly strained optimism".

One factor that complicates the present day observer's view of the period is its outward mask. Conventional surface, enamelled over the cracks like the ladies' make-up, hid, or attempted to hide, the truth, that the apparently accepted standards of behaviour had become hollow, fixed attitudes of decorum preserved rather to safeguard stability than to state positive moral rightness. Institutions — the British Empire, established religion, public morals — mattered more than did the ideas they embodied. A shrewd American observer, Samuel Hynes, has pointed out that the forms of values had become the values themselves.

In its mixture of outward propriety and inner indulgence the age contrived to conceal the appearance during its span of phenomena that one still associates with the post-war years: psycho-analysis, wireless telegraphy, the cinema, aircraft, modern writing and painting, the rise of the Labour Party. Rutherford's work on radiation, Epstein's early sculptures and Eliot's early poems, the first books by James Joyce, Virginia Woolf, D. H. Lawrence and Ezra Pound, and all except one of E. M. Forster's novels, are Edwardian in date. That they were in advance of their time is beside the point: it was before 1914 that they appeared, like jazz.

One good clue to the underlying change is shown in the choice of Poet Laureate. By any standards Tennyson, the Victorian, is a great poet, and for some years after he died no successor was selected, neither Mr Gladstone nor Lord Rosebery feeling equal to the task of appointing any one. In 1895, however, Lord Salisbury picked Alfred Austin on his normal easy-going principle that one would do as well as another (he later answered critics by saying: "Well, he wanted it."). Austin was a diminutive white-moustached producer of dreadful verse whose idea of heaven was to sit in an English garden receiving news of British land and sea victories. When friends kindly drew his attention to linguistic errors in his work, he replied simply: "I dare not alter these things. They come to me from above." Whether or not he was the author of the famous lines about Edward VII's illness:

Across the wires the electric message came,
"He is no better, he is much the same,"

is uncertain, but his first effort as Laureate was an embarrassing piece celebrating the ill-fated Jameson Raid, published in *The Times* on 11 January 1896. It ended:

We were wrong, but we aren't half sorry,
And, as one of the baffled band,
I would rather have had that foray
Than the crushings of all the Rand.

The lady who presumably was *the* Edwardian lady was far from typical in many ways, entirely so in others. Alexandra of Denmark was the reluctant choice of Queen Victoria, who disapproved of the Danish royal family as "those fast Christians". Prince Christian was poor by royal standards and, for his time, rather Bohemian in tastes; worse, he was by his marriage heir to the impoverished Danish throne, then occupied by his disgraceful uncle-in-law, Frederick, three times divorced and currently living with a French ex-ballet dancer of no social pretensions whatever.

Prince Christian and his wife Louise had three sons and three daughters, all taught gymnastics by their father, so that the Princess of Wales later amused her friends in London by turning cartwheels, telling them that it was only a matter of speed. She and her sister Dagmar as girls shared a bedroom with two Spartan iron bedsteads in it, wore home-made dresses, waited at table when guests came, and spent idyllic holidays at their grandfather's palace at Rumpenheim near Frankfurt or in a modest villa on the Baltic coast. Their principal home was the Yellow Palace in Copenhagen, its walls peeling and shabby. Their mother said that she brought her children up in sackcloth so that they would wear the purple more gracefully later. There was more in this than met the eye at first: two of the daughters became empresses.

The need to marry off the Prince of Wales and his lack of interest in eligible German princesses combined to open the way for Alexandra, or Alix as her relations all called her. One of Queen Victoria's ladies, Countess Walburga von Hohenthal, had married the British Ambassador to Copenhagen, Sir Augustus Paget. She reported that Alix was fresh, simple, childlike, resembling a half-opened rosebud, and sent photographs for the Prince of Wales to see.

In September 1861 the Prince visited his great-aunt, the Duchess of Cambridge, at her home in Strelitz, where an "accidental" meeting with Alix and her mother was carefully brought about in the unlikely setting of the cathedral at Speier. The Prince was deeply impressed, his father approved, so, rather surprisingly, did the Prince's elder sister Vicky, Crown Princess of Prussia; and when the Prince Consort died three months later, Queen Victoria felt bound to honour her late husband's wishes and gave her approval after a visit of inspection carried out in the summer of 1862. Travelling as the Countess of Balmoral, an incognito that deceived very few, the Queen met Alix and her parents and sister Dagmar at the Palace of Laeken, where King Leopold of the Belgians told her that Alix was a ray of sunshine and looked for nothing but love, and Alix herself suggested that she was not important enough for the reputedly solemn English.

In *The Times* the betrothal was announced rather subduedly, provoking questions in Parliament to which Lord Palmerston rather splendidly replied that when Her Majesty's Government undertook the duty of selecting a consort for the Prince of Wales it insisted that she must be young, handsome, well brought up and a Protestant. The Queen declared that the wedding must be in St George's Chapel, Windsor, the first royal wedding held there since Edward I's reign. She also made Alix spend a month with her at Osborne during which she told her not to meddle in politics, not to let the Prince meddle in Danish affairs, and to persuade him to give up cigar-smoking. Parliament voted to increase the Prince's annual income from £60,000 to £100,000 and to give Alix £10,000 a year with the promise of an extra

£20,000 if she were widowed during the Queen's lifetime.

In March 1863 Alix set out for her wedding. The ship's boiler blew up in harbour so the Danish party transferred to another ship for the crossing to Belgium, where they stayed for a few days with King Leopold. He gave Alix a Brussels lace wedding dress which was indignantly refused in a telegram from the Queen, who insisted on Honiton. Alix boarded the royal yacht *Victoria and Albert* at Flushing, escorted in silence by HMS *Resistance* amd *Warrior*: the Queen wanted a quiet reception because of her state of mourning. The yacht reached Gravesend where the citizens gave Alix a wildly enthusiastic reception, decorating the pier with orange blossom and banners reading "Welcome thou chosen one" in Danish, and employing sixty "maids of Kent" to strew rose petals in Alix's path to the royal train, which was driven up to London very slowly through bitterly cold sleety weather with the Earl of Caithness at the controls of the engine. Emerging at the Bricklayers Arms terminus, Alix, now accompanied by the Prince, and the rest of the party went in a carriage procession to Paddington. By the Queen's orders few soldiers were present as escort and the crowds got out of hand, so that a number of people died in the crush.

The wedding day was frosty and fine for the Queen's first public appearance since the Prince Consort's death. In deep black, with her ladies by order wearing grey, mauve and lilac, she watched what to her was the "sad dismal ceremony" which appeared beautiful to others. Alix was late — a lifelong characteristic — having taken four hours to dress. The Chapel was crammed with royal personalities, among them the Crown Prince and Princess of Prussia whose four-year-old son, the future Kaiser, bit the knees of his uncles and threw an aunt's muff into the street, and the town was jammed with people, so that afterwards a most undignified scuffle took place, everybody mashed up together in a scramble for trains back to Town. The Archbishop of Canterbury reached Slough station only by hanging for dear life on to the back of somebody's carriage.

Bizarre events occurred to and around Alix for years. Her first child, Albert Victor Christian Edward, Duke of Clarence and Avondale, was born prematurely on 8 January 1864, signifying his imminent appearance while Alix was sitting in a sleigh on the ice at Windsor watching the skating. She was rushed back to the Castle where, without a nurse, cot or baby clothes available, the baby was delivered three hours later by the Windsor physician, Dr Brown, assisted by Lady Macclesfield. On 3 June 1865 her second child, George Frederick Ernest Albert, later George V, was born orthodoxly enough at Marlborough House; but a few days later fire broke out in the nursery. The Prince of Wales promptly pulled off his coat, prised up floorboards, flooded the nursery and the stairs and wrenched his knee, but saved the situation.

In February 1867 Alix was ill in bed with rheumatic fever when her first daughter, Louise, was born; she had to stay in bed for four months and was left with a limp that was sedulously imitated by fashionable ladies, just as they copied the high "dog-collar" she always wore to conceal an operation scar. Her interest in hospitals dates from that illness. Daughter Victoria was born in July 1868; in 1869 the Waleses visited Egypt where Alix smoked a hookah and ate with her fingers among the ladies of the Khedive's harem; daughter Maud was born in 1870 just as the scandal of the Mordaunt divorce case broke, involving the issue of a subpoena to the Prince. Alix went off to Denmark where she might have stayed had not the Queen ordered her back because of the outbreak of the Franco-Prussian War. In April 1871 her last child, Alexander John Charles Albert, died at birth, and from that time on Alix and her husband led increasingly separate lives, though he was unfailingly punctilious in giving her every honour that could outwardly attach to her position, and there seems no doubt that he remained devoted to her in his own way.

During her married life, especially its early years, Alix often took part in events of the boisterously hilarious kind typical of the publicly inhibited society of the day. When Tennyson at her request read aloud his "Ode of Welcome" in which he stated that Saxon and Norman and Dane were we, but all of us Danes in our welcome of the sea-king's daughter from over the sea, she shrieked with laughter. She did the same at Sandringham when the lively Lord Charles Beresford doped a cockerel and hid it under the bed of a pompous guest who was awakened in the dawn by loud cacklings from the chamber-pot, And when he with Alix and the Prince attended a séance at Mrs Cust's villa at Cowes, Lord Charles flitted about the room in stockinged feet sprinkling the company with flour. The Prince Imperial, who was also present, then joined with the Prince of Wales in dragging a donkey through the window and putting it to bed in one of the spare rooms.

In the spring of 1885 Alix accompanied the Prince to Ireland which was bristling with anti-English feeling. The Prince was determined to go to show his disregard for the fact that the Fenians had set a price of £2,000 on his head, dead or alive. The University of Dublin gave Alix an honorary Doctorate of Music: the Cork nationalists redoubled their threats and Queen Victoria telegraphed to order that the royal route be changed, but the telegram was never delivered. The train journey was enlivened by shouting, fist-shaking crowds carrying black flags bearing the skull and crossbones, and throwing stones, and a mob holding a pair of miniature coffins awaited the party at Mallow Junction.

Alix passed unflinchingly through the tour, as she did five years later through the state visit of the Shah of Persia, who took one look at her ladies in waiting and told the Prince that if those were his other wives he had better behead them and find new and pretty ones. Perhaps she did not hear him — she was growing deaf by this time — or perhaps, knowing how many new and pretty ladies littered the Prince's path, she merely smiled wryly to herself. She was not unloved. Her personal comptroller, Sir Dighton Probyn, VC, worshipped her all his life, and her devoted friend Oliver Montagu openly adored her. The word "friend" has almost got out of hand, so it is essential to say that their relationship was an idealistic, romantic one, like the "amour sans amitié" of medieval chivalry.

With the assassination of Tsar Alexander II in 1881, Alix's sister Dagmar, who had married the Tsarevitch in the same year as Alix had married the Prince of Wales, became the new Empress Marie Fedorovna. Alix and the Prince went to Russia for the funeral. In England then it was estimated that thirty per cent of the population were living below the poverty line, but that seeemed like the Earthly Paradise compared with Russia. Alix noted that the enclosed courtyard of the Anitchkoff Palace, where the Russian royal family took their daily walks was worse than a London slum. The sisters retained all their old devotion and met every year for increasingly long spells at the Danish royal villa on the Baltic coast.

It will not have escaped notice that Alix lived almost up to her ruby wedding in the shadow of Queen Victoria. The very names given to her children reveal that. In 1897 important statesmen begged Alix to use all her influence in persuading the Queen to come out of black at least for the Diamond Jubilee procession. Alix tried and received what she called (at the age of fifty-two) the snub of her life. Actually, whether out of sentiment or her unfailing sense of the effective, the Queen was well advised not to change. On that spectacular day, among all the brilliant uniforms and flowery colours, all the glittering gold and sparkling silver, the focus held steady on the one dumpy little figure in black. Small wonder that when Alix actually became Queen she could hardly believe it. She hesitated before advancing to the centre of the stage, refusing to let anyone call her "Your Majesty" until after Queen Victoria's funeral. Then, however, she took a deep breath and began to clear away the mountain of undisturbed clutter that had piled up around her predecessor for sixty years. The new King would perhaps have liked to leave her to it, but goodhumouredly joined in with increasing enthusiasm, often working in his shirt sleeves like a foreman and shouting comments in Alix's ear. He seemed particularly to relish throwing out the pictures and souvenirs of John Brown, whom he had always disliked. Alix, like a true Edwardian, collected her own clutter, cherishing stacks of old letters and theatre programmes, menus, books, photographs, bits of china ranging in value from exquisite pieces of Meissen to Earls Court china pigs, and filling her rooms with ornaments to that extent that young relations demurred at playing the piano because they said it would take an hour to replace all the stuff crowded not only on the piano top but on the stool as well.

Alix's first public appearance as Queen was at the State Opening of Parliament on 15 February 1901, where her enchanting good looks — despite her fifty-six years, her limp, and her deafness — drew gasps of admiration from an assembly used to attractive women. Two days before, the King had created her a Lady of the Garter Order, the first such distinction since the reign of Henry VII four hundred years previously. Faced with the first coronation for more than sixty years, court officials dug out information, most of it smilingly ignored by Alix, who said she was going to wear what she liked and that she would be attended by four duchesses, all tall and beautiful. She had her way and was hailed as the loveliest queen ever crowned in Westminster Abbey.

When Alix was forbidden to do something on which her heart was set, she usually did it any way. On the King's birthday he told her to watch the Trooping the Colour from a window. She said nothing, which he ought to have known by then was a bad sign, waited until he had set off, stated simply: "I go," and ordered her carriage. All her life she was incurably unpunctual. She would slip gracefully into rooms asking: "Am I late?" at which the King was seen to swallow but did not speak. She detested over-formality, rigidity, and pompousness. She loved animals, including unusual ones like parrots, monkeys, baby bears and tigers which she kept at Sandringham, and exotic dogs of which in her lifetime she possessed dozens, including Japanese spaniels, Russian wolfhounds, basset hounds, chow-chows, collies, even St Bernards. She adored her children and made them all (and their eventual partners) call her Motherdear. She was sentimental, and her emotions were easily stirred. Moreover, she was generous, impulsive, sweet and loving, lively and enthusiastic, inspiring genuine devotion in those who looked after her, tiresome and unpredictable, vague and outspoken. Not the conventional Edwardian lady: or was she?

CHAPTER TWO

The Golden Age

There is in it that ache we all have for lost times, when the sun was warmer, the days and nights longer and everything was cosy and safe . . . against the dewy background of a world that nearly was.
— Richard Winnington

William Morris is reputed to have said that, of all people who took it upon themselves to bring up children, parents were undoubtedly the worst. He should, therefore, have been rather pleased than otherwise about the upbringing of the Edwardian lady and of the Edwardian lady's children, because these came to official maturity without much direct parental influence at all.

Relays of other people — nannies, nursery maids, domestic servants, governesses — filled, regulated and managed the daily lives of little girls of wealthy houses as they had done for generations and still do among the dwindling band of those who can find helpers. Yet for these children there was an element of freedom that was painfully lacking in the lives of daughters whose parents could not afford a houseful of servants. In big country houses little girls could run wild to a degree impossible to the present-day child in a suburban dwelling. If at any moment a child can be with any one of a couple of dozen people in a score of rooms, she can very easily be with none: a net of wide dimensions is easier to slip through than a single gate.

The fundamental differences between the Edwardian girl of good family and the modern one are four in number. First, childhood was not considered a desirable state in itself with its own rights; it was merely a preliminary to be got through in order to assume adult privileges. Second, children were not individually catered for in the scheme of things; they had to fit in as best they could. Third, child psychology was non-existent to parents; to admit it would be to admit that they were

The archetypal Edwardian Lady—hat, hair, pearls, lace, facial expressions: one can almost smell the Parma violets. (*Publishers' collection*)

Drawing by Simont originally captioned "The King as dancer: His Majesty portrayed for the first time in this
He is joining in the Quadrille d'Honneur at a summer ball at Apsley House, with the Duchess of Willington, wh
Queen partners the Duke. The pastel-tinted silk, satin and lace dresses show off all the jewels. (*The Mansell Col*

Queen Alexandra playing cards. Her companions are her sister Dagmar, Empress Marie Fedorovna of Russia; her father, King Christian IX of Denmark; and the Duchess of Cumberland (with her back to the camera). The crammed, lavish room with its elegant chairs, clutter of screens and mass of flowers (the ladies are wearing flowers, too) are typical of the Queen. (*The Mansell Collection*)

The Edwardian lady in full fig: (*top left*) Queen Alexandra bejewelled for the opera with her daughters the Duchess of Fife and Princess Victoria in pearls, sequins and a feather boa; (*top right*) Princess Marie of Edinburgh, future queen of Ferdinand of Roumania; (*bottom left*) the Duchess of Fife with her daughters Princess Maud and Princess Alexandra, showing what the well-dressed young girl wore in 1905; (*bottom right*) the princess who had a bomb on her wedding day, Princess Ena with her Fiancé King Alfonso of Spain, and their two mothers, Princess Henry of Battenberg and the Dowager Queen Cristina. (*Publishers' collection*)

"Her First Season: a Study of Society" —drawing by Charles Dana Gibson. (*The Mansell Collection*)

The debutante's big moment: the Presentation at Court, drawn by W. Hatherell. (*The Mansell Collection*)

Edwardian sentimentality about childhood in characteristically elaborate Edwardian magazine lay-outs. (*Publishers' collection*)

not divinely appointed guardians of the young. No Edwardian parent agonized "Where did we go wrong?" And fourth, no doubt occurred as to what the daughters' future life was likely to be.

These attitudes applied more to girls than to boys. Barrie's Peter Pan (the play first appeared in 1904) did not want to grow up. Everywhere that the boys looked, they saw men whose lives seemed less attractive than the boyhood they had left behind. But the girls saw that women, real grown-up women, had the best of it in the feminine world.

Whether or not the parents of these daughters consciously thought out the idea that it is hardly possible to enjoy childhood and adult life equally and that, therefore, since one is an adult for far longer, it is the grown-up state that had better be preferable, is not clear. Probably they did not. Certainly it is true that leaving a child to be brought up by servants has many disadvantages; but not all parents are fit to look after anybody's children either, as court records dispiritingly show. It is also true that if children see their parents at intervals — instead of being under their feet all day — they are able to idealize and admire them, wish to make a good impression and live up to them, far more readily than if they see these fallible humans at close quarters. And remote, authoritative parents do provide a solid wall for the children to bang their heads against as they start to think for themselves. The debate is endless and rendered incapable of solution because of all the personal prejudices, experiences and opinions that complicate argument and darken counsel. Perhaps it is best simply to record Edwardian girlhood as far as one can and leave it at that.

Various portraits of contemporary childhood have become famous and it is unnecessary to insist too precisely upon the dates of the period, for wealthy households remained essentially consistent in their treatment of children from the closing years of the nineteenth century until the Great War. One writer whose books spanned the time was Kenneth Grahame, whose masterpiece, *The Wind in the Willows*, appeared in 1908, but who had already set down his recollections of childhood in *The Golden Age* (1895) and *Dream Days* (1898). In these two books he writes as an adult (male) looking back before it is too late to recapture the full flavour of what to him was a happy time. His five children — Edward, Selina, the nameless narrator, Harold, and Charlotte — live in the country under the care of shadowy aunts and uncles. These elders hand down implacable dictates from time to time: a governess leaves, an uncle arrives, Edward must go to boarding school, visits of ceremony must be paid, the toys are to be sent away to poor children. Few matters are ever explained.

The real life of the five is lived away from these Olympians, a life crowded with play and pretence, free alike from the questioning adult or the trained psychiatrist, no one ever wonders whether what they are doing is normal, or abnormal, or right, or whether they are making progress in their lessons. They have few toys, and these are mostly old, handed down from one to another until even Charlotte is generally considered too old for them. A new toy is an event. Harold goes through all sorts of financial, physical and moral difficulties in order to give Selina a doll's tea-set that she has coveted for weeks in a shop-window. Most of their games are "let's pretend", with the boys' tastes firmly in the ascendant. Sometimes such games demand solitude. Harold is discovered sitting in an old pig-trough in the tool-shed, wielding a shovel as though it was an oar, and when challenged by Edward ("What rot are you playing at now?") replies that he is Jason, and this is the *Argo*. The other fellows are here too, "only you can't see them; and we're just going through the Hellespont, so don't you come bothering". But all Harold's games were solitary, like "muffin-man" and "clubmen". It is impossible to gauge the exact ages of these children, particularly the girls: Selina plays with dolls yet peacocks about in the moonlight in a new dressing-gown, puzzles the boys by her long babbling chats with the vicarage girls, and makes a bonfire in Nelson's memory on Trafalgar Day because her pet subject is naval history, although she has never seen the sea. Charlotte is unquestionably babyish, prattling stories to her dolls (out of *Alice*) and spanking the one that is not paying attention. But she knows all about King Arthur's knights, and, when Edward goes off to school and the bereaved four are walking away from the railway station, "the girls in front, their heads together, were already reckoning up the weeks to the holidays". It is a boy's world predominantly. Some observations however, apply to the girls equally well:

> Certain spots always had their insensible attraction for certain moods. In love, one sought the orchard. Weary of discipline, sick of convention, impassioned for the road, the mining-camp, the land across the border, one made for the big meadow. Mutinous, sulky, charged with plots and conspiracies, one always got behind the shelter of the raspberry-canes.

Judging by Selina, not all young Edwardian ladies spent holidays at the seaside, but those who did found advantages less readily discoverable today. Miles of uncontaminated sand, free alike of oil and litter; no speedboats; a free view framed in dunes or cliffs with gorse and heather and sandy grass, with perhaps a bungalow or two beginning to show, but not many; and the unaccustomed joy of going barefoot. Perhaps a pigtailed girl in her school blazer would be allowed to help her brother in his white school sweater to man a small sailing dinghy; more often, she would spend long hours on the beach, hours enlivened by watching the pierrots or the Punch-and-Judy, if the place was big enough to provide these treats.

The resorts were growing. Aiming to attract a good class of resident rather than a flood of trippers, they were developing exclusive suburbs: Hove beside Brighton, Broadstairs close to Margate, Westcliff by Southend, and, best of all, perhaps, Frinton along the coast from Clacton. Other watering-places emphasized eventless Sundays in order to encourage ratepaying stayers and put off fly-by-night one-day visitors: no trains ran to Bournemouth on Sundays before 1914, allot-ment-holders were forbidden to dig on Sundays in Eastbourne, piers were closed on Sundays as a rule, the park or promenade bands did not play on that day. (Though in Kipps's Folkestone there were sacred concerts on the pier.) A comment in *Punch* gave a few more details about Bournemouth, stating that it was a blithe place during the week, with coastal steamers plying to and fro, and, on the beach itself, "donkey-riding, al fresco refreshments, clowns, niggers" (meaning, of course, the seaside nigger-minstrel, the Edwardian equivalent of the Black and White Minstrel Show); the streets bustled with wagonettes and coaches, the strains of music welled forth from the public gardens, the Bournemouth Symphony Orchestra conducted by Sir Dan Godfrey played in the Winter Garden, but all this liveliness was Cinderella's:

> Every Saturday night, long before the stroke of twelve, bands, lights, cocoa-nuts, niggers, donkey-boys, and all things and people that make quiet life impossible, vanish as if by magic, not to be heard of or seen again till Monday morning. Sunday papers arrive late from town. At Bournemouth on Sunday there is no four-horse coach, no horn-blowing; I saw no motors, nor heard the raucous cries of journal-vendors.

Bournemouth, like other resorts, was expanding fast, increasing its rateable value sevenfold in the forty years between 1878 and 1918. The growth of the railways pushed seaside holidays forward: by 1911 Fleetwood, virtually none-existent in 1836, had a population of over 12,000, and St Anne's, planned on a drawing board and the first sod cut in 1875, was approaching 7,000. In the period 1871–1911 Blackpool multiplied its size by nine, and so did Southport. But apart from Blackpool, which set out to be a holiday resort on the grand scale, capable of swallowing whole towns at a time, the seaside places pre-ferred to plan for residents rather than for transient visitors.

Some children had relations who lived on, or close to, the coast. Angela Mackail, later Angela Thirkell, remembered staying with her grandparents at Rottingdean. Years before, in search of a house near

Brighton — the air of which was splendidly tonic for Mrs Thirkell's grandfather — they had bought a three-storey cottage, one room thick, on the village green, adding to the purchase that of the house next door, and the two buildings were joined together in a way that was maddeningly hard for a housekeeper to manage but enchantingly interesting for a child to explore. The annual summer visit started with the train journey from Victoria to Brighton (in 1901 this took 53½ minutes, hardly different from the time it takes today), and then came the drive out to Rottingdean in an open-topped horse-bus drawn by four horses. The family luggage, including the baby's bath filled with all the baby's belongings and sewn into coverings of hessian and mackintosh, was piled on top, and the bus set off past Castle Square and Sussex Square (where Roedean School was situated in those days), with the sea on the right and the open downs before it, until the black sails of Rottingdean windmill showed that the journey was near its end. Between the road and the sea was the grass-grown Old Road, which had crumbled away in places. Mrs Thirkell's mother used to make the children get out and walk up the last hill, to save the horses, and they would scramble up the steep embankment flowery with scabious and yellow poppies, and wait at Greenways House looking lovingly at its pigsties until the bus reached the crest. There the drag was put on and the bus skidded downhill into Rottingdean with the conductor blowing blasts on his long coaching-horn.

Holiday recollections usually remain clear in the memory. Sonia Keppel and her sister paid a visit every September to Duntreath Castle, situated below the Campsie Fells in Strathblane. The journey was fascinating, with the luncheon basket taken on the train at Carlisle and put out again, empty of its huge chicken rolls, Cheddar cheese, and unripe pears, at the next stop. It was dark by the time the party changed to the wagonette at Blanefield station for the last part of the journey. Duntreath swarmed with relations, some of them a bit peculiar, like Cousin Gladys who believed that she was the reincarnation of Bonnie Prince Charlie and who therefore wore a kilt and a gentlemanly jacket and asked to go to the gentleman's cloakroom at every hotel she visited, or Aunt Frances, who followed her brother's advice and planted male and female hollies together so that they would berry and then was too shy to look and see whether they had.

During the holidays at Duntreath the Keppel children were taken to Glasgow to be fitted with tweeds, taken for picnics on the banks of Loch Lomond where they could call softly over the water and hear the echo come softly back, taken to eat enormous, delicious teas with Mrs Strachan at the Lodge, and guided up and down hills on ponies by a bald middle-aged keeper named Dingwall who, like his pony, smelt of sweat and peat and with whom the eight-year-old Sonia fell in love, though she normally had only a back view of him.

But there were more exotic holidays than these. In spring the Keppels usually went to Biarritz. This meant an experience that Mrs Keppel and her elder daughter Violet enjoyed to the full, Nanny and Sonia not at all. The journey was thrilling for the one pair, disagreeable or frightening for the other. Both girls were provided beforehand with bottles of what Nanny called "Oh Dick Alone" in case they felt seasick; at Calais they had double-bedded sleeping compartments, Nanny and Violet in one, Mrs Keppel and Sonia in the other. Sonia lay awake in the upper berth, not daring to stir lest she might disturb her mother, an unlikely occurrence as Mrs Keppel had taken a sleeping-pill.

Being Alice Keppel's daughter was not something in the common way. It was noticeable how Mrs Keppel was treated like royalty throughout the journey. The *chef de gare* himself met her off the Calais packet and escorted her to the train, including the passage of the Customs, and the *wagon-lits* attendants could not do enough for her. Of course, as soon as the tickets were bought in the first place every single person on the line would know that the King's favourite was travelling, so naturally she was wafted effortlessly through her journey. At Biarritz they stayed at the Villa Eugènie, hired every year by Sir Ernest Cassel. The villa, in the little girls' recollection, resembled a big conservatory in which people happened to be living. Sir Ernest's sister was always there, and his daughter Mrs Ashley, with her two little girls Edwina and Mary. The Keppel nanny often lamented that Mrs Ashley's daughters had real lace on their knickers while her two charges had to make do with imitation. It was Edwina Ashley who grew up to become Lady Louis Mountbatten.

King Edward turned up at Biarritz for Easter, too. He visited the villa regularly, bringing with him his dog Caesar, which had no consideration for the chair-legs and curtains. Easter gifts came with the King, who included the children: Sonia Keppel, now the Hon. Mrs Cubitt, still possesses a specimen of that arch-symbol of the Edwardian lady at her peak, a tiny Fabergé Easter egg, this one in royal blue enamel with a letter E in diamonds and a tiny gold and ruby crown on top.

On Sundays there were picnics, reminiscent of the memorable fleet-of-limousines picnic in the film *Citizen Kane*. At the chosen spot selected by the King, always, surprisingly, at the side of the road, the footmen unpacked the table and chairs, linen, silver, glasses, and plates, and loaded the whole thing down with huge quantities of cold food and iced cup. After three weeks or so of this film-set existence, the Keppels went back to London, stopping on the way in Paris where Mrs Cubitt's doll Julie was fitted out with new clothes by Mrs Keppel's Paris dress-maker, the great Worth himself.

Holidays at Rottingdean were far simpler. Mrs Thirkell and her brother spent hours in the garden, a space not much bigger than a tennis court but so cleverly laid out in sections that it appeared en-ormous. Here they collected the hundreds of snails that daily infested the garden and dropped them into a tin bowl full of salt water; they watched the garden boy burning rubbish in the brick incinerator, interrupted in his labours from time to time by their grandmother, who kept coming out and reading bits of Ruskin aloud to him; they sowed penny packets of mustard and cress and nasturtiums and then neglec-ted the results, if any; they went through the tiny orchard with its ten apple trees to the summer-house with its ground-floor tool-shed and its upper room containing several unbelievably uncomfortable wooden chairs designed by Burne-Jones for the William Morris Round Table tapestry; they ate waspy windfalls and the delicious russet cooking-apples that grew behind the sweetbriar hedge, where the children pitched a very small rickety tent, stuffy in the extreme but ideal for dozens of let's pretend games.

In these games they were joined by their young cousins from The Elms across the green — Josephine, Elsie, and John — and quite often by the cousins' father, Rudyard Kipling. All the children were allowed to go barefoot at Rottingdean, whether on the brick paths, which felt pleasant, or on the shingle paths, which did not. Mrs Thirkell envied the Kipling children who, going barefoot half the year, had the soles of their feet so hardened that they could run effortlessly over the grass of the downs which was full of little flat thistles, whereas she and her brother, with only six weeks' holiday, had to proceed more cautiously.

It was for his daughter Josephine that Kipling wrote the Just-so Stories, and it was his happy practice to read these aloud to Josephine and the small Angela in his study. He had a special way of reading them, with certain emphases and vocal changes, that made magic of them. It is Josephine who is Taffimai and Kipling who is Tegumai in "How The First Letter Was Written" and "How the Alphabet Was Made". Kipling took the children's games with complete seriousness, acting Roundhead to their Cavaliers, replying to their written challenges in correct style (though, of course, he corrected their spell-ing), and at the end of the summer holiday he always gave Mrs Thirkell a sheet of paper covered with autographs that she could trade with her friends for stamps and other coveted objects. The Elms was a mecca for sightseers and the children had a splendid time telling them, or letting them go on believing, a mass of misinformation about the illustrious author. Their neighbouring Ridsdale cousins (one of whom, Cissie

Ridsdale, had married Stanley Baldwin) went one better than this, Mrs Ridsdale in particular. Whenever a tourist stopped her to ask where Rudyard Kipling lived she invariably demanded to know whether he had read any of Kipling's works, and if the answer was No she would simply refuse to point out the house.

Another little girl who had stories made up for her was Loelia Ponsonby. Her strange name, pronounced, she explains, Leelia, was supposedly a Russian version of Lily. Her father, Sir Frederick Ponsonby, was the son of Queen Victoria's private secretary, Henry Ponsonby, and, so to speak, inherited the post, so that the small Loelia and her brother Gaspard were brought up in that most appealing of royal residences, St James's Palace. Sir Frederick had struggled to marry the lovely Miss Ria (short for Victoria) Kennard against the combined opposition of his parents, her parents, and Queen Victoria; they were married in 1899, and one of their wedding presents was a table fitted with bottles, glasses, sugar bowl and tongs "for the smoking-room" — an early version of the cocktail cabinet — from the Prince of Wales.

Little Miss Ponsonby's father was a joy to her, but he was away so often on the King's business that she seldom saw him; when she did, however, he told her wonderful stories in which she was personally involved in a situation of cliff-hanging peril. At a climax he would stop and ask her to work out how she would escape. His brother Arthur told stories too, about his own children Elizabeth and Matthew and about Gaspard and Loelia, when they were all grown up; in one of these he had Loelia married to a Lord Wimbledon who drank port. Sometimes Lady Ponsonby would provide a story, and excellent these were, though hers were read aloud (very well) out of books: *Black Beauty*, *King Solomon's Mines*, *At The Back of the North Wind*, *Treasure Island*, and she would stop reading at all the most thrilling places, so that the children would long for the next instalment.

The Edwardian period was in many ways the apex of the nanny power and influence. Mr Jonathan Gathorne-Hardy places the dates of what he calls the Classic Nanny at 1895–1914. During this time the English nanny was so admired and valued that aristocratic European families made every effort to secure one. The fact that every nanny thought poorly of foreigners in general only made her more desirable. Nanny Eager went in 1899 to St Petersburg, where she naturally taught the Tsar's little girls to embroider, to be familiar with English nursery rhymes and tales, to sing English songs and hymns (their favourite was "Rock of Ages"), to hang up their stockings at Christmas. Only the advent of the heir in 1904 ended her nursery reign, for the court officials felt they could not permit her influence to be exercised over a future

Tsar. It is one of history's fascinating "ifs" to wonder how different the life of that unfortunate little boy might have been had the English nanny stayed.

Some nannies, of course, were cruel, and even lofty social rank was no safeguard. The late Duke of Windsor recorded in his autobiography how his nanny used to pinch her charges till they cried just before they were due to appear in their parents' drawing-room, in order, presumably, to emphasize her power over them. Little Loelia Ponsonby suffered bitterly: her nanny married when Loelia was four years old, and her parents decided that a series of foreign nursery-governesses would do. They were a horrid lot who tormented the children: one Belgian woman pulled Loelia's hair by dragging a comb through its tangles with both hands, held her face down in a basin of water, and, knowing that she was frightened of the dark, sent her to fetch things from the other end of the house. One nursery governess dressed her in a frock made out of a smelly old piece of sacking; when, at a party, Loelia was given a jig-saw puzzle, she also brought home a pencil, one of several left over, and "Mademoiselle" made her confess to her mother, return the pencil with a letter of apology, and live for weeks with a notice reading "I am a liar and a thief" above her bed. Every time another child visited her, she had to explain this awful statement over again. Eventually her mother caught sight of it and told her to take it down.

This incident reads like something out of Dotheboys Hall or Lowood, certainly not like a twentieth-century upbringing by supposedly progressive parents, and so does the fact that the young Loelia was almost certainly the last girl in England to wear a backboard, which was made of mahogany and strapped on. Later a violin string was tied tightly round her shoulders so that whenever she leaned forward it cut into her arms, and when it snapped, she was expected to buy a replacement. Her pocket money was threepence a week, one penny of which had to go into the money-box and one into the bag in church on Sunday; a new violin string cost one shilling and twopence.

Quite a few children were put through physical tortures in order to improve their posture. Dame Edith Sitwell's parents noticed that her thin ankles were weak and that she stooped slightly, so they sent her to a London orthopaedic surgeon, who appeared to her to be carved out of frozen margarine, and who put her into a kind of steel brace. She referred to it as a Bastille. It was fastened round under her arms and extended to her feet, and she had to sleep in it. She also had to wear a band round her head from which two pieces of steel, padded thickly at the ends, reached down the sides of her nose, in an attempt to force it straight.

These punitive measures were the choice of parents, not of nannies, and mostly Nanny was archetypal — powerful to be sure, firm, decided, but kind, cosy, eternally there, ruling over the separate little nursery world, providing the essential feeling of permanence that every child requires. That world contained, as a rule, the day nursery, the night nursery, either with a room opening off it for Nanny or with her own bed in it, a room or rooms for the under-nurse or nursery-maid or maids, and a pantry or still-room.

Both nurseries had coal fires, secure behind massive fireguards. There would certainly be a rocking-chair, and very probably a dilapidated old rocking-horse and an equally shabby old dolls' house; both these objects passed on through several generations until they literally fell to pieces. More often than not there was an old upright piano. A stout door covered in green baize nailed on with small brass studs barred the way between this set of rooms and the rest of the house. The nursery might well be approached by a separate staircase and even a separate door leading out into the grounds, with a store-room close by for the perambulator and the rows of wellington boots. A small, stable, shut-in, cosy, safe world, apart from the great big grown-up world outside.

In his profoundly interesting book, Mr Gathorne-Hardy advances the theory, for which there is a vast mass of documentary evidence, that it was to the existence of the nanny that the well-bred Englishman of the nineteenth and early twentieth centuries owed his undoubted taste for lower-class girls as sex objects. The nanny, lower-class herself, was the one who kissed, cuddled, fed, comforted, disciplined and played with the little boys during the crucial formative years. Certainly this theory appears to hold up. But what about the little girls? The nanny gave them, too, the kisses and hugs, the food and comfort, the stories and discipline and games. Would they not be expected therefore to reveal a similar preference for lower-class *men* when they grew up?

If the little girls had had a man-nanny, this might well have been so. Indeed, there are debatable examples. Lady Chatterley, with her *tendre* for Mellors the gamekeeper, has seemed to several eminent critics a piece of wish-fulfilment on the part of D. H. Lawrence. But there are quite a few instances of rich and high-born young ladies decamping with their chauffeurs, or even with a footman, in twentieth-century literature, alongside less idyllic scenes of other young ladies only finding true surcease in the arms of a docker, or coalheaver, but the interesting thing about these literary examples is that they come almost entirely in post-war works, when women had stopped being Edwardian ladies and had become Bright Young Things, addicted to driving in fast cars, attending bottle-parties, smoking in public, drinking cocktails, and shocking their parents. Most of the nanny-controlled young girls of the Victorian and Edwardian periods did not display these symptoms. Nor did most of them search for sex from among those outside their own circle. Those who did, to judge by the novels featuring them, were little girls during the later part of the Edwardian period alone: the closing years of the Classic Nanny epoch.

In the first place, ladies were not officially supposed to have any sex feelings. In the second place, Nanny was a woman, too. In the third place, little girls were treated differently from little boys from the very beginning. Nanny's admonitions usually included remarks like: "Young gentlemen don't do this," and "Ladies don't do that." The boys were expected to play with toy soldiers, the girls with dolls, or, at the very least, with cuddly toys. Also, although it was possible for Master George or Master Algernon to take up one of several careers when he grew up, there was no doubt in anyone's mind that Miss Daisy or Miss Dolly would get married, setting up a new nursery in which a new nanny, or, more likely, the old one, could again reign supreme. What today is called the climate of opinion showed to all children that in most grown-up ways men and women led quite different lives, with different standards, different expectations, different basic attitudes.

Nanny permeates every recollection written down by ladies who were once Edwardian children. Each one remembers watching with fascinated interest the spectacle of Nanny getting dressed. The soft pink body inside its tentlike nightgown was rapidly pushed and squeezed into layers of starch and whalebone, most of the process being carried on under the cover of various garments. And there were so many of those — clicked into place by stays, pins, buckles, comparable with the riveting of armour, and all at astonishing speed. Nurseries smelt of Brasso, soap, and perspiration. Being washed in a hip-bath made one's behind boiling hot while one's back felt cold. Going out with Nanny was a daily occurrence, whether in London, in the country, or at the seaside. In London one went to Kensington Gardens, where all the prestigious nannies went, and they all knew one another. Gossip rose in clouds above the park benches, yet every nanny unfailingly kept an eye on her charges. In the country one walked in the park of the great house, regularly visiting chosen spots. At the seaside the ritual was perhaps most picturesque.

Every morning (except, of course, on Sundays) a great procession of nannies and children would set out for the beach. The nannies, wearing their summer boaters and stiff white piqué dresses, pushed per-ambulators in which the babies were almost hidden behind bathing dresses, towels, wooden spades (iron ones were forbidden because you might cut your toes off), and small children with their feet dangling over the side. The bigger children walked close by, clutching a shilling for buns in one hand and perhaps a green shrimping net in the other, a net in which it was in the highest degree unlikely that anything would ever get caught.

All the way along the street to the beach there were friends to speak to and fresh reinforcements of nannies with perambulators and children all well acquainted, with here and there a slightly dim-witted nursery-maid who was graciously permitted to listen to the nannies' gossip, though the sky would have fallen had she attempted to join in. The children were always delighted if one of the nannies had to stop at the post office, or the bakery (where the shilling would purchase thirteen buns, the baker's dozen), or the tiny fruit shop where someone with a spare penny could buy a bar of Fry's chocolate cream. Then, if the shore had modest cliffs, the perambulators had to be lifted, each one by two nannies, down a cleft to the beach, where the encampment for the morning had been selected by the senior nanny.

The bigger children were allowed to paddle, after a lengthy pre-liminary in which the girls' sleeves were rolled up to the elbows, their skirts pulled up and back and twisted into a bundle which was then stuffed into the seat of their serge knickers, their shoes and stockings taken off and their sand-shoes put on, their knicker legs rolled up as far as possible (they always fell down again), and awful warnings were issued against getting wet. Then at last they were turned loose on the sandy or shingly shore, with the sun glaring blindingly off the chalk cliffs or brightening the red ones or gleaming on the grey, and the water icy cold, to amuse themselves by digging in the wet sand and in-vestigating the rocks and the small rock pools, until the grown-ups came strolling down to the beach and the children were permitted to bathe. They changed inside the snug, salt-scented little bathing-machines, ventured bravely into the chill sea, while their mothers sat watch in hand counting the minutes and finally waving a handker-chief to signal that time was up.

Back in the bathing-machine came the thrill of feeling it move as it was winched up by wire ropes fastened to a capstan turned by a donkey. The immensely heavy blue serge bathing-dresses had to be laboriously wrung out, the little girls' hair was dried and brushed by the nannies, then the buns were joyfully devoured. After that perhaps some kind older person would take the children for a walk along the pier, or to watch the fishing-boats, or, if like Mrs Thirkell they were at Rottingdean, to look at the curious train that ran on rails laid on vast concrete blocks in the sea all the way from Brighton, sometimes stick-ing en route.

At last the nannies called all the children back and packed everything up and returned in procession to the various houses, where the wet bathing-dresses and towels were spread out to dry on sweet-smelling hedges and the children were all sensibly put to bed for a noonday nap.

Parents were usually remote and left Nanny to it. Sometimes one's mother came into the nursery for a few minutes in the morning to coo over her offspring and then rustle away again, and every afternoon when they were at home both parents would receive their children in the drawing-room for an hour after tea—children unnaturally clean, brushed, polite, the little girls frilled up, shepherded downstairs for a short time into the grown-up world. If the parents were loving and demonstrative the children would thaw out, begin to romp and show off; if any of the dogs had got into the drawing-room the children would flop down on the rug to hug and pat them. At the end of the hour Nanny would whisk the children away upstairs again, no doubt to the relief of some parents. Occasionally mother might come quickly into the night-nursery before setting out for a ball or a dinner party when the family was in town. Many men and women retain clearly in their memories the picture of a beautiful woman in evening dress and jewels sweeping across the room in a cloud of scent to say goodnight — "Funny little monkeys."

Sometimes both parents went away for weeks or months at a time, if father had the kind of interests that took him abroad or on a round of country house visits of social importance. But always there was Nanny — permanent, secure, pouring out her inexhaustible flow of monitory wisdom: it was rude to point, it would all end in tears, a bit should be left for Miss Manners, if you wanted any more you could have a plain piece of bread and butter, patience and perseverance brought the snail to Jerusalem, all joints on the table were to be carved (so take your elbows off at once), those who asked didn't get and those who didn't ask didn't want, somebody had got out of bed the wrong side, and it was high time to go up the wooden hill to Bedfordshire. For so many children, such a safe and comforting world; for the girls, a background often so loved that they kept up their confidences to Nanny throughout their teens, rejoicing in her approving statement that *that* would make a nice picture for the *Tatler*.

Not all girls had a happy childhood. Young Miss Ponsonby suffered through a miserable time on the whole, largely because Lady Ponsonby was always rather cold towards her daughter, so that Loelia found her natural shyness deepening into a frozen reserve that in the end took years to thaw. She noticed that all the parents she ever met seemed either chilly and severe, like her mother, or absurdly over-sentimental and emotional, dressing their little boys as girls and lovingly combing their long curls, having their daughters photographed in gauzy wisps, and expecting a hothouse atmosphere of sloppy demonstrativeness. No one seemed to strike the mean of the loving but sensible and bracing middle way. It never ceased to astonish Miss Ponsonby that she grew up to become the Duke of Westminster's third wife; his first marriage, to Shelagh Cornwallis-West, ended after the First World War, and his second, to Violet Nelson Rowley, ended in 1926. His country home was the enormous Eaton Hall in Cheshire, about which a guest once said, as he came in to breakfast, that it was a surprise to eat bacon and eggs in a cathedral. The Westminster fortune, drawn largely from wide tracts of land in Belgravia, was assessed at sixteen million pounds when the Duke died in 1953.

But all that was a long way off for the unhappy little girl in St James's Palace. Her happiest hours were spent with her brother exploring the roofs. These were reached by squeezing through an attic skylight, and then there were ups and downs with small iron ladders. A good game was to fill the bath sponges with water and drip them on to the sentries in the street below to persuade them into believing it was raining; complete success was gleefully achieved if the sentries retired inside their sentry-boxes. Of course, such a ploy could not go on for ever: a complaint to Sir Frederick put the roof out of bounds.

Another very eminent lady who looked back on her nursery and growing days with undisguised hatred was Dame Edith Sitwell. She was born in September 1887, two days after a most colossal row between her mother's parents, Lord and Lady Londesborough, had broken out in the bedroom where the beautiful eighteen-year-old Lady Ida Sitwell lay awaiting the birth of her first child. Lady Londesborough had just discovered that the splendid gifts of emeralds she had been receiving from Lord Londesborough were gestures of remorse following his periodic forays after musical comedy actresses, and the subsequent explosion was of vast proportions. But, Dame Edith quietly pointed out, she kept the emeralds.

Dame Edith's parents never understood what she felt and thought; they seemed not to be aware that she thought anything. Her father in particular could not forgive her for being a girl; her mother was troubled by her looks, that Plantagenet appearance inherited from the Londesboroughs that in later life gave Dame Edith some of her matchless distinction. In addition, Lady Ida resented the fact that after a few days of marriage to Sir George Sitwell she had run away to her parents, who promptly sent her back. Of course, it is not easy for a young, pretty and somewhat brainless woman to have a born poet for a daughter, especially when her own wish was, as she wistfully confided to that daughter years later, that she could get Sir George put into a lunatic asylum. The epitaph on Lady Ida uttered by Sir George's valet,

Henry Moat, was superb, as so many of his remarks were: he commented that at least Sir George would now know where Her Ladyship spent her afternoons.

At least Henry Moat was a friend to Dame Edith throughout his life. So was her old nurse, Davis. But much of her childhood was solitary — or, rather, spent in the company of animals and birds, who were beautiful, and who always seemed to understand. Her special pet at the Sitwells' Derbyshire house, Renishaw, was one of the peacocks, which waited for her in the garden every morning. They walked together, her arm round his neck. The peacock's crown made him taller than the little girl. Her other special pets included a puffin with a wooden leg that reminded her of an old sea-captain in some book by Dickens, and a baby owl that slept with its head on her shoulder and tried to attract mice by pretending to snore. She was on reasonably friendly, though not truly intimate, terms with the two little daughters of Colonel Hume (the original of *Old Sir Faulk*). When they were all about five years old Mrs Hume died, and Dame Edith could not understand why the little Hume girls were crying.

Dame Edith mentions going to tea with other little girls, but never refers to children's parties. This is not surprising: such a phenomenon was almost unknown. The party that brought Loelia Ponsonby so much trouble was an exception. The daughters of the Earl and Countess of Abingdon, Lady Betty and Lady Gwendoline Bertie, who were brought up in Oxfordshire (Lady Gwendoline, indeed, grew up to marry Jack Churchill, brother of Winston), knew a neighbouring family named, perhaps fittingly, Brassey, who actually gave a children's party every year. This caused scandalized clucks in every nursery for miles around. The Brasseys' parties were organized according to age-groups, with the youngest children invited from three in the afternoon to six, the older children from six to eight, and the ones in their teens from eight to ten. For seven mortal hours a stream of carriages, pony-traps and motors fetched and carried, dropped and picked up, and inside the house there was lemonade, there were cakes, there were balloons. The Bertie girls were never allowed to go and never quite recovered from their disappointment. They begged and pleaded every year in vain: the Countess said that all the excitement would be bad for them, and that settled the matter. It quite probably would have been. On the other hand a lifelong regret is unfortunate also.

The idea of entertaining for the young virtually did not exist. "Showing off" was bad for young people. (Is that why their elders, and they in turn, so much enjoyed showing off for the rest of their lives? And is it a twisted kind of reflex of this attitude that made Lady Ida Sitwell say, in an odd piece of advice to her children, three future writers: "Never put pen to paper"?) Daughters were permitted, nay encouraged, to train horses, but strictly forbidden to show them: this was competitive and vulgar. It was part of the general principle that indulgence spoiled children. It was also part of the superb assurance of the late Victorians and Edwardians: if one is assured enough there is no need to compete.

If there were no parties, there were plenty of visits. Going to the houses of friends and relations was a regular thing, carrying with it impressions of rooms crowded with furniture, flowers, and people, of sometimes actually having tea in the drawing-room (Mrs Cubitt recalls one aunt's house where the children had tea at a tiny table with everything to scale), or of having nursery tea which might or might not be nice according to what the other children and nannies were like. Other people's houses were always fascinating: Mrs Cubitt knew one where, if you went to the lavatory, the door was so situated that if you opened it without thinking you fell down the stairs, and one where she heard her aunt summon a maid by blowing into a speaking-tube.

These were, of course, afternoon visits, but children went to stay with relations whose houses were invariably a source of interest. Again the children simply fitted in, they were regarded rather like the luggage — room was found for them, but no special arrangements were made for their entertainment. It was the grown-ups who had the big parties: children lived their nursery life interspersed with visits to the drawing-room just as they did for the rest of the year.

Some of the nicest visits were to grandparents, who usually lived in agreeable places and who were often eminent people. Because Mrs Thirkell's grandfather was Edward Burne-Jones, the inside of his home at Rottingdean, North End House, the walls of which were all whitewashed, contained many murals painted by him, some of them purely to amuse his grandchildren. One afternoon he came up to the nursery and found his granddaughter in the corner, having been put there to repent of some sin in accordance with the usual rule laid down by Nanny. The next day he brought his paints up and decorated the corner with a cat and kittens and a flight of birds to keep his granddaughter company (it is clear that he was sure of her being put there again). He had already painted an angle on the wall at the foot of her bed and a water-mill with its mill-pool on the sloping attic wall, facing another mural of a peacock in a tree.

North End House was one of those furnished almost entirely in the Pre-Raphaelite style, as were the houses of many of the Burne-Joneses' friends. Mrs Thirkell recalls it as acutely uncomfortable. It was not, she said, that the Pre-Raphaelites despised comfort as that the concept of comfort conveyed nothing to the brotherhood as a whole. The characteristic sofa, for example, was a hard flat low table with a little wooden balustrade round two or three sides, the table part covered with iron-hard squabs upholstered in chintz or linen, with perhaps a small concrete-like bolster or one or two thin stiff cushions. The beds had wooden slats running lengthwise. Sometimes one would find an overstuffed and therefore very hard sofa, short in length, covered in velvet so thick that it clung to one's clothes. Sometimes the lighter pieces of furniture, like towel-horses, were designed so aesthetically that they fell over at a touch, and sometimes perfectly good sash windows had been removed and replaced by others that slid sideways and constantly stuck in the grooves.

The dressing-room at North End House was always known as The Bower. There was nearly always a bower in an aesthetically planned house of the period. Sometimes it was the principal lady's bedroom. The true Pre-Raphaelite followed as keenly as money allowed the neo-medieval ideas put forward by William Morris, calling the living-room The Hall and filling the smallish windows with tinted glass to keep reality out. Beams and walls and chimney-pieces were often decorated with mottoes worked in a rounded, vaguely Celtic style. One architect ironically remarked that these ought to be rather illegible and it helped if the words were in a foreign language, and some Edwardian children had quite a time puzzling over something carved over the fire that apparently read "oost woost hooms boost". The general effect seemed to aim at a special type of poverty, all too often called quaint by its less experienced practitioners, featuring light waxed natural woods, wool or cotton rather than silk, bright colours against white or Morris-papered walls, and a general hand-made look. In contrast with the dark shining surfaces, heavy gilding, rich-looking upholstery, furniture deriving from Tudor, Jacobean, or Queen Anne models, and general air of over-stuffed satiety of the late Victorian house, it was certainly startling.

Visits to Dame Edith Sitwell's grandmothers provided a few gleams of ironic humour to relieve the cold loneliness of her early life. Her grandmother Sitwell collected curates, who were, on the whole, apparently of the same type as the ineffable Mr Slope, along with a suffragan bishop, with whom she would drive in her carriage round Scarborough, searching for disreputable young women. These were captured and shoved into the Home, run by a deaconess called Sister Edith who, Dame Edith said, reminded her of a station poster advertising tomatoes. In The Home the young women were forcibly bathed and then expiated their sinful disreputability by maltreating the Sitwell family washing. One young inmate of The Home proved particularly recalcitrant, refusing to have a bath on arrival and generally behaving in a defiant way that annoyed the deaconess very much, but in due time it was clear that every one of the other inmates was pregnant, and that the problem one was really a young man in disguise who detested the suffragan bishop and had worked out this method of making his opinion plain.

Both grandmothers had hair trouble. Grandmother Sitwell owned two coils of false hair, frequently kept in the back pocket of her maid, Leckly. Leckly often forgot they were there, and would go out shopping with the hair still in the pocket. Sometimes the long curls would start to escape, making the unfortunate Leckly look as if she had a tail.

Embarrassing though this was, the contretemps of Grandmother Londesborough was far worse. One day at the beginning of November she appeared abruptly at the breakfast table wearing a white wig. Her family and servants, long trained to affect complete unawareness of any quirk in the Countess's looks or manner, gave no sign of surprise. After breakfast, as usual, the Countess was wheeled out in her bath-chair by one of the footmen, and, accompanied by several of her daughters, taken to a favourite spot, at the entrance to the gardens of Londesborough Lodge. Here, habitually, she sat, watching the road. A very small clergyman with a wife and brood of children came by, observed the motionless white-wigged apparition in the bath-chair, the daughters in attendance, and the silent footman, and walked up to the group, saying cheerfully, as he dropped a penny in Lady Londesborough's lap: "Remember, remember the fifth of November."

Dame Edith does not know precisely what happened after that, except that her grandmother, after a long pause, recovered her voice sufficiently to demand the butler, and to order him to round up a pose of all the footmen and gardeners to chase the clergyman and his family away. (They had walked innocently on into the Lodge gardens, which, of course, were private.) Implicit in Dame Edith's account of this magnificent incident is the feeling, never put into words, that she wished she *had* known what happened.

Young Miss Ponsonby had happier recollections of her grandmother. She recalls sitting on her grandmother's bed and cutting out coloured pictures from magazines with her grandmother's gold nail-scissors. This was especially delightful because if one of the horrid nursery-governesses opened the door and told Loelia to come at once, "Granny" sent her packing without hesitation, and it was a rare joy for Loelia to see one of her tormentors sharply dismissed.

Ladies who came to tea with her grandmother or with her mother provide one of the clearest of little Miss Ponsonby's scenes from childhood: the ladies at tea in the garden. They wear big hats, pretty dresses, and gloves, they hold parasols, they sit in basket-chairs with cushions

covered in jap silk, grouped round a table. The table has a white
embroidered cloth on it, and a silver tea-tray loaded with silver tea-
things that include a strange object like a hunting-horn, which extin-
guishes the flame under the kettle. Flowered china plates hold thin
bread-and-butter, cucumber sandwiches, hot scones, seed-cake and
sugar-cakes and home-made biscuits, and there is iced coffee as well as
tea to drink. The ladies lean forward so that their hats cluster together
like a huge bouquet above the table as the gossip becomes more exciting.
The sun shines, there seem to be no midges, hardly even a wasp.

Considering the upbringing of children in the Edwardian period, the
researcher cannot fail to be struck by the pinch-penny attitude towards them as compared with the extravagance and luxury of their
parents. Over-lavish treatment of children is still the mark of the
parvenu among the reduced ranks of the "real" aristocracy. Some
critics have suggested that this is a selfpreserving cover for the fact that
many parvenus are much richer than most old-established grandees.
But there is no denying that the little Edwardian lady had no regular
pocket-money, or, if she had, it was a matter of a few pence, most of
them earmarked, and just because a toy was dropping to pieces was no
reason for buying a new one. Much was made of small treats. The
notion of buying an expensive present for a child to give anyone else
was unheard of. Nannies made sure that some lopsided little drawing,
smudgy painting, or wavering bit of needlework greeted a parent's
birthday; and "unsuitable" (that is, too elaborate, or too grown-up)
presents were firmly removed, with no possibility of argument, from
the child's grasp at once.

Mrs Cubitt remembered the joy of the Christmas shopping walk
along Oxford Street, and one occasion in particular, when she gazed
longingly into a shop window at a beautiful baby doll. A dirty, ragged
little girl of about Mrs Cubitt's age was standing beside her, similarly
riveted. Mrs Keppel made sure which doll it was, went into the shop,
bought the doll, brought it out, put it into the dirty little girl's arms,
smiled, and told her to call the doll Alice. The little girl gasped, clutched,
and darted away. Alice Keppel smiled down at her furious daughter
and calmly remarked that she thought the other little girl needed the
doll more than Sonia did.

But sometimes there was a real financial treat. Mrs Cubitt recalled
going with her mother to the Westminster Bank near Albert Gate,
where Mrs Keppel would be bowed in by the manager in person and
invited into his private office. Sitting down, Mrs Keppel would lay her
umbrella or parasol on the table, raise her veil, take a gold sovereign
out of her purse, and ask if it would be a very great trouble to change
the sovereign into threepenny bits for Sonia. The manager would

allow the little girl to watch the cashier as he counted out eighty threepenny bits (in those days, of course, small silver coins) into a pink canvas bag.

Even the King knew better than to be lavish with money when he was anywhere near children. Mrs Cubitt was not very big before she realized that one person whom she was sure to meet in various houses, including her own, was the King. Nanny had told her always to curtsey to the King, but at first she was too shy to look right up at the face of a portly gentleman, so if she saw a ringed hand holding a cigar, and obtained an impression of a beard somewhere above, she curtseyed. It was not always the King, but Sir Ernest Cassel seemed not to mind.

Later the shyness evaporated, and she learnt to refer to Edward VII as "Kingy". When he came to tea she played a game with him that, remembering his immense reputation for always being perfectly turned out, astonishes the modern reader. He would stretch out one leg on which she would place two bits of bread-and-butter, butter side down. He would bet a penny on one, she a penny on the other, as to which would reach the bottom of the trouser-leg first. The secret was plenty of butter. It is interesting to know that she never dared to play this game with Sir Ernest Cassel.

Sometimes, by accident or design, a child would run away from home. Dame Edith Sitwell did this, deliberately, when she was five. She was, however, hampered by having no money, and by being unable to fasten her buttoned boots, so a kindly young policeman quickly rescued her and took her home. Mrs Cubitt, considerably younger, once walked out inadvertently. One day she toddled out into Portman Square and climbed up on the water-cart which was spraying the roadway. She stayed in her precarious place, getting steadily wetter, while the water-cart crossed the square. When it halted a policeman saw her, lifted her down, set her on her feet, and asked her name. She could only reply: "Baby". He noticed her tiny gold bangle with its pendant S in diamonds and took her in his arms to the Marylebone Lane Police Station. When her father arrived to collect her an hour later he found her having a marvellous time — sitting on the table in the charge-room wrapped in a blanket being fed with bread and jam and hot milk by two policemen, who had washed her face and dried her hair and hung her wet pinafore to dry in front of the stove. Another policeman had lent her his whistle, on which she was blowing shrill and crumby blasts. Back safely at the house in Portman Square, the order was reinforced that the nursery gate must be kept shut and baby kept in.

Mrs Cubitt never attempted to run away again, but Dame Edith did, successfully. Her childhood recollections have a nightmare quality: her education was planned on, one supposes, the orthodox lines of the time,

presumably very suitable for young ladies who were going to marry and
move in fashionable society, but distasteful in the extreme to a sensitive
poet and writer to whom her parents' friends appeared to resemble
either unpleasant vegetation or cheap dolls, to whom the process of
(as she saw it) grinding her down so that she would become like everybody else was agonizing.

Neither the middle-class grinding of the governess nor the upper
class grinding of her family ever mastered her; but she suffered a great
deal for all that, finding her freedom only when she was old enough to
leave home without the risk of being brought back by a policeman, and
making it clear to her scandalized parents that she would prefer to live
on twenty-five shillings a week in Chelsea, working in the Pensions
Office, and renting a small flat in Bayswater, rather than continue to
exist at either of her parents' houses, Renishaw and Wood End, Scarborough. So precisely did she see her freedom at this time (at the
beginning of the First World War), that she described herself uncompromisingly as a ticket-of-leave woman.

By now, of course, the worst of her loneliness was long since over.
When she was five her brother, now Sir Osbert Sitwell, was born, and a
few years later her other brother, Mr Sacheverell Sitwell, completed
what was to beome a formidable, and utterly devoted, literary trio.
But those long early years had left their scars, the years of confiding
in the peacock, the puffin and the owl, of reading voraciously, mostly
fairly tales, which frightened her sometimes, particularly those of Hans
Andersen, because of their pervading cold and loneliness, echoing her
own.

If Dame Edith is the rule-proving exception, it is because there are
few great poets. Yet it is interesting, if sad, to find that all three Sitwells,
as children, were unable to make friends with any of their immediate
blood-relations. On the other hand, the long-established family servants were genuine lifelong friends. Perhaps the Sitwells would not
have been the writers they were, had matters stood otherwise. And no
one can blame them who reads, for example, the comment of Mr Henry
Moat who, when told by Dame Edith some facts about religious fan-
atics, suggested that she should look at the stars, and then, with a
deep sigh, said simply: "Well, Miss, if it's all the same to you, I think
I'll stick to the bacon and eggs."

Most of the little Edwardian girls, not being poetic, were able to look
back more cheerfully. They saw straw laid in the street outside great
town houses to deaden the sound of traffic when someone lay ill inside
or was having a baby; they saw the great rooms filled with flowers,
orchids, malmaisons, lilies, in drifts of delicious scent; they were photographed in the traditional way at the age of six months, naked and

sitting on straw; they learnt to know the smell of their fathers' hair-oil and cigars; they loved going downstairs in the morning to their parents' rooms. Mamma, breakfasting in bed, might let a small girl play with the beautiful jewels she had worn the night before; papa might permit her to watch him curl his moustaches with special tiny tongs, or sit with him while he polished off an enormous breakfast, letting her crack his eggshells with a knife and spread jam or marmalade on his toast.

They resented a prettier sister: when Mrs Cubitt was born her parents already had one daughter, Violet, a charmingly pretty child of six. Mrs Cubitt says, in defiance of her delightful photographs, that she was the plain one, born with a fuzz of hair resembling strawberry jam, and the naughty one, who would not stay where she was put. As a child she had to wear a mouthful of braces to correct the splay of her teeth.

It was several years later that Sir Osbert Sitwell came to know the Keppel girls, and he was much impressed by them. Violet, he says, had an exotic, cosmopolitan personality, and was an excellent mimic in her low-pitched speaking voice. Sonia, still in the schoolroom, with her long golden hair hanging down her back, and tall for her age, expressed decided opinions in a charming, caressing voice. Both girls had exquisite manners.

Mrs Cubitt opens her memoirs of childhood by saying that her mother always told her that she celebrated the relief of Mafeking sitting astride one of the Trafalgar Square lions, two weeks before Sonia was born. She explains that her parents were not wealthy. George Keppel was one of ten children and Alice Keppel one of nine, but they moved in the most admired circles in the land, and were related to, or friendly with, people securely placed in aristocratic spheres. They had a butler, a cook-housekeeper, three female servants and a boot-boy, as well as the nanny, the nursery-maid and (later) the French governess. Nine people not, as Shaw pointed out, to wait on four, but to look after thirteen. The Keppels were strikingly handsome: Mr Keppel was six feet four inches tall, well built, with blue eyes, black hair, and a splendid moustache; Mrs Keppel had a mass of chestnut hair and a lovely face with turquoise blue eyes. Sir Osbert Sitwell found her memorable. He comments on her frank good nature, free from any trace of pettiness, her humour, her insight, her vivid way of expressing herself. He liked to persuade her away from the bridge-table, not an easy thing to do, so that he could enjoy her conversation. While she talked, she smoked cigarettes in a long holder.

The house in Portman Square was tall and narrow, each floor distinct in atmosphere and function. By the time Sir Osbert met the Keppels, they had moved to an impressive house in Grosvenor Street, whose lofty façade concealed the full size of the building. Inside was an air of splendour, luxury, light and space. The grey walls, thick carpets, eighteenth century English portraits, red lacquer cabinets and enormous porcelain pagodas demonstrated Mrs Keppel's ability to run her house like a work of art.

While the Keppels were still living in Portman Square "Kingy" died, shortly before Mrs Cubitt's tenth birthday. The atmosphere of anxiety and shock, percolating through the household, terrified Sonia, principally because nothing was explained: her parents suddenly became remote and serious, then abruptly left the house without a word; Nanny and "Moiselle" evaded questions; then the Keppel daughters were taken round to the house of Mrs Arthur Jones in Grafton Street, where they found all the blinds drawn and black clothes set out. The girls were told that Mrs Keppel was in bed and must not be disturbed; somehow Sonia found her father, and on his always consoling shirt-front burst into tears, confiding to him all her terrors. Her father comforted her tenderly and then said that it was true, that nothing would ever be quite the same again, because "Kingy" had been such a wonderful man.

Mrs Keppel had been sent for to the Palace. When she knew that her husband was dying, Queen Alexandra sent, in warmly friendly terms, for Alice Keppel — a gesture of revealing thoughtfulness. All his life the King had liked to be surrounded by pretty women: when Alix's father died and court mourning prohibited the usual lady guests at the Ascot house-party in 1906, the King remarked: "What tiresome evenings we shall have!" Now, in 1910, she did not let him die without his latest favourite pretty woman beside him. She did not allow his death to interfere with beloved Ascot: the consequence was the famous "Black Ascot" with all the ladies dressed in beautiful new confections — but every one of them black.

One point that strikes the present-day reader about the upbringing of Edwardian children, at any rate of the children in high places, is their utter seclusion inside the circle of their families. So seldom did they see anything of the world in general. Glimpses might show to them from the windows of a carriage or a motor; or on the way to the zoo with Nanny; or at the railway station; or on a shopping expedition. But only glimpses. On 25 February 1901 *The Times* carried a small-print advertisement announcing:

CRYSTAL PALACE.
GREAT ASSOCIATION FOOTBALL TO-DAY.
NORTH v SOUTH (Amateurs and Professionals) Kick off 3.30.
Seats 1s., 2s. 6d., and 5s.
Café Chantant: Twice daily at 4.0 and 8.0.

Bay of Naples, Lilliputian Theatre, Natural Colour Photography,
Bicycle Polo, Roller Skating, &c., Daily.
FANCY DRESS SKATING CARNIVAL, THURSDAY
NEXT, 8 p.m.

For the little Edwardian lady, this advertisement, and others like it,
were compiled in vain.

CHAPTER THREE

To Market, To Market

There is nothing more wounding to our sense of human dignity than the husband hunting that begins in every family when the daughters become marriageable; but it is inevitable under existing circumstances; and the parents who refuse to engage in it are bad parents, though they may be superior individuals. The cubs of a humane tigress would starve.
Bernard Shaw (1908)

The world of the Edwardian lady centred to a surprising degree around horses. It began with the great moment, the long looked-for arrival, the first pony of one's very own, an experience common to boys and girls alike. When the pony appeared, plump and sleek with its tail touching the ground, then began the series of lessons in charge of the groom. The whole idea was aimed at the eventual competent management of a horse in the hunting field or in the Row, and gradually the daily sessions would expand to include the first canter, the first tiny jumps. Very quickly the little girl would learn that, if she let go of the reins and the pony refused to be caught, there followed the humiliation of seeing the pony trot away towards the stable leaving the child to trudge back, hot and cross, to find that the groom had captured and stabled the pony. The groom would make no comment, thereby providing in addition a lesson in good manners.

This horse-centred society produced quaint inconsistencies in what was permitted and what was not. If a young girl wished to hunt with a different pack she was allowed to travel by train, so one of the grooms would go with her to the station and see her installed in the horse-box, where she could pass the journey with everyone's approval, but she was absolutely forbidden to go into a railway compartment. It seemed odd to many girls that they might be out alone in the dark with a horse but for a morning walk to visit a girl friend they must have a maid or footman in attendance.

Throughout the years of youth this horsy existence went on all the time in the big country houses, interrupted only by visits to London, as far as the daughters of the house were concerned. The sons, of course, departed to boarding-school at (usually) the age of eight, returning disruptingly for the holidays over the next ten years and emerging at eighteen with a relaxed, assured manner that effortlessly proclaimed their twin beliefs: that they were natural leaders of men, and that their code of honour was all-important. They left their sisters to the routine of the schoolroom, that part of the house set aside for lessons under the tutelage of a governess.

Perhaps the most unfortunate of all women other than the destitute in this period were the governesses. Neither fish, flesh, fowl, nor good red herring, they led lonely lives in these huge households, unable to mix with the family on the one hand, too superior to mix with the servants on the other, and often despised by the nanny as the woman skilled in baby care all too often despises the woman who lacks that experience even to this day.

Nanny was a permanent fixture compared with the governess, it was implicitly realized that the fear of doing something that Nanny would think shabby restrained both gentlemen and ladies all their lives, and it was much easier to behave badly to the governess than to anyone else. The governess of fiction is almost always a sad character: Ruth Pinch in *Martin Chuzzlewit* is having a wretched time. Visited condescendingly by the Pecksniffs, covertly sneered at by the footman ("Missis's compliments to Miss Pinch, and begs to know wot my young lady is a learning of just now"), sneaked on by her horrid little charge to her critical employers ("for the lady of the establishment was curious in the natural history and habits of the animal called Governess, and encouraged her daughters to report thereon"), yet she could still speak with cheerfulness: "You will be able to tell him how more than comfortably I am situated here, and how unnecessary it is that he should ever waste a regret on my being cast upon my own resources."

Perhaps the most famous of all governesses in English literature is Jane Eyre, and she is entirely untypical, the heroine of possibly the most blazingly romantic tale ever written: but she is treated atrociously by the female guests at Thornfield, and her romance would have been impossible had she been in a house with a lady in charge of the supervision of a daughter and the entertainment of a husband.

These, to be sure, are Victorian examples. But the Edwardian governess still occupies a solitary, awkward position in the confident society of that time. This holds good even when there was more than one governess in a house, when the poor creature, handicapped by gentility added to poverty, was reinforced by the mademoiselle or the fräulein, or even both, when the time came for the daughters to learn French or German.

More often than not the little girls knew how to read and write before the governess came. They might have had a nursery governess for this purpose, or the nanny might have taught them. The school-room in a big house was a somewhat bleak apartment, containing a large table, several upright chairs, a few pictures of an uncompromis-ingly moralistic nature and unexciting technique, a few bookshelves and possibly a cupboard, and perhaps, though not often, a blackboard. Here for seven or eight years the future great ladies of England would spend several hours a day, yawning and fidgeting and longing to get out to the horses, or back into the warm cosy nursery, or downstairs where there was always something going on. What they were taught was hardly exacting. Most parents were not interested in girls' education, or strongly opposed to the whole idea. To produce a bluestocking would be dreadful. Nothing could possibly be more calculated to put off eligible young men.

Women's education was just beginning to break through the pre-judice of centuries with the foundation of a few schools, since then growing into places of glittering eminence. Miss Dorothea Beale at Cheltenham Ladies' College, Miss Frances Mary Buss with her double foundation of the North London Collegiate and Camden School, were the pioneers who had grasped the truths that, as Mrs Pandit later said, if you educated a boy you educate a man but if you educate a girl you educate a family, and that it would not be at all a bad thing to equip girls to earn their own living in the professions, seeing the way the world was undoubtedly going.

But to the people who led society, these were awful middle-class establishments in which girls were taught nothing of the slightest use and a great deal that was positively harmful — habits of manners and speech that sapped their essential femininity. Miss Buss struggled for years against parental prejudice when it came to gymnastics and games (evidently no one knew about the Princess of Wales's cartwheels), and the few boarding-schools for girls that did exist, the great Roedean among them, often produced a somewhat hothouse atmosphere. The girls for the most part had two ambitions when the time came for them to leave: to go back as soon as possible in order to knock everyone's eye out with the dazzling spectacle of their grown-up clothes, and to get engaged before anyone else.

By the beginning of the century, most girls' schools had Classics, mathematics and science on their list of subjects, as well as some games. But often these were treated as rather smudgy carbon copies of boys' learning, so that most girls played cricket if they played any summer games at all. Often there was a contempt for domestic subjects. A really clever girl had to fight every inch of the way to reach a university, and her life there was not much fun either, as witness one of the most depressing portraits in literature, the character of Miss Heydinger in *Love and Mr Lewisham*.

It comes as a surprise to find that in 1901 there were 212 women doctors and 140 women dentists in England (in that year eighteen out of every hundred office clerks were women, a figure that would almost double in the next ten years). Schools like the boarding-schools founded by the Religious Society of Friends, which were co-educational right from the start in most cases, made decided breaks in the conventional pattern. But it cannot be overemphasized that all these educational establishments for girls were hopelessly middle-class in the eyes of the Edwardian lady and her daughters.

What was acceptable, and what the governesses were employed to teach, was a knowledge of some of the English classic works, a little history, some French or German or possibly both, and the accomplishments of playing the piano, singing a little if the voice was at all musical, and painting in water-colours. Good speech was essential. Girls were trained to keep their voices low and never to raise them in excitement, and to laugh in such a way that the ear was not offended. Queen Mary once said that she always tried never to laugh out loud because she had such a vulgar (that is, hearty) laugh. The result of all this training was, for most ladies, a clear soft silvery tone that lasted unimpaired through a long life: a lady was known by (among other things) the charm of her speaking voice. Certain words were often pronounced in a manner that has now almost died out: "blooze" for "blouse", "lahndry" for "laundry" and "lahnch" for "launch" were usual, and ladies with a liking for country as opposed to town life dropped the final g as their brothers did, saying "ridin', huntin', doin'." These are now collectors' items in speech, though the diligent researcher may still find some elderly lady who unselfconsciously uses them.

Most girls, if they thought about it at all, seem to have felt vaguely that what they were taught by the governesses was reasonably adequate, but here and there an exception appeared, like a young Scottish lady who actually took a course in laundry. Her patrician family, utterly bewildered, wondered why any one should do anything so odd, so unnecessary: one could always get someone in to do that, why bother to learn it oneself? Queen Mary, while still the unmarried Princess May of Teck, attended courses in Elizabethan literature and social hygiene in 1891, and was already deeply committed to one of her life-interests, the London Needlework Guild.

It was characteristic of the period that the elderly and the middle-aged, in all ranks of society, freely handed out masses of advice to the young, all of it based on the firm belief that everything was going to go unchanged for ever. In the world of the lady, life was full of terrifying dowagers resembling, in the young girls' recollections, Lady Catherine de Bourgh and Lady Bracknell. These old ladies had, it was said, been beautiful and often scandalous in their own youth, but had now settled for being tough and — a popular word of the day to describe them — "alarming". Expensively dressed in styles that the young thought ugly and unbecoming, they stared implacably through their deadly lorgnettes and united in creating one indispensable element of highly organized family life, the family bugbear. "Whatever would Cousin Mary (or Aunt Margaret or Great-Aunt Augusta) say if she knew?" put the brake effectively on high spirits. The girls moved, all too often, through an air of frosty disapproval.

It touched so many aspects of life. Every big house had its library, so a girl who enjoyed reading could find plenty of books. These stood ranked in their rows of calf binding, often neglected and badly arranged unless the house happened to be grand enough for the master to employ a librarian. The musty volumes were often out of date, and some sets were incomplete. Always, or nearly always, there was somebody to say that certain books were "unsuitable" for young ladies to read. Curious taboos existed. Most French books were banned except for a few harmless examples, Daudet's *Lettres du Mon Moulin* or Halévy's *Mon Oncle et Mon Curé*, a really splendid specimen like the elder Dumas whose *Count of Monte Cristo* and *The Three Musketeers* no one could ban (though naturally the elders forbade the younger Dumas with his deplorable *Dame aux Caméllias*), and Stendhal, for the peculiar reason that he was so difficult any way that the impropriety of his work would pass unnoticed. Balzac, Flaubert and de Maupassant were for married women only, and, as for Zola, he was not mentioned even by them.

Girls might, and did, read such English works as *The Mill on the Floss* or *Silas Marner*, but not *Adam Bede*. They were permitted various rather stuffy biographies, for the age of the debunker was not yet, and historical novels, in which they revelled — Stanley Weyman, H. Seton Merriman, Maurice Hewlett, Captain Brereton. Most of these were relished by young Miss Susan Grosvenor, though her future husband, John Buchan, considered the style of Hewlett "superheated".

Miss Grosvenor also devoured everything she could find by a very mixed bag of writers including G. K. Chesterton, Andrew Lang, A. C. Benson, Anthony Hope, and Somerville and Ross. She said that there was a great family discussion as to whether she should be permitted to read Elinor Glyn's *The Visits of Elizabeth*. The verdict she does not

TO MARKET, TO MARKET

reveal, but she seems to have read the book any way. According to her, the genuine atmosphere of Edwardian England can be recaptured in such contemporary books as *Elizabeth and her German Garden* by Elizabeth von Arnim, Countess Russell; *The Waif's Progress* by Rhoda Broughton, *Red Pottage* by Mary Cholmondeley, and, rather surprisingly in that company, *The New Machiavelli* by H. G. Wells.

Susan Grosvenor's father was Norman, third son of Lord Robert Grosvenor, later Lord Ebury; her mother was Caroline Stuart Wortley, daughter of the Recorder of London. Both families owned land in London, Cheshire, and Yorkshire. Susan's grandparents lived at Moor Park in Hertfordshire, where Susan and her parents lived for much of her childhood. She remembered the beautiful surroundings which include a pleasure ground (now built over), where there were five camellia trees in a wood. Caroline Grosvenor did not much like living among a crowd of in-laws in someone else's house, and took refuge in painting water-colours. Norman Grosvenor worked for the Sun Life Insurance Company, and composed music in his spare time. An uncle, the second Lord Ebury, was the first chairman of the Army and Navy Stores, most lavishly provisioned of shops. The grandmother, Charlotte, was the niece of the Duke of Wellington, no less, and was believed to be a tremendous rebel, declaring herself both agnostic and Liberal; Caroline was Conservative, and detested Gladstone, an odd fact as she was part Scotch and distantly related to the People's William.

Eventually the Grosvenors settled more or less full-time in London, living in a house in Green Street (then Upper Grosvenor Street) on the site of the present-day Grosvenor House Hotel. The Green Street house had a completely pre-Raphaelite drawing-room with Morris willow-pattern wallpaper, chintzes, and de Morgan plates round the walls. When Norman Grosvenor died at just over fifty, his widow was drawn into the more conventional and worldly orbit of the rest of the family. Susan remembered how her sister wrote to say that she expected the Boer War would ruin the London Season.

At least reading was possible. An early opinion poll to name the greatest living novelist was carried out in 1914 and put Hardy first, Wells next, and Conrad third: a fair enough choice. Miss Grosvenor cherished a passion for a book called *Fragment d'un Journal Intime* by Henri Frédéric Amiel, whose gentle Swiss melancholy exactly suited her youthful taste. (In the same period Dame Edith Sitwell sat up in bed for hours, poring lovingly over Pope's *Rape of the Lock* with a sense of ever-deepening joy and enchantment.) Miss Grosvenor's mother told her that she could scarcely expect to amount to much in the world if she sat rapt in Amiel to the exclusion of real life. Miss Grosvenor went on dwelling upon Amiel and reading Pascal and Goethe as well, and grew up to receive years later honorary degrees from the universities of McGill and Toronto.

There were several literary quirks in the Grosvenor family, including that of Aunt Mary's husband, Ralph Lovelace, a godson of Byron. Far from relishing the connexion with one of England's most eminent poets, Ralph Lovelace positively detested him, so much so that the young Susan was warned never to mention Byron at meals. This was less of a hazard than it might have been because Mary Lovelace kept little green parrots that walked about under the dining-table pecking people's ankles. When Miss Grosvenor jumped and squeaked her aunt stated coldly that she did not like cowardice about parrots, which would seem to settle the matter. In addition to hating Byron, the Lovelaces disliked the Prince of Wales, and, if they happened to be at Marienbad when he was staying there, attempted to avoid him by dodging behind skinny little trees. As the Lovelaces were stoutly built, the vision conjured up by this reduced Miss Grosvenor to ill-suppressed giggles. Mary Lovelace also advised her niece never to wear green in the country.

But on the whole the Edwardian lady, whatever her age, was not bookish. The comparative dreariness of the schoolroom routine encouraged her to look forward, with increasing longing, to the day when she would escape from it for ever. The rest of the house seemed exciting in comparison: life was bustling away in the kitchens, the stables, the servants' hall, thrilling and pulsating through the drawing-rooms; even the meals were more fun elsewhere. In the schoolroom, afternoon tea appeared at five, consisting of plenty of milk to drink, bread with butter *or* jam but seldom if ever both, and one slice of cake each. Not even Nanny was there to remind one to say one's grace and to speak up, don't mumble, remember you're talking to God.

In sharp contrast to the enormous meals downstairs, this Spartan tea was the last meal of the day for the girls, unless they could contrive to creep out on to the stairs leading down to the servants' hall and cadge something later from a kindly-disposed maid or footman. This was frequently successful, but could never be absolutely depended upon. The governess subsequently received a solitary tray later still, rather grudgingly brought up by an under-servant who thought that waiting on the governess was beneath his or her dignity, and containing a selection from the immense delicious dinner served in full fig in the dining-room below.

When the family removed from the country to Town for the season, the whole working apparatus of the house went too. The carriages in the care of the second coachman, the horses in the care of the first, the riding-horses with the head groom, two other grooms, and a mountain of luggage; the butler with several chosen footmen, the housekeeper with several chosen maids; the nanny with the smaller children; the governess with the older girls. The reduced staff left behind put the furniture in the drawing-rooms under holland covers, took the chandeliers to pieces and washed the crystal in warm soapy water, rolled up the carpets and polished the floors, knowing that they had plenty of time in which to clean the whole house from top to bottom before the family returned. The agent was able to make a thorough inspection of the estate; the gardeners could cherish their flower-beds and greenhouses in happy freedom from the daily demand for cut flowers.

In the London house the nursery and schoolroom routines effortlessly re-established themselves: the children lived their upstairs lives, the girls doing the same lessons as before. The main differences were that walks were more exciting in the London streets and parks than in the huge peaceful grounds of the country estate, and that there were more guests, much more varied, to glimpse from the top of the stairs as dinner-time approached than there had been in the country.

There were, of course, finishing schools, mostly abroad — France, Germany, and Switzerland were the favoured countries — where the girls in their teens spent a year or two learning fluent French or German and a certain amount of social poise; and there were a few — a very few — small London schools in Mayfair and Belgravia to which a number of carefully selected girls might go. They went, as a rule, for three hours every morning, to sit at long tables in elegant rooms that had been built in the eighteenth century. The girls were all mixed up together regardless of age, and the mistress in charge would start every morning by introducing the topic for the day, speaking from notes. She then walked round the room pulling books off the shelves and suggesting where each girl should start reading up her topic. The morning sessions ended with a general discussion. The girls were taught to focus their thoughts quickly on a subject, to find those parts of it that were entertaining, to be articulate, to hold opinions and yet be able to express them in a civilized way, and to read good books, well written. By contemporary European standards these girls were only half educated — nearly all their topics were drawn from history or literature — yet some of them became some of the most influential women in the world later on.

There were long periods of boredom while the girls sat around at home and waited, daydreaming, playing word games or card games, and kept on guessing the time: three o'clock? better — three-thirty? not so good — three-fifteen? wishing the time away, as athletes wait for the summons to the track, or footballers for the signal that sends them out into the roar of the stadium, or actors for the call-boy's word.

These comparisons are valid. Sportsmen and actors alike practise, train and wait for what matters most: the action. The young girls did not practise in the same sense — indeed, they were mostly inexperienced to a ludicrous degree — but they had thought and dreamed and imagined and listened and waited, all for the same thing: the signal for action.

Unsympathetic, or possibly deeply sympathetic, observers referred to the action as the marriage market.

For that is exactly what it was. At the age of eighteen, each girl put her hair up, which might be described as coming under starter's orders. Perhaps it is useful to have some visible signal that says unmistakably that a young woman is open to offers. The Edwardians certainly thought so. No man so much as bothered to address himself with other than the merest passing courtesy to a girl whose hair hung down her back, whether that hair was plaited, tied, or loose. As soon as it was pinned up, however, everything changed, or could change. And it stayed pinned. For the rest of a lady's life, only inside her bedroom, or in fancy-dress, would her hair hang down over her shoulders.

If pinned-up hair marked the frontier between childhood and the grown-up world in a girl's personal circle, the sign for the rest of society was the Court presentation.

Queen Victoria held her presentations at what was known as the Drawing Room, at three o'clock in the afternoon. Her son changed all that, preferring the evening court ceremony, usually held in June. Each debutante was presented by her mother, if available and a former debutante herself; if not, by some acceptable lady. It was possible for one lady to present more than one girl.

The etiquette was iron-clad. To begin with, the girls' dresses must be white, and each girl must wear the correct headdress of three curled white ostrich feathers, which rather gives an impression of a circus horse. The long procession of carriages approached Buckingham Palace along the unfinished stretch of the Mall, moving so slowly that the watching crowds could have a good look. Inside the carriages the girls sat nervously, hoping that their dresses were not getting too creased and that their feathers would stay in place, feeling hot with apprehension and the quantity of garments they wore, which as a matter of course included long white gloves. The carriages passed through the Palace gates, under the central archway and round the courtyard to the carpeted steps where their passengers alighted, and the impeccable Palace staff marshalled them in order of precedence in the ante-rooms. The Throne Room, where the King and Queen sat on gilded chairs on the dais, was lined with onlookers, most of them capable of merciless criticism. As each girl's name was called, she advanced with the correct slowness and the proper five curtseys, and re-

1908

Still in the Edwardian schoolroom: her hair is not up and in her sailor blouse she is ready for a game of hockey—the New Girl, in fact. (*The Mansell Collection*)

Celebrated Edwardian ladies: (*top left*) The Duchess of Devonshire; (*top right*) Lady Duff Gordon; (*centre left to right*) the King's three favourites Lillie Langtry, Frances Warwick and Alice Keppel; (*bottom*) Mrs Patrick Campbell. (*National Portrait Gallery*)

Jennie Churchill, the "Black Panther". (*The Mansell Collection*)

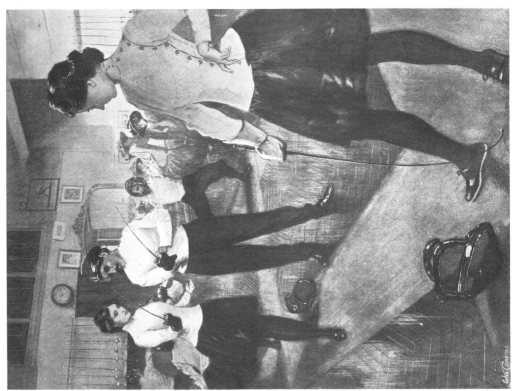

A famous Maître d'Armes teaching a lady pupil to hold the foil. Fencing became a fashionable sport for ladies around this time. (*I.L.N.*)

Hockey, like fencing, entered the list of standard sports for young ladies at the girls' schools. (*I.L.N.*)

Some celebrated American beauties of the day. Styles and standards remained remarkably close to Britain. (*Illustrated London News*)

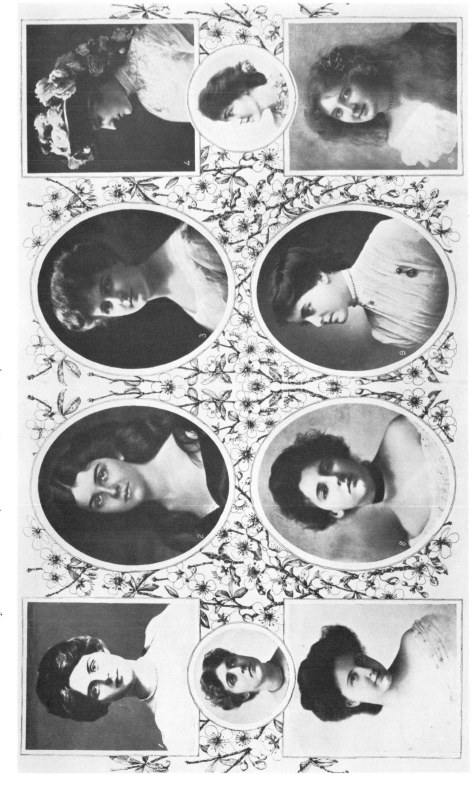

1. MISS ETHEL McDONALD. NEW YORK.
2. MISS JEANNETTE WILSON. MISSOURI.
3. MRS. EUGENE H. SCHLANGE. MISSOURI.
4. MISS MAE BOVEE. NEBRASKA.
5. MISS FLORENCE CLURE. COLUMBUS.
6. MISS GABRIELLA WORSLEY. WISCONSIN.
7. MISS PEARL SEBOLT. CLEVELAND.
8. MISS MILDRED A. BALDWIN. MICHGAN.
9. MISS NELLIE HUNT. WISCONSIN.
10. MISS PEARL MEYER. BUFFALO.

Lord and Lady Dufferin's garden party at the British Embassy in Paris.

On the beach at Biarritz—the fashionable Edwardian resort.

The Edwardian round: (*top left*) "Riding on the Row", a painting by Ernest Prater;
(*bottom left*) The King's picnic party on the roadside on Monkey Island; (*centre*) The
Hunt Ball; (*top right*) boating party on the Thames; (*bottom right*) the "motoriste" on
the Promenade des Anglais at Nice. (*centre and bottom from the Mansell Collection*)

treated backwards to the door, not an easy thing to do in a dress with a train. But all this was the essential overture to the marriage market, and as such perfectly understood by everyone concerned.

Now began the round of dinners and balls of the girls' first season. Young women, who only a few weeks before had been in the school-room, suddenly found themselves mingling with the Establishment in its full panoply. At her very first dinner party a girl might well find a distinguished statesman next to her, and the rule was inflexible: she must keep up a conversation with him. There was no compromise, the girls were thrown in at the deep end and expected to swim, and they usually did. They must display adult manners; young people's parties did not exist, the young were merely allowed to attend the splendid grown-up ones. On most evenings during the season there was a ball to go to after a dinner party, so that no girl could depend upon arriving at the ball with any of the people with whom she had dined. Of course, she could not go to the ball without a chaperone, who spent a vigil within the ballroom as long as that of the family coachman outside the house.

At a ball, each girl would ascend the stairs to be greeted by her host and hostess at the top, with their debutante daughter standing beside them, and, once inside the ballroom, would stand or possibly sit with her parents or her chaperone until the young men came up to ask for a dance. The dance programmes, specially printed with tiny pencils attached, had a space beside each dance for the man's signature, and the great thing was to have one's programme as full as possible before joining in the dancing.

Here again it was necessary to be careful. The supper-dance was the most important because it was an understood thing that one's partner for the supper-dance then took one down to supper, which gave him a good long innings. At the same time the critical eyes all round the room would miss nothing, so that to dance more than once with the wrong person — especially if one of these dances came very near the end of the ball — would be instantly noticed and the information flashed from one pair of eyes to another. The same thing happened if a girl was seen to romp, especially in the galop, or, indeed, to make herself conspicuous in any way.

Dancing was a skilled art: many of the dances of the period were elaborate set pieces like The Lancers, or bravura effects like the Viennese waltz. There could be only a remote thrill of contact, for everybody wore gloves, and it was a finger-tip, arm's length business. The girls wore white, with no jewels except perhaps a little string of pearls, and the flowers that they wore or carried were white or very pale pink.

The young men whom the young girls might meet were always carefully inspected and discussed beforehand by their mothers, aunts,
grandmothers and indeed the whole circle of older ladies. Meetings
were seldom if ever a matter of chance. Daughters who might be expected (because of their fathers' status) to become good political
hostesses in their turn were deliberately placed in the way of eligible
political bachelors so that these could soon see the range of possible
choice. The same thing happened with the daughters of great landed
estates who could expect to live for the most part in the country. The
acceptable choice was limited, but at least it was clear.

Most mothers with several daughters to bring out hoped to get each
daughter settled by the end of her first season. There was a convention
about this too. In order to understand it, it is necessary to look at the
social code in general as it applied to unmarried young girls.

Edwardian England was not just a man's world: it was an *old* man's
world. (The group photographs of the time are full of old beards.)
Society was patriarchal. Daughters were part of the patriarch's
property, his show window, and must therefore do him credit and
reflect his values. His wife was set on a pedestal, at least to outward
view. This proprietary, protective attitude helped to create an atmosphere far more favourable to older women than to young girls. Property
was all-important and must be seen to be in excellent condition: well-
run houses, well-cooked meals perfectly served, good furniture and
pictures, well-kept grounds, fine horses and carriages all in trim, good
clothes and jewels, a good reputation, the right sort of friends, and, as
part of this splendid estate, charming wives and virtuous daughters.

For virtuous one must read ignorant. It is true that in 1897 and 1899
appeared the first two volumes of Havelock Ellis's *Studies in the Psychology of Sex*, in which he declared that ignorance and superstition
spoilt sex relations and impurity flourished behind the veil carefully
held up at all times by the prudish. It is also true that in 1908 appeared
Sigmund Freud's *Essay on Infantile Sexuality*, but neither of these
works was read by the landed gentry, who would have cast them aside
in irritated disagreement if they had.

The Edwardian code of social behaviour really developed before
Edward VII became king. It dates from the time when he first began
to have love affairs, or at any rate affairs, after his marriage and grew
gradually into the code that is recognizable as Edwardian.

Briefly, its principal commandment was: Thou shalt not be found
out. That was the core of the matter: to drag out the facts into the light
of common day, to have recourse to the law, to feature in an un-
desirable way in the newspapers, these were unforgivable. A perfect
screen of manners and composure must always shelter the privileged.

What actually happened behind that screen was something else again. Consequently, it is easy to see why mothers wanted to marry off their daughters quickly: it was essential to hand over the daughters to their future husbands in a completely untouched state — in mint condition, in fact, and the longer they were "out" in society the harder it was to keep them unaware of what was going on.

Some older ladies had effortless poise enough to deal with any contretemps. There is an enchanting example of this given by Miss Anita Leslie, who tells how one great lady took a few guests to look at one of the pictures in the library during a ball in her house. When she opened the library door, a man and a woman sitting on the floor in front of the fire started guiltily apart. The lady of the house at once whisked the young girls out of sight, but one of them asked — and one can hear the high clear puzzled tone — "But what are they *doing*?" Quick as a flash, smooth as cream, the answer came back: "Mending the carpet — so kind."

Throughout recorded history there have been only two kinds of society as far as sex is concerned. Either there is prostitution or there is permissiveness. No third pattern has ever yet shown, apart from temporary expedients (a group struggling for survival, for example). The permissive society speaks its mind, brings out facts into the open, and discards its corsets. The prostitutional society hides its true feelings, conceals the facts, and clings to tight lacing. (It is perhaps of added interest that tight lacing goes with an expanding economy and non-lacing with a static or variable economy or a slump.) But in a society where prostitution thrives, its reflex thrives also: the carefully preserved virgin bride. And therefore the girls were told nothing or as near nothing as possible.

The usual, and often the only, counsel given by a mother to her daughter on the eve of the wedding was that whatever John did to her was right and she might not like it much, but it was one of the things women just had to put up with. It was tacitly understood that no really nice women could possibly enjoy sex: only immoral women did that. Equally it was assumed that all men were potential if not actual seducers, ready to pounce the minute they got the chance. Consequently, it was out of the question for a young girl to be alone with a man even for half an hour in somebody's drawing room. This is why the chaperones kept their eyes so fixedly on their charges: if a girl passed out of sight for an hour it meant that something could have happened, and this awful suspicion would deter possible suitors. Such an event, never investigated, never explained, would be put in words absolutely characteristic of the age: "Dolly (or Rose or Daisy) has got into a scrape."

All this is the code, and all codes are broken. Many girls did manage to find out something of what it was all about. They asked their elder sisters, some of whom remarked that such things were too sacred to talk about but who later allowed a gleam of light to break through, if, that is, they were happy with their husbands. They heard partially enlightening comments from brothers home from school; they kept their eyes open in the country, where animals, tenants and estate staff provided bits of information that could be pieced together; they could hardly fail to notice that some of the married ladies they met were obviously enjoying life, radiating happiness, in some glowing way. They could, and did, find specific details in books on dog-breeding or even, like Miss Nancy Mitford's Hons a generation later, duck-breeding.

None of this helped, however, when they ran up against a real aberration. What exactly had Oscar Wilde *done*? His own son was eighteen years old before he even realized that his father was Oscar Wilde, let alone the reason why he had been disgraced. And so many girls were held in check by the deterrent of terror. Danger and demons lurked everywhere. What was a girl to think when she could not visit a cathedral in broad daylight with the man she was engaged to unless she took a chaperone along? Was it indeed true that no man could be trusted? She was sternly cautioned against any vigorous exercise, she must always ride side-saddle, she must avoid a frank look into people's faces because "no man would want to marry a girl with a bold eye". A great many married ladies unaccountably developed a bold eye surprisingly quickly, she noticed. How strange, how difficult it all was — and how wonderful it would be when she was married and could enjoy herself as all the married ladies seemed to be able to do, free of chaperonage, free to wear lovely colours, free to criticize, in a position to *know*.

Every circumstance worked to inhibit and prevent action outside the accepted pattern. At all costs the strict rules, whereby the flawlessly polished surface of family life must at all times be presented to the public with a confident air of smooth and gracious dignity, had to be seen to be kept. Any sort of casual affair was not just unthinkable: it was quite impossible. Young girls had, for one thing, servants around all the time, they were woken up in the morning by maids, dressed by maids, put to bed by maids; their own coachman drove them home from dinners and balls; their entire lives were led in public. Not for them the secluded opportunities of the closed car, the midnight coffee-making in the kitchen of somebody's flat, the walk home from the theatre or cinema or dance, of all of which their successors (today's grandmammas) took such startling advantage. Above all, there were the clothes.

The woman of today, wearing perhaps four garments at any time
during the year, must find herself brought to a standstill at the thought
of what dressing and undressing meant in the first years of the twentieth century. For the wealthy and fashionable woman it was almost
unbelievable. To begin with, there was a garment known as "combinations". This was a kind of vest and pants in one piece, made of fine
wool, or a mixture of wool and silk, its legs reaching to the knee.
Sometimes the top had short sleeves, sometimes shoulder-straps. In
answer to the obvious question, it had a back panel that unbuttoned
below the waist. Over this went the corset, or stays, made of pink
coutil more often than not, boned and shaped to produce the admired
swanlike silhouette, its busks fastened with metal clips down the front,
its back laced to produce the slender waist. This had to be made to
look slenderer still by attaching silk pads to the hips and under the
arms. Then came the camisole, or petticoat-bodice, a kind of under-
blouse that buttoned down the front, was gathered at the waist and
was trimmed with lace round the neck and the diminutive puffed
sleeves.

The knickers had lace frills at the knee; sometimes they buttoned at
the waist, sometimes they were tied with tapes. Knickers and camisole
were made of very fine material, lawn, nainsook, nun's veiling, always
white. Silk stockings, black, white, or steel grey, were fastened with
suspenders clipped to the corset, or held up by garters. The waist-
petticoat, which might be of lawn or of rustling silk, was laid on the
floor in a circle, the lady stepped into the centre of the circle and the
maid lifted the petticoat up and tied it round the waist.

Then at last came the dress, or the skirt and blouse. The Edwardian
period was a great one for blouses. The junction of blouse and skirt was
concealed by a stiffened belt that fastened in front with a clasp, and at
the back was pinned to the undergarments so that there could never be
a gap. How on earth, one wonders, did any woman ever get to the
lavatory in a hurry? All those layers, all those tapes and buttons and
boning! Before going out, there was the hat, a fantastic creation of
flowers or feathers or even half a stuffed bird,* balanced carefully on
the pinned-up hair, tilted forward over the brows, skewered into place
with steel hatpins ten inches long. Ankle-high buttoned boots for walking, black slippers with cut steel buckles for the house, gloves, of course,
if one were going out of doors — and the gloves were buttoned too. No
wonder that one of the indispensable tools of the Edwardian lady was a
button-hook.

There was also the jewellery. A brooch at the centre of the high

* Mrs Cornwallis-West, for example, had a hat made from a ptarmigan which the
Duke of Fife sent her as a present.

stiffened collar, earrings, rings, a watch pinned to the bosom like a
soldier's medal — wrist-watches were extremely newfangled — a necklace, or indeed several necklaces with a low-cut gown for the evening;
and then the accessories, a bag and parasol in the daytime, fan and
flowers at night, and a wrap of some kind, furs if one's husband were
wealthy and generous enough. (No furs for young girls as a rule.) Any
hopeful seducer would blench at the thought of unwrapping so
elaborate a parcel. A present-day woman breathes thankfully that she
need not fasten herself inside all these complicated coverings.

Miss Monica Baldwin, who entered a convent of a closed order during
the First World War, when clothes were beginning to liberate their
wearers, and left it during the Second World War, did not even recog-
nize the modest undergarments brought by her sister for her to put on
when the day came for her to leave the convent. (The clothes of 1940
seem needlessly elaborate to the readers a generation later.) The dress
of 1900–1914 explains a lot about the way of life for any lady during
that time.

Let us take a look at the marriage market at its worst, its most unhappy. This can be seen in a contemporary bestseller: *Moths*, by Ouida.
Like all Ouida's work, it is wordy, florid, melodramatic, exotic, and
utterly readable. The opening sets the whole atmosphere at once:

> Lady Dolly ought to have been perfectly happy. She had every-
> thing that can constitute the joys of a woman of her epoch.
> She was at Trouville. She had won heaps of money at play. She
> had made a correct book on the races. She had seen her chief rival
> looking bilious in an unbecoming gown. She had had a letter from her
> husband to say he was going away to Java or Jupiter, or somewhere
> indefinitely. She wore a costume which had cost a great tailor twenty
> hours of anxious and continuous reflection. Nothing but *baptiste*
> indeed! but *baptiste* sublimised and apotheosised by niello buttons,
> old lace, and genius. She had her adorers and slaves grouped about
> her. She had found her dearest friend out in cheating at cards. She
> had dined the night before at the Maison Persanne, and would dine
> this night at the Maison Normande. She had been told a state secret
> by a minister which she knew it was shameful of him to have been
> coaxed and chaffed into revealing. She had had a new comedy read
> to her in manuscript-form three months before it would be given in
> Paris, and had screamed at all its indecencies in the choice company of
> a Serene Princess and two ambassadresses as they all took their
> chocolate in their dressing-gowns. Above all, she was at Trouville,
> having left half a million of debts behind her strewn about in all
> directions, and standing free as air in gossamer garments on the

planks in the summer sunshine. There was a charming blue sea beside her; a balmy fluttering breeze around her; a crowd of the most fashionable sunshades of Europe before her, like a bed of full-blown anemones.

What is bothering Lady Dolly is that her sixteen-year-old daughter is due to arrive at any moment. She confides her worry to her companion, Jack, Lord Jura, son of Lord Shetland and an officer in the Guards, who is cheerfully unsympathetic, saying that she must simply marry the daughter off, and then she will be a grandmother.

"I suppose you think that witty," said Lady Dolly with delicate contempt. "Well, Hélène there is a great-grandmother, and look at her!"

Hélène was a Prussian princess, married to a Russian minister: she was arrayed in white with a tender blending about it of all the blues in creation, from that of a summer sky to that of a lapis lazuli ring; she had a quantity of fair curls, a broad hat wreathed with white lilac and convolvulus, a complexion of cream, teeth of pearl, a luminous and innocent smile; she was talking at the top of her voice and munching chocolate; she had a circle of young men round her; she looked, perhaps, if you wished to be ill-natured, eight and twenty. Yet a great-grandmother she was, and the "Almanach de Gotha" said so, and alas! said her age.

Lord Jura says that Lady Dolly will not wear as well as that, because she does not take care of herself.

"You smoke quite awfully too much," pursued her companion immovably. "It hurts *us*, and can't be good for you. Indeed, all you women would be dead if you smoked right; you don't smoke right; you send all your smoke out, chattering; it never gets into your mouth even, and so that saves you all; if you drew it in, as we do, you would be dead, all of you. Who was the first woman that smoked, I often wonder?"

The daughter, Vere, arrives. She is the child of the first marriage, between Lady Dolly (herself the daughter of the lively little Countess of Caterham) and her cousin Vere Herbert, younger son of the Duke of Mull and Cantire. Left a very young widow with a baby daughter named after the father, Lady Dolly leaves her baby with its strictly moralistic grandmother in Northumberland and goes off to the south of France with her own mother, where within the statutory year of mourning she has met, and immediately the year is over married, the wealthy Mr Vanderdecken, he who is always conveniently going off on business to far-away places. Vere, aged sixteen now, is very beautiful, in a tall, fair, statuesque way, very serious, and, to her mother, impossible.

> "Oh! pray do not send away the Fräulein! We are now in the conic sections."
>
> "The what?" said Lady Dolly.
>
> "I mean I could not go on in science or mathematics without her, and besides, she is so good."
>
> "Mathematics! science! why, what can you want to make yourself hateful for, like a Girton College guy?"
>
> "I want to know things; pray do not send away the Fräulein."

Worse is to come. Vere says that she likes Greek better than anything else, and, after that, music, and her mother thinks despairingly that she has not the smallest trace of *chic*:

> "You look like a creature out of Burne-Jones's things, don't you know, only more — more — religious-looking. You really look as if you were studying your Bible every minute; it is most extraordinary!'

And when Vere produces her bathing-dress, "the long indigo-coloured linen gown — high to the throat and down to the feet — of the uneducated British bather, whose mind has not been opened by the sweetness and light of continental shores," Lady Dolly gasps that it is indecent:

> "Indecent," reiterated Lady Dolly, "If it isn't worse! Good gracious! It must have been worn at the deluge. The very children would stone you!"

The next morning Vere gets up at five and goes for a walk along the shore. She meets Corrèze — full name Raphael Marquis de Corrèze — a world-famous opera singer, who reveals himself as serious, chivalrous, and noble, asking a nearby peasant-woman not to allow the nearby larks to be captured for sale, and admitting that he hates seeing cut flowers left to die. He is about to leave on a concert tour, but before he goes he gives Vere some advice:

> "Try and keep yourself 'unspotted from the world'. Those are holy words, and I am not a holy speaker, but try and remember them. This world you will be launched in does no woman good. It is a world of moths. Half the moths are burning themselves in feverish frailty, the other half are corroding and consuming all they touch. Do not become of either kind. You are made for something better than a moth."

Lady Dolly is advised by her friend Lady Stoat to try to marry Vere to the immensely wealthy, dissipated, middle-aged Prince Sergius Zouroff, and to this end takes her on a visit to his seaside chateau, Félicité. On the drive there she gives her daughter some advice in her own turn:

"Now, dear, this will be quite going into the world for you. Do remember one or two things. Do try to look less grave; men hate a serious woman. And if you want to ask anything, don't come to me, because I'm always busy; ask Adrienne or Lady Stoat. You have seen what a sweet dear motherly creature she is. She won't mind telling you anything. There is a charming girl there, too, an American heiress, Fuchsia Leach; a horrible name, but a lovely creature, and *very* clever. Watch her and learn all you can from her. *Tout Paris* lost its head after her utterly this last winter. She'll marry anybody she chooses. Pray don't make me ashamed of you. Don't be sensational, don't be stupid, don't be pedantic; and, for mercy's sake, don't make any scenes. Never look surprised; never show any dislike to anybody; never seem shocked, if you feel so. Be civil all round, it's the safest way in society; and pray don't talk about mathematics and the Bible. I don't know that there's anything more I can tell you: you must find it all out for yourself. The world is like whist, reading can't teach it. Try not to blunder, that's all, and — do watch Fuchsia Leach."

This paragon is hardly the person to impress Vere with anything but disdain, which she is very quick to feel. Here is Vere's first sight of Miss Leach:

She saw a very lovely person of transparent colouring, of very small features, of very slight form, with a skin like delicate porcelain, an artistic tangle of artistically-coloured red gold hair, a tiny impertinent nose, and a wonderful expression of mingled impudence, shrewdness, audacity, and resolution. This person had her feet on an ottoman, her hands behind her head, a rosebud in her mouth, and a male group around her.

Vere, naturally, thinks Miss Leach deplorable, but is forced to admit that she has a point when she tells Vere how frequently the nobility of Europe falls all over itself to obtain American money by marrying American heiresses. Then, by her very coldness, Vere has the ill luck to attract Prince Zouroff, who has been madly pursued for years by women who want his money and position — "a man that all Europe has been wild to marry these last fifteen years past: Insult you! A man who offers you an alliance that will send you out of a room before everybody except actually princesses of the blood!" — and is pressured, in a scene of deepening melodrama, to marry him. Lady Stoat tries the pressure first, and gets into difficulties.

> "What answers to the boy's Iron Cross, I suppose, is to dance in the Quadrille d'Honneurat Court. Princess Zouroff would always be in the Quadrille d'Honneur."
>
> "Princess Zouroff may be so. I shall not. And it was of the Cross you wear, and profess to worship, that I thought."
>
> Lady Stoat felt a little embarrassed. She bowed her head, and touched the Iona cross in jewels that hung at her throat.

So it is left to Lady Dolly. She begins fairly lightly:

> "You think of love," she said. "Oh, it is of no use your saying you don't; you do. All girls do. I did. I married your father. We were as much in love as any creatures in a poem. When I had lived a month in that wretched parsonage by the sea, I knew what a little fool I had been. I had had such wedding presents! — *such* presents! The Queen had sent me a cachemire for poor papa's sake; yet, down in that horrid place, we had to eat pork, and there was only a metal teapot! Oh, you smile! it is nothing to smile at. Vere used to smile just as you do. He would have taken the cachemire to wrap an old woman up in, very probably; and he wouldn't have known whether he ate a peach or a pig. I knew; and whenever they put the tea in the metal teapot, I knew the cost of young love. Respect your father's memory? Stuff! I am not saying anything against him, poor dear fellow; he was very good — in his way, excellent; but he had made a mistake, and I too. I told him so twenty times a day, and he only sighed and went out to his old women. I tell you this only to show you I know what I am talking about. Love and marriage are two totally different things; they ought never to be named together; they are cat and dog; one kills the other."

But then she is driven to the melodrama's stock resort, the tear-stained visit in the night to the daughter's bedside, where she confesses a pack of lies, as Vere explains three years later to Zouroff:

> "She told me that she was in your debt; that she could not pay you; that you had letters of hers to some one — she did not say to whom — that placed her in your power; and you had threatened to use your power unless I — But you must know all that very well; better than I do."

Vere, of course, agrees to marry Zouroff, and, filled with fear and revulsion, does so, falling in a faint at the altar of the Russian church, and she is pictured after one week of marriage pacing the terrace of the Zouroff palace-like villa in the south of France, and frozen into the icy cast in which she spends the next three years:

> She herself had not known what she had done when she had consented to give herself in marriage . . . An unutterable depression and repugnance weighed on her always; she felt ashamed of the sun when it rose, of her own eyes when they looked at her from the mirror. To herself she seemed fallen so low, sunk to such deep degradation, that the basest of creatures would have had full right to strike her cheek, and spit in her face, and call her sister.

> Poets in all time have poured out their pity on the woman who wakes to a loveless dishonour: what can the few words of a priest, or the envy of a world, do to lighten that shame to sacrificed innocence? — Nothing.

This is good strong stuff, and there is plenty more of it to come because Ouida never let her heroines off without the full gamut of suffering. But all comes right, or fairly right, by the end. The book throughout is heavily loaded with symbolism: Vere receives an anonymous wedding present of a necklace:

> It was an opal necklace of exquisite workmanship and great value, and, as its medallion, there hung a single rose diamond cut as a star; beneath the star was a moth of sapphire and pearls, and beneath the moth was a flame of rubies. They were so hung that the moth now touched the star, now sank to the flame. It needed no words with it for Vere to know whence it came.

In a later dramatic scene Zouroff flings this necklace on the floor and grinds it under his heel, not an easy thing to do with real stones, but he crushes the whole lot to pieces except for the moth.

Now there were very few Veres, and few Zouroffs, but the loveless marriage with the girl abysmally ignorant (not only of the so-called facts of life but of the true character of her husband) was by no means infrequent. Indeed, the loftiest of families could provide examples, some of them years later than the Edwardian period. But equally there were some marriages that started unfavourably and then, because of the qualities of those concerned, turned into genuine love-matches. In all, however, as will appear later, it was the outward look of the matter that counted.

One important point that no one concerned with marriage ever forgot was the necessity for producing an heir to all the great estates, That was why careful enquiries were always made about the health of the families, why a whisper of rumour about some hereditary weakness was enough to give parents pause.

One illuminating example of this is shown in Dornford Yates's novel *Lower Than Vermin*. The story spans more than fifty years, and traces the lives of a brother and sister, Philip and Vivien Brabant. Lord Ringwood (Philip) discovers, in the Edwardian section of the book, that Vivien's husband is being pursued by a very beautiful but unscrupulous Frenchwoman, and, to spare his sister, tells this Frenchwoman that Hubert has gone abroad. In time, of course, the thwarted lady finds out the truth and looks about her for a way of revenge. She has observed that Philip is in love with a beautiful Scotch girl, Ildico Ross. Ildico has an attractive and impressionable brother, Andrew. Accordingly the Frenchwoman, Claude, makes a dead set at Andrew, without the slightest difficulty captivating him entirely. Then, working from a position of strength, she hesitantly and untruthfully tells Andrew that Philip has been her lover, that her little son is Philip's child, and that the baby is . . . *not very well*. In fact he has a twisted leg: but, put that way, it can be, and of course is, taken to mean the worst. Andrew, naturally horrified, reports this to his father; Colonel Ross forbids the marriage; Ildico wants to know why; in the end, after a good deal of careful enquiry with the family lawyer (for Andrew, of course, cannot reveal his informant's name), the truth comes out. All is well for Ildico and Philip, but a barrier has risen between Andrew and his sister that can never be quite broken, and he settles abroad. Mr Yates stresses that the least suspicion of an hereditary taint was dreaded in that period as nothing else was.

The existence of the marriage market brought out a new social phenomenon, or, rather, revived and expanded an old one: the lady of more or less secure social position without the money to keep it up, who for an excellent fee would guide a debutante through the Season and contrive to get her eligibly engaged by the end of it. On a small scale this practice had existed in previous periods, notably in the first quarter of the nineteenth century. However, the stolidly middle-class propriety of the Victorian heyday had reduced its scope.

Now, at the end of the century, it flowered out again, on a much bigger scale this time. For into accepted society now was coming money, money unaccompanied by nobility of blood, and the daughters of great financiers, of men who had made a fortune in the colonies, of emigré Europeans who were unfamiliar with the English scene, were often taken over by these "professionals". It was a custom frowned upon by the old families, who spent a good deal of time lamenting the vulgarity of modern life. Yet the wealthy patrons of the system were grateful for it, and the children of the marriages achieved in this way grew up with all the assurance that the old establishment could show, and a lot more financial security into the bargain.

In all periods of history there seems to be one age group that has the dull time. In the Victorian age it was probably the widows. Today it looks remarkably like the wives with no employment outside their homes. But in the Edwardian period it was emphatically the girls in the marriage market. They were spectators, not participants; they were hemmed in by rules; they had to tread the prescribed measure, and an uninteresting measure it was compared with the lives their mothers led, let alone the lives of the young married women. No wonder they were eager to escape into comparative freedom. The key of the door was the wedding ring.

CHAPTER FOUR

Much Noise on the Stairs

There is much noise on the stairs, but no one enters the room.
— old Chinese saying

At the beginning of the century, the magazine *Ladies' Realm* printed a piece by Marie Corelli in which she stated her special dislikes. They included "the modern marriage market", want of sympathy with little children, lack of enthusiasm in a great cause, materialists, sneerers at faith and aspiration, moral cowardice, the priest who preaches but does not practise, cynics and pessimists, low conduct in high places, and pretended friends who are secret foes. She disliked the man who thinks that every pretty woman he sees is, or ought to be, in love with him, and the woman who finds charm in every man except her own husband, the man who is his own God Almighty, the woman who cannot consecrate her life purely and faithfully to one great love-passion, and the man who has outlived romance. She had no time for "the new poet who curls his hair with tongs and writes his own reviews", "William Archer and his god Ibsen", or the scandalously best-selling novel *The Woman Who Did*. She disapproved of "ladies of title who allow their portraits to be on sale in the shops for any cad to buy", "tuft-hunters and worshippers of royalty", and "society noodles".

She included several items behind which no doubt, lay some irritating personal experience: "music — when it isn't wanted"; "the hostess who interrupts conversation between two friends merely to introduce a bore"; "being taken in to dinner by an uncongenial partner as old as Methuselah"; and "the 'funny man' at a party". She detested fuss, hurry, and lack of courtesy, and, for some reason, American millionaires, which seems a little sweeping. She abominated "the health-faddist and consumer of tabloids" (presumably this last is a pill-taker on a large scale), and "women bicyclists and he-females generally".

In this last she was not alone. Since the eighteen-eighties voices had been lifted in complaint that young women had no sense of morality, with their outdoor sports, bloomers, slang, and smoking; that even plain looks such as red hair and green eyes were admired, along with square-set eyebrows and sunburnt complexions; and that the New Woman (an ageless phenomenon), with her objectionable habit of lounging on sofas, wearing tailor-made suits of checked tweed, ties, and hard pork-pie hats, was really deplorable in comparison with the satin-clad beauties with their scooped-out décolleté necklines blossoming with roses. The vogue of the bicycle was the final abomination.

The bicycle had become possible for ladies with the discovery of the pneumatic tyre by the Belfast veterinary surgeon, John Boyd Dunlop. Soon smart ladies were posing for photographs standing primly with their hands resting on the handlebars, or even cycling in the park, wearing straw boaters. Young girls were given baggy serge knicker-bockers to wear over their frilly white drawers, which Mrs Gwen Raverat remembered as rather grand, if horribly improper at first. Ladies of the more radical élite put their bicycles on top of a growler and went to Battersea Park, where masculine breeches and feminine knickerbockers could sedately progress side by side without chaperones. Sometimes, when invited out to dinner, the ladies could even tuck up their trains and go on the bicycle. There was no doubt that the modest bicycle was a powerful element in the liberation of women.

Indeed, the reign of Edward VII was a time of revolution in transport generally. Electric propulsion was acknowledged as an alternative to steam (one remembers Mrs Cubitt's description of Mrs Keppel's electric brougham pinging through Hyde Park), the submarine came in as a war weapon, battleships were driven by turbines, man started to fly, and, bringing in the biggest change of all, the petrol engine got into the motor-car. The trade of motor-maker was first listed in 1901 (though dictionaries still stated that "garage" was a foreign word and that "automobile" was an adjective). The Red Flag Act had been repealed in 1896, but its existence in England had given European cars a head start, and Edward VII's first cars were a Mercèdes and a Renault. The first road death caused by a petrol-driven vehicle in England occurred in 1899, when the legal speed limit was twelve miles an hour.

At first every car chassis was made by coachbuilders who were accustomed to building high. The driver sat on the right because the coachman sat on the right in a carriage, though both drove on the left; the word *chauffeur* was the French word for a traction-engine stoker. Car lights were carriage lamps, burning gas or acetylene: the re-chargeable battery did not appear until 1911. As we have seen, tyres were fragile to begin with; one militant suffragette was able to puncture a tyre on a police car with nothing more powerful than a safety-pin.

But the car caught on. In 1903 there were 8,500 of them registered, at the statutory fee of one pound, in London alone: the British total passed the hundred thousand mark six years later. Licences cost five shillings and the driving test did not exist. The famous racing track at Brooklands in Surrey was opened in 1907. Car prices spread over a wide range: the 1910 Morgan runabout cost £65, the 1911 Rolls-Royce Silver Ghost cost £1,154.15s. Efforts were made to improve road surfaces, which were muddy in winter and dusty in summer, by trying out tar and bitumen. The steam-drive car proved a disappointment, breaking down easily, requiring constant topping-up with water, having to be pushed up steep hills, and all too often blowing up in a cloud of orange spray from the boiler. At first cars had neither hoods nor windscreens.

The obviously all-pervading dust, wind, rain, and mud, not to mention the orange spray out of the boilers, forced early motorists, male and female alike, to wrap up against these. Only the chauffeur wore, as he contines to wear, a flat cap with a peak (apart from the armed services, and various other uniformed officials, only yachtsmen have ever taken to this style of headgear in England), and the chauffeur also adopted the breeches and gaiters worn by coachmen. Other men wore cloth hats with ear-flaps, and both sexes swathed themselves in long dustcoats or capes with slits for the arms, and protected their eyes with goggles.

Ladies' hats, ordinarily large and decorative, were small for motoring, and a veil that smoothly covered face and hair and was firmly anchored with pins was essential if they were not to arrive with matted locks. As it was there was a considerable risk of presenting themselves at their destination with reddened cheeks and noses, speckled with smuts or powdered with dust, and eyes streaming with smudgy tears.

But the ladies who took motoring seriously did not allow themselves to get into such a deplorable state. Miss Dorothy Levitt, the first Englishwoman to enter for an official non-stop drive (from Leeds to London in one day, starting at five in the morning, having come from Glasgow the day before), and who, in the same four-cylinder Gladiator, drove from London to Warwick and back in a day with luncheon in the middle, wrote a book, *The Woman in the Car*, in which she recommended tailored coats and skirts with specially made gaiters:

Under no circumstances must you wear lace or fluffy adjuncts to your toilette — if you do, you will regret them before you have driven half a dozen miles. Tweed, frieze, or homespun lined with "Jaeger" or fur. For summer, the ideal coat is of cream serge, which does not crease like silk, alpaca, or linen. A cloth cap to match the tweed should be pinned securely, and over it put a crepe-de-chine veil, of length a-plenty. Alternately, a close-fitting turban of fur. A long scarf or muffler, good soft kid, fur-lined gloves, made with just a thumb. Don't wear rings or bracelets. Indispensable to the motoriste is the over-all, butcher blue or brown linen, fastening at the back. . . . If you are to drive alone, it is advisable to carry a small revolver. I have an automatic Colt and find it easy to handle as there is practically no recoil — a great consideration for a woman. . . . In a little drawer in the motor-car is the secret of the dainty motoriste. In its recesses put clean gloves, veil and handkerchief, powder-puff, pins, hair pins, and a hand-mirror.

Disarmingly, she adds: "Some chocolates are soothing sometimes."

Miss Levitt knew what she was talking about. In 1902 she set up a world record for women of 91 mph, and she was for ever being fined for breaking the 12 mph speed limit, which caused her to recommend membership of the Automobile Association, whose scouts would kindly warn members of nearby police traps and thereby save them the amount of the annual subscription (two guineas) several times over.

Miss Levitt was not alone. Other "dainty motoristes" of the day included the first British lady owner-driver, the Baroness Campbell de Laurentz, the president of the Ladies' Automobile Club (founded in 1903), the Duchess of Sutherland, who drove a Mercèdes, Mrs George Thrupp whose baby son had the first "motoring christening", Mrs Bazalgette who took part in the 1900 one-thousand-miles trial run, and Miss Vera Butler, who raced balloons as well as cars and whose father was a racing balloonist. Shops sprang up to cater for these ladies and their rapidly growing crowd of imitators, providing, among other garments, tailor-made, flannel-lined leather motoring knickers, three-quarter length leather coats with storm-fronts and sleeve wind-guards, tussore silk head-veils, and tweed coats lined with vicuna, squirrel, mink, or "camel fleece", and trimmed with nutria or astrakhan.

For the equally intrepid there was yachting for ladies, though it must be admitted that many of them were content to relax on deck in harbour, or attend shipboard dances. Women, however, were more and more moving into active participation in sports: cycling as we have seen, roller-skating which was called "rinking" in those days, hockey, tennis, and golf. Thomas Burberry designed a golf suit with a skirt that could be looped up clear of the ankles and a jacket with "Patent Pivot Sleeves"; Harrod's supplied golf knickers and cycling knickers and a special cycling skirt that divided at the back to fall modestly on either side of the saddle, as well as something less practical, starched golf collars and cuffs.

The enchanting sporting photographs and advertisements of the period, showing the ladies posing demurely in boaters and long skirts by the tennis-net or the bicycle, force the reader to realize how uncomfortable these clothes were, yet how easy in comparison with the ordinary fashionable dress of the day and of the preceding epoch. Women *were* becoming more liberated. True, it was a slow process, and much acrimony, struggle, and violence occurred before it was on the way to completion, but it had started, which meant that it would go on. It is often overlooked that all the keenest agitation for social reform takes place when the basic situation has improved: periods of great oppression generally see little positive stir for reform. Those women who approached the closest to liberty fell into two groups: the wealthy marrieds, and the creative artists. Of this second group the majority were writers.

Elinor Glyn perhaps caused the greatest commotion. She began to write with the laudable, and entirely liberated, idea of paying off her husband's debts, and her first novel came out in 1906. It was called the *Vicissitudes of Evangeline* and contained nothing more shocking than a description of the heroine looking very becoming in bed, which, however, earned the horrifying rebuke that no nice woman wants to look becoming in bed. But in 1907 the roof fell in: *Three Weeks* appeared.

Three Weeks (and no one has bettered the delicious account of its plot by Mr S. J. Perelman in one of his "Cloudland Revisited" essays called *Tuberoses and Tigers*) is a somewhat florid account of a love-affair in Switzerland between an incognito European noble-woman, an expert in the romantic, and an inexperienced young Englishman named Paul Verdayne. The story includes a trip to Venice, where the couple dine in a bower of roses and lilacs with a sofa of solid roses in the background, but after three weeks the lady vanishes, leaving Paul to collapse with brain-fever and then to return to make his mark in politics and the social world of England, though he apparently never looks at another woman again. The book ends with the lady's murder by her husband, his murder by the lady's devoted groom, and the coronation of their little boy — or, rather, of Paul's and the lady's little boy — a ceremony attended, in a complete hearts and flowers atmosphere, by Paul.

On publication this book set off a storm of reaction. The head master banned it at Eton, the Lord Chamberlain refused to license a stage adaptation, the *Daily Telegraph* reported that it avoided "only by a hair's breadth the accusation of proving positively squalid". Of course, it was a roaring success. Within nine years it had sold two million copies, a room in the Cavendish Hotel was named the Elinor Glyn

Room, and, because of the celebrated scene where the lady lies stretched out on a tiger skin, *Punch* carried a rhyme that became famous overnight:

> Would you like to sin
> With Elinor Glyn
> On a tiger skin?
> Or would you prefer
> To err with her
> On some other fur?

It was, of course, Elinor Glyn who coined the word "It" to mean sex-appeal, having made the same discovery as J. M. Barrie that, if a woman has it, she does not need to have anything else, and, if she does not have it, it doesn't much matter what else she has. In due time, after the First World War, she took herself off to the one place where tuberoses and tiger skins were everyday items in a cloudland of perfection: Hollywood.

But other women were writing less sensationally but with a clear eye for feminine appeal and personality in their stories: for example, a Hungarian expatriate who, in the unlikely setting of Gloucester Road underground station, where she was waiting for a train, had a vision. The vision was of a tall, fair, elegant Englishman, with a drawling voice and a rich laugh, perfectly dressed in the full fig of a late eighteenth-century dandy, levelling his quizzing-glass, and concealing behind this foppish appearance a keen brain, a deep compassion, a love of sport for its own sake, a zest for risks and a wish to save victims of the French Terror. She saw him, in her mind's eye, whole, complete, even to his name — Sir Percy Blakeney, the Scarlet Pimpernel. She was Emmuska, Baroness Orczy, born in 1865.

Baroness Orczy was born in Tarna-Ors in Hungary and was educated in Paris and Brussels. At what point in her life she fell in love with the archetypal Englishman is uncertain, but it was an unwavering, lifelong love, and, what is more, she married one of them. Her own account of her marriage, in her autobiography, *Links in the Chain of Life*, is idyllic. She broke into print first with short stories, later published in book form under the title *The Old Man in the Corner*. This is particularly interesting because they were detective stories, early and by no means undistinguished examples in one literary field in which women have been predominant. These stories came out in 1900; five years later *The Scarlet Pimpernel* achieved print, and flourishes still, enshrining one of the most famous of all English fictitious characters.

The Scarlet Pimpernel has been dramatized, filmed, adapted for broadcasting; the books have run into dozens of editions in hardback and paperback, and Mrs Montague Barstow knew what it was to spend the last forty years of her life as a celebrity. She and her husband made their home in France, where they survived the German occupation in the Second World War, but only a few weeks after the publication of her autobiography in 1946 Baroness Orczy died. Her photographs reveal a dumpy little woman with a lively face and something decidedly Edwardian about her dress thirty years after that era had ended.

Famous as she became during the Edwardian period, and surely as she outlived most of her literary contemporaries in popularity, Baroness Orczy was not nearly as celebrated in 1905 as was Marie Corelli, the best-seller of her day. Born in 1864, the adopted daughter of a writer named Charles Mackay, Miss Corelli was educated in France and brought out her first book when she was twenty-two. This was *A Romance of Two Worlds* in which she stated one of her basic creeds:

> Believe in anything or everything miraculous and glorious — the utmost reach of your faith can with difficulty grasp the majestic reality and perfection of everything you can see, desire, or imagine.

The key word here is "miraculous". Its glorification, as Shaw pointed out, is the sure sign of romantic religion. Miss Corelli designed her book as a vehicle for something she called Electric Christianity, which, she said, was not her own invention:

> Its tenets are completely borne out by the New Testament, which sacred little book, however, has much of its mystical and true meaning obscured nowadays through the indifference of those who read and the apathy of those who hear . . . I merely endeavoured to slightly shadow forth the miraculous powers which I *know* are bestowed on those who truly love and understand the teachings of Christ.

The miraculous powers sounded impressive enough. They included knocking people down at will with electric shocks, playing the piano at angels' dictation, walking on water ("Walking on the sea can be accomplished now by anyone who has cultivated sufficient inner force"), living for ever, and taking journeys round the solar system. In *The Sorrows of Satan*, published in 1895 and appearing in its fifty-sixth edition in 1911 (besides being adapted for the stage), Miss Corelli made her Satan immune to seduction by her villain, Lady Sybil Tempest; made him reveal his supernatural character by flashes of lightning; made him, like Wagner's Flying Dutchman, redeemable if he can find one soul faithful to the death; and, indeed, after various scenes in which Satan steers the ship dressed as a cardinal, and a young nobleman play-

ing baccarat suddenly stakes his soul (at which point Shaw, the re-
viewer, said that he missed Meyerbeer's music to *Robert le Diable*
rather badly), flourished up to the climax, borrowed (presumably)
from Wagner also, of the ship sinking and the redeemed man rising to
heaven in a suit of armour. In spite of Miss Corelli's verbal squeamish-
ness (in one of her books she refers to Ishtar as "the Queen of the Half
World of Babylon"), or, perhaps, because of it, she succeeded pro-
digiously, even to the extent, in her book *Barabbas*, of rewriting the
New Testament story so popularly that it was obvious that her readers
considered it an improvement on the original.

Critics were not quite so tolerant: they considered her works the
victory of a powerful imagination over a careless and somewhat
commonplace mind, or, more unkindly, the pretentious treatment of
lofty subjects by the illiterate for the illiterate. She is scarcely read at
all now, but she was a huge success among the Edwardian ladies, and
(hardly surprisingly) reputed to be the favourite author of Alexandra,
Empress of Russia and devotee of Rasputin.

Other Edwardian best-sellers included *Three Weeks*, as we have
already seen, and *The Rosary* by Florence Barclay, who created a
sensation by deliberately making her heroine plain yet destined for a
happy ending. The book, which came out in 1909, was warmly praised
by a woman editor, Flora Klickmann, whose *Girl's Own Paper and
Woman's Magazine* enjoyed marked popularity among a respectable
public who, whatever their private conduct, approved of her clear-cut
moral tone. In 1910 Miss Klickmann stigmatized "false work", by
which

> I mean the sort of work that strives by cheap tricks to look like
> something that it isn't! I recently saw a blouse that a girl had trimmed
> with some indifferent, machine-made coarse cotton insertion, which
> she had embellished in coloured wool and a little gilt thread run in
> and out around the pattern. She told me she had done it herself, and
> asked if I didn't think it had a rich Oriental effect!! She said she had
> got the idea from Paris — as though that necessarily stamped it as
> artistic and desirable!
>
> Sometimes it is very hard to be kind as well as truthful! I didn't
> want to hurt her feelings by telling her exactly what I thought: viz.,
> that it utterly vulgarized her blouse and revealed a deplorably
> "common" streak in her personal taste. I did the best I could under
> the circumstances by saying that I thought the blouse material
> (which was a pretty, simple pattern) didn't need the trimming to set
> it off.

And in one of her magazine articles appears this typical comment:

I wonder if you, like myself, feel sometimes there really isn't time to do an insignificant bit of mending properly, and proceed to cobble up the tear with any cotton that is near at hand, or catch the button to the stuff with half-a-dozen hasty stitches? And all through these lapses one has an uneasy sense of guilt, and even degradation, as if one has quite consciously offended against an innate standard of refinement. On the other hand, what a delightful sense of peace, freedom, and satisfaction in right doing comes when one has re-sisted the temptation to be in a hurry, and has carefully unravelled threads from a piece of stuff, chosen a fine needle, and completed a well-nigh invisible darn. That inward feeling is proof positive of right or wrong doing; and it ought to show us that even in a simple thing like needle-work there is a "narrow path" to follow.

The maddening thing is, of course, that the writer is right: a quick poll of young women on whom this passage was tried shows a virtually unanimous response. Here is Miss Klickmann again in full flood, though less apt to carry her readers with her now on this point, when the "ready-made" is no longer inferior nor morally distasteful:

The girl who will don badly-machined, ready-made underwear, gaudily trimmed with cheap imitation lace, and garnished with bows of papery ribbon, is not only wasting her money in buying such garments, but is actually pandering to dishonesty, and encouraging herself to tolerate and condone what is false and bad — hopelessly bad.

The girl who takes a pleasure in making her own things (if she has the time) as nicely as they can be made (whether by machine or by hand), putting fine, even feather-stitching and such-like work into them instead of the "cheap and nasty" imitation lace and ribbon, is fostering a love of truth and sincerity, as well as cultivating a sense of beauty and fitness.

The ostensible morality of the time caused the emphasis on clothes that covered women from throat to instep, yet its innate contradiction showed in the strong hour-glass silhouette. The Anglo-Saxon Protestant ethos held (outwardly) that sex morality was the core of all morality, that woman was the source of all temptation as Adam had found, and, in consequence, society taboos must be upheld to protect men against themselves and to guard the tender plant of chivalry towards women, who otherwise would, presumably, be immoral at a moment's notice. The fear of the flesh was at the root of these beliefs; yet fashion was dictated by the *grandes cocottes*. Again, paradoxically, it favoured older women, who according to official opinion ought to be able to behave themselves.

Humbler women were breaking into the hitherto masculine worlds of business, without apparently the need to behave like Miss Sally Brass to do it. In 1901 eighteen per cent of office clerks were women, a figure that had almost doubled by 1911. In 1900 there were 3,000 women telephone operators (there were 775,000 telephones in Britain by 1914), and the first London telephone exchange was set up in 1902. When Gordon Selfridge opened his great shop in 1909 he asked the National Telephone Company to install a public exchange, which they refused to do, but as a consolation offered him a prestigious number — Gerrard 1 — which soon had 120 main lines with more than 600 extensions. It is a surprise to find that the first automatic telephone exchange was set up as early as 1912, at Epsom.

It is also a surprise to find that one Edwardian lady of unquestioned status interested herself in the working conditions of her time. This was Lady Florence Bell. The daughter of Sir Joseph Olliffe, MD, Florence Eveleen Eleanor married, in 1876, as his second wife, Sir Hugh Bell, then aged thirty-two, an ironmaster and colliery owner. He was a Justice of the Peace, Sheriff of the West Riding of Yorkshire in 1895, and Lieutenant of the North Riding from 1906; he was also the father of Gertrude Bell, whose collected letters were edited by her stepmother in 1927. Lady Bell was a writer, and many of her works — novels including one called *The Story of Ursula*, plays for children, even translations from and into French, some adult plays including *L'Indécis* produced by Coquelin at the Royalty Theatre in 1887 and *Time is Money* produced by no less a person than Charles Hawtrey — seem orthodox enough. But she wrote, in 1895, a text-book called *French Without Tears* still available today, and so successful that its title was used by Sir Terence Rattigan for the first of his brilliant stage comedies (produced in November 1936); and she wrote *At The Works*.

At The Works is a remarkable book by any standards: as the product of an Edwardian lady it is positively astounding. It is a careful, thoroughly documented, deeply analytical study of conditions in an industrial town at the time, 1907. Its chapter titles give its thesis: "The Genesis of the Town", "The Process of Ironmaking", "The Expenditure of the Workman", "Illness and Accidents", "Old Age — Joint Households — Benefit Societies", "Recreation", "Reading"; "The Wives and Daughters of the Ironworkers", "Drink, Betting, and Gambling". Pages of clear figures give details of the weekly budgets of families of three with incomes ranging from nineteen shillings and sixpence to one pound three and ninepence a week, families of six or seven on a similar scale. Lady Bell did not rely upon the reports of others for her statistics: she went to see for herself, visiting homes under normal conditions, homes struck by bereavement or sickness, and, of course, the works themselves, where she asked pointed questions about such matters as possible canteen arrangements, because

> many of their wives practically do not know how to cook at all, or at any rate do not wish to do so, and get their food ready cooked from an eating-house or a fried-fish shop; and some of the others who do cook in the home do it so badly that it might be almost better if they did not attempt it. . . . But the question of catering for the men during their day's work is not as simple as it looks, given the varied hours and different lengths of time available for the various workers. This is the kind of matter on which it is not always easy in this country to meet the views of the workman. He may possibly be aggrieved if he is not arranged for and helped a little; but he will certainly be angry if he is arranged for and helped too much. One learns after long experience that what he wants is that the next step that is of any concern to him and that he chooses to take in his own way, should be facilitated for him; but one has to be very careful not to go a little further and make superflous suggestions, which he then, much to the discomfiture of the suggester, absolutely negatives and dismisses.

It was becoming easier, though only by degrees, for women to squeeze their way into the world of art and letters: some still followed the example of Charlotte and Emily Brontë over half a century before, and wrote under masculine pen-names (there were volumes of love lyrics by "Laurence Hope"). But the success of Marie Corelli, Baroness Orczy, and Elinor Glyn encouraged other women to step forward boldly. Lucy Kemp-Welch's horse paintings were widely admired; Ethel Smyth wrote the *March of the Women* to be played at suffragette parades; Gertrude Bell was acclaimed as remarkable linguist, explorer and traveller, naturalist, historian and archaeologist.

The women's suffrage movement tried hard to recruit such a glittering example, but failed: not only did she not join, but in 1908 she went over to the opposition, joining the Women's Anti-Suffrage Committee. In this body, later expanded into the Anti-Suffrage League and gaining such well-known adherents as Lord Curzon, Lord Cromer, Lord Milner, Rudyard Kipling and Joseph Chamberlain, one active woman was Mrs Humphrey Ward. A granddaughter of Arnold of Rugby, she was born in 1851 and died in 1920, after inspiring such witticisms as "Virtue is its Humphrey Ward", and after making a name for herself as a writer of novels with religious doubts and perplexities as their theme.

The campaign for women's rights was launched as far back as the eighteen-eighties by two redoubtable persons, the professed agnostic

Charles Bradlaugh and the theosophist Annie Besant. At first they linked the fight for the vote with a call for birth control, socialism, and liberation from religious orthodoxy, but, as time went by and the suffrage movement tied itself more firmly to the slightly more sympathetic Liberal Party, which was immovably churchgoing, the latter three points were dropped. It is interesting, though profitless, to speculate about what might have happened if the socialist idea had persisted, for it has been carefully assessed more than once that, if women had never had the vote, Britain would have seen the Labour Party in power consistently since the twenties: the majority of women vote Conservative.

In the thirty-eight years up to 1905, Parliament had debated the suffrage question no fewer than eighteen times. It was still undecided, and possibly the slowness of its progress prompted the leading spirits to alter the traditional feminine way of getting what they wanted by indirect methods and determining to attack head-on. It is a difficult matter to assess, but it does appear that the militancy of the later campaign did more harm than good to the cause. When Mary Richardson slashed a Velasquez painting in the National Gallery, when other women set fire to buildings, smashed shop-windows, tore the clothes off Cabinet Ministers, jabbed their ten-inch steel hatpins into police-horses and laid open policemen's faces with their finger-nails, it was hard for those involved to react with moderation; and when imprisoned hunger-striking women were put through the dreadful business of forcible feeding it added fuel to the already blazing fire.

More nonsense has been talked and written about one incident than about any other: the death of Emily Wilding Davison, who ran out on to the Epsom racecourse in the middle of the 1913 Derby and was trampled to death by one of the horses. It happened to be the King's horse, Anmer, ridden by a jockey called Herbert Jones. Many people who ought to know better have declared that Miss Davison deliberately *selected* the King's horse: anyone watching a race will know that the horses, regardless of the breadth of the track, always bunch. Miss Davison may have hoped to pick out Anmer, but she could never have had the time to make sure.

Actually the 1913 Derby was the most sensational of all Derby races. The winner, Craganour, was disqualified: its owner was Mr Bruce Ismay, head of the White Star Shipping Line, who had been disgraced, and subjected for ever to public contumely, for having been rescued from the *Titanic* the year before. A mist of rumour that such a man could not be allowed to win the Derby has clung round the decision ever since.

Be that as it may, Miss Davison, wearing the white, purple and green suffragette colours, made her gesture, the one that everyone remembers, and died of a fractured skull after four days, during which she never regained consciousness. Her fellow suffragettes paid tribute to her in the loftiest terms; Hertha Ayrton, for example, wrote:

Last week Miss Davison was asked to speak at a meeting to be held this week. Her reply was, "I have other work to do." Her other work is done. She went cheerfully, almost gaily, to certain death — or worse — offering herself as the sacrifice that should open the minds of men to the desperate needs of women and to their desperate determination.

I see that some of our journalists, measuring Miss Davison by their own petty, pint-pot standards, are calling her mad. Mad? Yes! with that divine madness that recreates the world.

In the Light Brigade there were six hundred — even at Thermopylae there were three — but she, *one*, alone, the Quintus Curtius of our Cause, has thrown herself into the gulf to set her sisters free.

Miss Ayrton was — one may think justifiably — infuriated by the newspaper reports, some of which took the line that the incident was a regrettable disruption of a great race, in much the same spirit as the Marquis de Saint-Evrémonde reacted to the dead child run over by his carriage: "How do I know what injury you have done my horses?"

But the suffragette movement did not become militant until after 1909. Before that the idea was to attract publicity and, if possible, support. When two suffragettes chained themselves to the Downing Street railings, Mrs Pethick Lawrence commented:

Doing something silly is the woman's alternative for doing something cruel. The effect is the same. We use no violence because we can win freedom without it; we have discovered an alternative.

From 1912 onwards the campaign mounted in violence. Fires were started in the ladies' waiting-rooms of Shields Road Station in Glasgow, in the goods yard at Nottingham, in three stores at Bradford causing £80,000 pounds' worth of damage, in the Methodist Chapel in Barn Hill, Stamford, and in the Stamford Hotel stables; Rough's boathouse at Oxford was burnt down, as was the grandstand at Hurst Park; an attempt was made to set fire to the Royal Academy, and Westwood Manor, near Trowbridge, was gutted the night after a Trowbridge meeting from which several suffragettes had been forcibly turned out. Telephone and telegraph wires were cut, purple dye poured into a reservoir, acid poured on golf greens and small bombs put into letter-boxes.

Now in the eyes of the Edwardian lady, the suffragettes were — for the most part — not ladies at all. Many of them were graduates, or business men's wives, which put them out of account at once; the whole movement seemed middle-class in tone and temper. When a lady did take part it often came to nothing: in 1900 Mrs Garnett Fawcett created the National Union of Women's Suffrage Societies (instantly nicknamed "Votes for Ladies"), but it failed to establish terms with the trade unions and with women working in industry, and thus petered out.

Mrs Emmeline Pankhurst became Manchester's Registrar for Births and Deaths when her husband, who had previously held that post, died. Aided by her elder daughter Christabel, a law graduate, she formed a more militant splinter group, the Women's Social and Political Union, in 1903. The first planned interruptions of political meetings really began in 1905. The Union often seemed to go out of its way to antagonize the very people who had shown some sympathy: the Liberal, Labour, and Irish Members of Parliament, the unions, the Independent Labour Party which had been continually friendly to the cause, and even individual Members who, if not in favour of votes for women, had at least never shown any antipathy.

The forces that really created women's liberation — or as much of it as exists today according to one's viewpoint — were, on the whole, forces outside the movement. Writers who never withheld criticism put forward solid arguments. Shaw said it was possible to object to the extension of the franchise on more or less reasonable grounds (such as holding that the whole business of voting was a delusion) or objecting to change, or believing it would upset a convenient division of labour between the sexes. But it was quite another thing to support a Prime Minister (Asquith) who placed one's mother on the footing of a rabbit.

Wells wrote *Anne Veronica* in 1909 and the *Spectator* said it could poison the minds of its readers; the redoubtable Wells stated explicitly that women could only be free if they had control of their persons, by which he meant birth control, easy divorce, and the end of money-contracts as a basis for marriage. Many suffragettes bitterly opposed all these ideas. Then there were those women who made their own unchallengeable place in the world without violence, without campaigning, but by sheer ability and work. Of these one was a most eminent Edwardian lady, Beatrice Webb.

Eighth daughter of Richard and Laurencina Potter, Beatrice was born in 1858. She always maintained that her childhood was unhappy partly, if not principally, because she never got on well with her mother, and was a solitary child by nature. She later summed herself up as conservative by temperament and anti-democratic by social environment. Brought up at Standish House, ten miles from the Severn estuary, she spent hours wandering alone in the grounds or curled up among the warm rough-dried sheets in the laundry, and preferred to educate herself, through her own choice of books and notebooks filled with personal reflections, rather than attend lessons in the schoolroom with her sisters.

By the time she was eight she was noting in letters the appearance of local political candidates and severely commenting on their limited vocabulary, as they did not (apparently) know the meanings of such words as demonstration, hustings, and nomination. She was charmed with the raffish glamour of American railway magnates who visited her father, puzzled by her sisters' young men who seemed to her most peculiar, and aware of Swedish timber-merchants and British business-men who also frequented the house, along with such celebrated indivi-duals as Julian Huxley and John Bright. Beatrice showed off, as children do who feel compelled to assert themselves against a mass of elder sisters and a less than affectionate mother. Outsiders found the Potter daughters, with their short rough black hair, pretty and original.

The dominant visitor, whose influence did more than anything else to mould Beatrice's entire life, was the splendidly eccentric philosopher Herbert Spencer. Listening to him expounding on all subjects, pro-testing against accepted theories of education, explaining this, illus-trating that, was always stimulating, and, although Beatrice disagreed with much of what he said, she was a devoted disciple because it seemed to her that he was the only person she knew who took her seriously. From him she learned how to argue and how to do research.

When the older sisters went to London for the season, Beatrice cadged tickets for the Ladies' Gallery of the House of Commons from their suitors and spent hours listening to debates. In 1872 Richard Potter took her with him on one of his periodic trips to America, where she saw Niagara (and felt drawn to hurl herself over it), Chicago (then rebuilding after its great fire), San Francisco (where she was poorly impressed by Chinatown), the Yosemite Valley (which made her long to paint) and Salt Lake City (where the Mormon women seemed dull and dejected but the city, with its wide streets edged with clear streams and white houses, looked celestial).

Beatrice "came out" in 1876, and enjoyed it immensely, going to dozens of functions including those early versions of the cocktail party, crushes and drums. These were gatherings of people all talking at the tops of their voices in drawing-rooms, held for the purpose of "sweeping-up" acquaintances to whom one owed an invitation of some sort, but, unlike the cocktail party, took place late in the evening after dinner. She went to Ascot and Hurlingham, paid calls, and took part in those everlasting late Victorian and Edwardian home entertainments, charades and amateur theatricals. Then she lay awake half the night reproaching herself for showing off, for being frivolous, and for having no aim in life.

To counteract this she gave up her third season to go on a European tour with her sister Mary and Mary's husband Arthur Playne. They visited Germany, Austria and Hungary, and Beatrice grew bored and irritable with Mary's and Arthur's company. Back in England she made up for it by taking the happiest holiday of her life, staying in the Lake District with her sister Maggie, her favourite sister, and, in many ways, her favourite person. After Maggie's marriage to Henry Hobhouse, Beatrice made a trip alone to Rome, where, lonely and purposeless, she wished that her temperament would permit her to become a Catholic. Her sister Theresa married Alfred Cripps (their youngest child was Stafford Cripps), and only Beatrice and the youngest daughter, Rosy, were left at home. Laurencina Potter died in 1882 and for the next ten years Beatrice was in charge of the house and of her gradually failing father.

But these ten years were not empty ones. She fell in love, for the only time in her life, with a man twenty-two years older than she, and twice widowered — the famous Member of Parliament, Joseph Chamberlain. He was everything she was unused to: a man who assumed that any woman must be subservient, both to him and to his career; a striking figure with commanding height, cold good looks, monocle, orchid in his buttonhole, determined on power and political prestige. He for his part found the beautiful, wilful, argumentative, windblown Miss Potter irresistible. He asked her to marry him, and she refused.

The trouble was that she knew perfectly well why. It was not in her nature to be a parliamentary wife — or, indeed, a wife at all. She was a born partner. Wretchedly she realized that she could not expect equal fulfilment in love and work; and she chose work. On refusing Chamberlain, she flung herself into social work, starting with house investigations in Soho for the Charity Organisation Society and going on to Octavia Hill's housing reform projects, in which she worked beside another eminent woman — Henrietta Barnett. She became convinced of the righteousness of socialism and she came, naturally, into contact with its intellectual stars — the members of the Fabian Society. Here she met Bernard Shaw — and Sidney Webb.

No greater contrast can be imagined than that between the man she loved and the man she married. Sidney Webb was a short, thin man with a beard, a big head, short-sighted eyes behind thick spectacles, untidy clothes, brusque manners, and imperfect speech. He was a year younger than she. His first impression of her was that she was too beautiful, too rich and too clever, but he was soon completely fascinated and slowly wore down her resistance until she married him in July 1892.

It is revealing that the two volumes of her autobiography are entitled *My Apprenticeship* and *Our Partnership*, for between them they laid the foundations for the British welfare state. From the moment of their marriage life for Beatrice stopped being a mixture of "interesting gloom and light" with mingled excitement and despair; it was all "warm flat midday sunlight".

Beatrice Webb is always held up as an example of women's liberation, yet she was never a suffragette. She preferred to work from the inside, so to speak, seeing with her great clarity of vision that society as a whole must be changed if women were to find a true increase of freedom.

Beatrice Webb might be said to have "married the job", but she was not the only woman to do that: to find through her marriage the outlet whereby she could fundamentally influence her world. Another woman who did the same, though in a very different way, was Olave St Clair Soames. But Miss Soames had something that Beatrice Webb never knew: perfect unclouded happiness in an idyllic marriage.

Theoretically it ought not to have been. Her husband was fifty-four when she was twenty-two, and had never really bothered about women. One day, however, he saw her walking in Kensington Gardens with her spaniel and, when he met her again two years later, he remembered. This second meeting was on shipboard, heading for the Caribbean; the two instantly fell in love. Miss Soames noted in her diary that she got up before dawn to see him and kiss him, that she was happy all day with him as they felt and thought alike about everything, and that even when they tried to be serious "the imp of mirth steps in. Perfect bliss". She was, above all, not deterred by the fact that he was a famous man, perhaps the most famous man alive: Robert Stephenson Smyth Baden-Powell.

Baden-Powell was already a legend. He had supervised the siege of Mafeking with his own blend of inventiveness, panache, humour and fizzing high spirits; it was not a storybook siege of privation and suffering but a wonderfully daft blend of the ludicrous and the resourceful (as shown in Mr Brian Gardener's superb account). But it gave Baden-Powell his chance: it made him a hero, and enabled him to launch the Boy Scout movement. So many girls joined alongside their brothers (6,000 by 1909) that the Girl Guides practically founded themselves, organized at first by Baden-Powell's sister Agnes. He was a completely happy man, a general in his fifties, apparently a confirmed bachelor with plenty of outlets for personal fulfilment in his work, when he boarded the *Arcadian* for her maiden voyage.

A last-minute cancellation provided places on the ship for Miss Soames and her father. She was quite unconscious of the age difference;

this slim, neat man, with his fair moustache and twinkling eyes, had never lost, and never did lose, the boyish quality that made his age irrelevant. Her own personality captivated him instantly, a fact that did not surprise an interviewer who talked to Lady Baden-Powell in 1971 and commented that it is rare to find a woman whose charm remains undimmed at the age of eighty-two.

They were married in October 1912 in the simplest of ceremonies and honeymooned first at Roche Castle in Pembroke and then in Algeria where they camped out in the desert, cooking in pans scoured out between courses with roots and sand. "Olave is a perfect wonder in camp," declared Baden-Powell in a letter to his mother, "thoroughly enjoys the life and is as good as a backwoodsman at it. She is a splendid walker, a good scout and never loses her way. You were so right, my dear Ma, when you said one ought to marry a young woman." (As a twenty-seven year old captain he had reported that he was being pursued by women, but stated that he was going to wait until he was a major "and then it will be a £50,000 girl at home".)

Lady Baden-Powell remained sure that it was fated. Why else would they have waited for each other? She had received offers of marriage before she met him; he had never cared for any woman until he met her. They had three children and a cloudless life together. After nearly sixty years his widow could say what a privilege, what an utter joy, it had been: "We never had a thought apart or a word apart and we were given those twenty-eight years of heaven together."

Another distinguished lady who experienced a blissful married life had to wait for it for more than ten years. This was Miss Jean Leckie, a slender, fair-haired young woman who fell in love with a married man, and he with her. His wife, Louise, was ill — in the early eighteen-nineties she developed tuberculosis and the doctors gave her only a few months — but her husband nursed her devotedly, prolonging her life until 1906, although he was as deeply in love with Miss Leckie as she with him. They longed passionately to be together, but her devotion and his code of chivalrous honour upheld them until Louise died in 1906. In 1907 they were married and Jean Leckie became Lady Conan Doyle. The creator of Sherlock Holmes had at last found his own true happiness. Lady Conan-Doyle had not precisely "married the job", but, like Lady Baden-Powell, she had assuredly married the legend.

The outward conventions of the day could, and of course did, cause more unhappiness than a prolonged and patient wait. The rather bizarre example of Mr and Mrs Hubert Bland proves this.

Hubert Bland was one of the founders of the Fabian Society, a group of literate, thoughtful, clever intellectuals who believed in pushing the reformation of society by well-publicised debates and tracts. An early tract, "Why are the Many Poor?" fell into the hands of Bernard Shaw, who read it and promptly joined the Society. Here, he said, the most fortunate event of his life happened: he met and, in his own word, grabbed Sidney Webb, his essential antithesis. Webb knew all Shaw did not know and Shaw knew all Webb did not know, which, he said frankly, was precious little. Webb, competent, English, experienced in politics and administration, immensely able, respectable, unchangingly solid, exactly complemented the lively, volatile, brilliant, Irish Shaw, who was capable of assuming a dozen different characters in an evening. Shaw realized that Webb was the collaborator he needed; Webb, after a while, realized that Shaw's genius for publicity would thrust the Society forward.

The leading Fabians now included a fellow clerk of Webb's in the Colonial Office, Sydney Oliver, a good-looking aristocrat of revolutionary ideas and a college friend of his, Graham Wallas. The Fabian aims were extraordinarily diversified in those days: the members individually promoted, or tried to promote, their pet ideas, which included currency reform, Christian socialism, the single tax, philosophical anarchy and an instant manning of the barricades. The new members, reinforced by the Tory Democrat Bland, proclaimed the sensible fact that with capitalism in full blast on Monday, to storm the Bastille on Tuesday and expect to find socialism in full blast on Wednesday was a delusion. The anarchist and insurrectionist members left the Society.

Bland and Webb never got on well and it took all Shaw's efforts to keep the peace. They were physically as well as temperamentally opposed. Bland was a gigantic man, so broad-shouldered that Shaw always avoided sitting beside him as the two would need three chairs. His great strength and vitality not only taxed his wife but required the assistance of two supplementary wives, whom Mrs Bland helped through their subsequent maternal difficulties. She relieved some of the personal tension by falling in love with Shaw, who, with all his kindliness and common sense, steered her without disaster through the rocks and shoals of her emotions until she emerged into calm water, settling finally for an enduring friendship. Much of her feeling she poured into her poems, but it is not as a poet that she is loved and remembered. Her name was Edith Nesbit.

Edith Nesbit was the same age as Beatrice Webb, a youngest daughter with two elder brothers. Her youth was spent in a succession of boarding schools in England, France, and Germany, in all of which she was more or less unhappy, principally because she was a born nonconformist. When at length her mother settled at Halstead Hall in Kent she was far happier. She loved the house and the flowery garden and the nearby railway cutting, she could swim, climb, run, and play

Boating on the Thames on a dreamy afternoon was a standard part of Edwardian courtship. Drawing entitled "Dolce far niente" by W. Hatherell (*The Mansell Collection*)

Carolus Duran pinx   *Swan Electric Engraving Company*

L. Marlborough.

The majority of portrait painting was of the conventional semi-classical type, such as Carolus Duran's portrait of the American Consuela Vanderbilt, Duchess of Marlborough. Her dowry amounted to $2 million and gave a substantial boost to the Marlborough fortune. There were, however, surprisingly early examples of acceptable eroticism in painting, so long as they were of classical subjects, such as (*above*) G. Spencer Watson's "Aphrodite" exhibited at the Royal Academy in 1905. (*Collection of H. A. Gordon*)

Edwardian ladies had dresses for all occasions. (*The Publishers' collection and the Mansell Collection*)

Edwardian *femme fatale* whose naughtiness was acceptable to Edwardian gentlemen. (*Publishers' collection*)

Edwardian magazine illustrations were of a high standard. This is
Maurice Greiffenhagen's drawing for a short story "Bianca's Daughter"
published in the *Windsor Magazine* in autumn 1909. It is captioned
"A number of young men had added themselves to the group."

Edwardian courtship: (*top left*) Afternoon tea, one of the few socially acceptable times for meeting, was often the starting point of love affairs; (*bottom left*) tea was also a meeting time for people not in the front rank of society; (*centre*) at Newport in 1901, the American Vanderbilts took part in a parade of decorated automobiles; (*top right*) punting was another favourite meeting spot for opposite sexes; (*bottom right*) and the pianola was also popular.

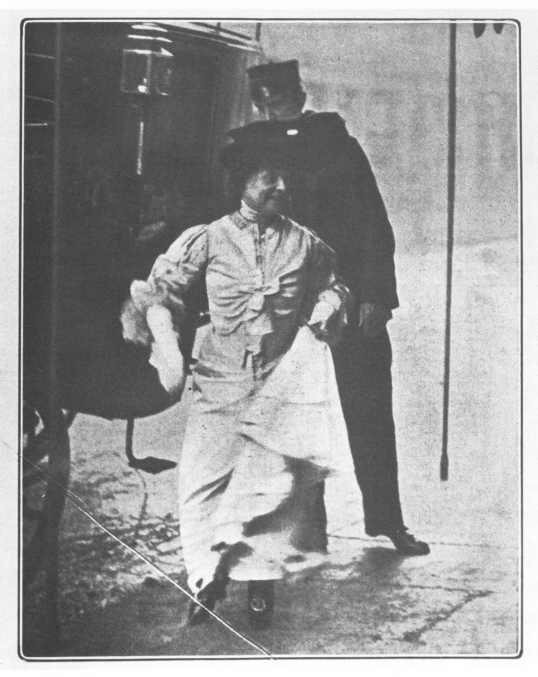

A rare action photograph of the period with the popular novelist Marie Corelli stepping out of a carriage. She hated photographers and refused ever to pose for them. (*Publishers' collection*)

tennis, and she wrote poetry and read everything she could lay her hands on. When she met Hubert Bland she was nineteen and he was twenty-two. She was instantly and for ever attracted. They were engaged for three years, and, when they married in 1880 at the Registrar's Office in the City of London, she was seven months pregnant. They lived at first in Lewisham and Mrs Bland began to write stories, to give recitations at smoking-concerts, to paint Christmas cards and to write the verses for them. She had three children and adopted the daughter of Hubert's second auxiliary wife. In 1886 Hubert became editor of a celebrated magazine, *Today*. Both the Blands were becoming well known through their Fabian Society contacts, and well liked for their sought-after home entertaining, an art at which both were highly skilled.

For years this curious life went on, revolving round three focal points: the intellectual Bohemianism of the Fabians and their acquaintances; Edith's poems and stories, still not great writing by any standards though she was making a name with them; and the sexual involvements of both Blands. No woman was safe from Hubert's advances and, perhaps in compensation, probably because her own nature was warm and passionate, Edith had love affairs too. Some of them were one-sided, short-lived infatuations, like the encounter with Shaw. Others were not. They included Richard le Gallienne and Dr Wallis Budge, with both of whom the affair came to the brink of elopement. Then everything, or at least a good many things, changed: in 1899 *The Treasure Seekers* was published.

Now at last, when Edith Nesbit was forty-one, came the fame, the prestige, the praise, and the money. The Blands moved out of London and went to live at Well Hall in Kent. It is described in *The Wouldbegoods*. Here all her best-known, best-loved books were written. Here, dressed in flowing robes and Turkish slippers and wearing silver bangles — each one a present from Hubert as each book came out — she entertained, worked on improvements to the house, wrote, made models that she called her "magic cities", played games, and smoked cigarettes. (Another of the very few points in common between her and Beatrice Webb.) Here Hubert Bland died in the summer of 1914.

It is not easy to establish any sort of common denominator among all these women who gained prestige through their work in the Edwardian period. Some of them deliberately wished to release women in general from the bondage of convention; some of them wanted to escape from such bondage for themselves, and be damned to all the rest; some turned to the arts or to social-political work as a compensation; some simply followed a private vision. Some worked, in the first place, for sheer financial necessity. But most of them, if not all, achieved a degree of independence and many gained fame and admiration.

One subject that still arouses a considerable amount of bitterness among women in Britain is the subject of divorce. In the Edwardian period it was immensely difficult, if not impossible, for unhappily married people to dissolve their miserable bond. In 1909 the Royal Commission on Divorce and Matrimonial Causes was set up, consisting of fourteen members, two of them women. Most men sincerely believed that such work was outside any woman's competence. (Yet none of them thought that marriage was.) The Commission called 246 witnesses, of whom 26 were women. The Commission found that men and women alike were forced into illicit unions because they could not afford to pay for a divorce.

The yearly average of decrees nisi in the five years from 1906 to 1910 was 638, of which about one-third were petitioned by wives. In 1910 there were 908 cases, 689 of them brought by men, of whom 344 were in trade or business, 267 in the professions, and 78 of independent means. A man could get a divorce on the grounds of his wife's adultery; a woman had to prove an additional offence, two years' desertion at least, cruelty, bigamy, incest or sodomy, none of which was particularly simple to prove. Divorce cases could be heard only at one court in London. An undefended suit cost from fifty to sixty pounds — over a year's average wages — and a suit that was defended cost anything up to five hundred.

The principal difficulty was then, as it still is, that the laws regulating marriage and divorce were usually framed by those who were contented with matters as they stood. Added to this, in the Edwardian period the social code implied that it did not matter what one did if apparent domestic calm and felicity were observed.

This will be seen in action in subsequent pages. It also helps to explain why so few people of independent means applied for a divorce: the open breach, clear to everybody, meant social ostracism. The "guilty" couple, who had asked to have an unhappy union dissolved so that one of them might marry someone else, legally, correctly, without ever having had a proper love affair, had to slink abroad and live in exile for years, sometimes for life, whereas the pair who were having casual affairs were received in the highest society provided that nothing was known officially. This conventional attitude has persisted for an astonishingly long time: as witness the example of the Duke and Duchess of Windsor, who, legally married, had to skulk abroad as though they were in perpetual disgrace.

The present-day reader may wonder why those who were striving for women's rights in the opening years of the century put all their efforts into campaigning for votes, rather than for a much fairer marital deal, which, after all, affects every married woman every day. The answer is partly that many of the campaigners were relatively uninterested in the marriage question. They were quite satisfactorily married, or quite composedly single, themselves, and did not feel affected: this may explain the point a little. It is also essential to emphasize the two separate attitudes among the campaigners.

They can be identified by their separate names. The original members of the National Union of Women's Suffrage Societies were called suffragists. They were moderate and respectable, holding meetings, writing tracts, and keeping the law. The Women's Social and Political Union, founded later by Mrs Pankhurst, were the suffragettes, and at first they were not militant either. Many of their members had been social workers, and had seen for themselves the conditions of life for thousands of women in slum homes, poor homes, sweated labour factories and workshops. They wanted to improve the general lot of women and came to believe that giving women the vote would greatly help this achievement.

As time went by, however, the leadership, and many of its adherents, saw more and more the vote as an end in itself. As opinions hardened on both sides, so the women came into a direct confrontation with the law and the men who made it, and the acts of violence started. Against all expectation they organized themselves brilliantly. Their courage was unquestioned. (It showed not only in their willingness to go to prison, but in some whole careers, like that of Emily Davison, who had at one time thrown herself down a stone staircase in Holloway to draw attention to the forcible feeding in women's prisons.) But where they went wrong was in not realizing quite how government works and they antagonized those who had shown themselves, if not precisely sympathetic, at least open to reason. Many far from hostile Liberal politicians wondered why the women did not harass the opposition meetings or at least try feminine blandishments, which might have worked better.

The full militancy did not get going during the reign of Edward VII. It started, with a campaign of smashing shop windows in Oxford Street, Regent Street, and Piccadilly, in March 1912. One couple — whose work had been invaluable to the cause, Mr and Mrs Pethick-Lawrence — resigned from the movement at this stage. It was now that the burnings and explosions and acid-pourings took place. With his usual admirable common sense, Shaw wrote a one-act play on the subject, *Press Cuttings*. It opens on the morning of 1 April three years hence (it was originally written in 1909) in the War Office, where General Mitchener sits opening letters at his writing-table. A cry in the street of "Votes for Women!" causes the General to snatch a revolver from a drawer in agonized apprehension, but nothing happens until an orderly comes in to say that a suffragette has chained herself.

MITCHENER. Chained herself? How? To what? We've taken away the railings and everything that a chain can be passed through.
THE ORDERLY. We forgot the door-scraper, sir. She lay down on the flags and got the chain through before she started hollerin. She's lyin there now; and she downfaces us that you've got the key of the padlock in a letter in a buff envelope, and that you'll see her when you open it.

After puffing protests from Mitchener and trembling reluctance on the part of the orderly, this is done. The suffragette appears, throws off her tailor-made skirt — revealing a pair of fashionable trousers — and presents himself as Balsquith, the Prime Minister.

Yes: it is indeed Balsquith. It has come to this: that the only way the Prime Minister of England can get from Downing Street to the War Office is by assuming this disguise; shrieking "Votes for Women"; and chaining himself to your doorscraper. They were at the corner in force. They cheered me. Bellachristina herself was there. She shook my hand and told me to say I was a vegetarian, as the diet was better in Holloway for vegetarians.

Asked why he did not telephone, the Prime Minister admits that all the telephones are tapped. Mitchener's solution is to shoot them down, which is his answer to everything until one of the suffragettes shoots the sentry, whereupon he demands indignantly whether anyone has any regard for the sanctity of human life. He groans with despair when he hears that the sentry, who "only got a stinger on his trousers", put down his gun and clouted the lady's head, which as a disciplinary measure appears to Mitchener perfectly deplorable.

The two men are waited upon by the secretary and president of the Anti-Suffragette League, Mrs Banger and Lady Corinthia Fanshawe. The manly brusqueness of the one and the romantic highfalutin of the other appeal to General Sandstone, Commander-in-chief of the Army, and to Balsquith. Sandstone offers marriage to Mrs Banger and Balsquith accepts Lady Corinthia's suggestion that she should be his Egeria. But both ladies terrify Mitchener so much that in self-defence he offers himself to his commonsense Irish charwoman, Mrs Farrell, who is capable of dealing with anything:

MITCHENER. When a man has risked his life on eight battle-fields, Mrs Farrell, he has given sufficient proof of his self-control to be excused a little strong language.

MRS FARRELL. Would you put up with bad language from me because I've risked me life eight times in childbed?

MITCHENER. My dear Mrs Farrell, you surely would not compare a risk of that harmless domestic kind to the fearful risks of the battlefield.

MRS FARRELL. I wouldn't compare risks run to bear livin people into the world to risks run to blow dhem out of it. A mother's risk is jooty: a soldier's is nothin but divilmint.

MITCHENER (*nettled*). Let me tell you, Mrs Farrell, that if the men did not fight, the women would have to fight themselves. We spare you that at all events.

MRS FARRELL. You can't help yourselves. If three-quarters of you was killed we could replace you with the help of the other quarter. If three-quarters of us was killed how many people would there be in England in another generation? If it wasn't for that, the men'd put the fightin on us just as they put all the other dhrudgery. What would you do if we was all kilt? Would you go to bed and have twins?

MITCHENER. Really, Mrs Farrell, you must discuss these questions with a medical man. You make me blush, positively.

MRS FARRELL (*grumbling to herself*). A good job too. If I could have made Farrell blush I wouldn't have had to risk me life so often. You n your risks n your bravery n your self-control indeed. "Why don't you conthrol yourself?" I sez to Farrell. "It's agen me religion," he sez.

The moral of the piece, according to the two leading characters, is that Generals must stop treating soldiers as if they were schoolboys and that Prime Ministers must stop treating women as if they were angels. The women have made rings round the men, but their militancy may be channelled into beneficial, or at least harmless, activities if they are sufficiently suitably tempted. It is Shaw's usual method of presenting a subject comically and allowing dozens of important ideas to emerge, forcing the audience to think afresh.

As matters turned out, however, the issue became academic. It was made so, curiously enough, by war. After the First World War, the vote was granted to women. True, it did not come all at once: it came in instalments, but it came without a struggle. And it was the war that enabled it to come.

One of the most frequently sung of music-hall songs in the opening years of the century was called "We all go the same way home". As August 1914 opened in brilliant bank holiday weather, the blue sky and the summer trees and the golden beaches shaped themselves into a landscape leading along a single road. The door of emancipation for the Edwardian lady swung open, and stayed open, because that road passed through Ypres and Passchendaele. Curiously enough, one part of that road ahead, dark and unknown and lit by shell-fire, was the *Chemin des Dames* — the Ladies' Road.

CHAPTER FIVE

The Colonel's Lady

The Colonel's Lady an' Judy O'Grady
Are sisters under their skins!
— Rudyard Kipling

The present-day reader, poring over statistics for 1901–1910, finds it all too easy to experience a rush of blood to the head, either because of the extremes of wealth and poverty revealed by these figures or because of the comparative ease and cheapness of hundreds of commodities. The Rowntree survey carried out in York in 1901 set the minimum possible income for a couple with three children at twenty-one shillings and eightpence a week, going on to point out that, on this sum, they could afford neither rail nor bus fares nor a halfpenny newspaper; no stamps, therefore they could send no letters; no contribution to the church collection, the trade union, nor the sick club; no tobacco; no beer; no tickets to a popular concert; no pocket-money for the children; no private funeral or medical care; no new clothes unless through sheerest necessity; and not one single day off ill for the wage-earner.

At this time, nearly half the men in the cotton industry and most farm workers got less than twenty shillings a week. Workers in ship-building and engineering trades received between thirty-two and thirty-six shillings, of which two-thirds was spent on food. Domestic staffs, who, of course, were provided with board and lodging, did better on the whole, though their wages look ludicrous on paper: cooks had from ten to twenty shillings a week plus their food, washing, and beer; housemaids from ten shillings and sixpence to fifteen shillings; a maid in London about eighteen pounds a year, eight pounds if she were under sixteen, plus keep and uniforms; washerwomen and charwomen were paid from half a crown to three shillings and sixpence a day, plus food and beer, and sometimes plus fares, though not by any means always. The lofty butler averaged upwards of fifty-eight pounds a year. It has been estimated by Mr John Gore that a dinner-party for twenty-four persons used 362 plates and 72 wineglasses in the dining-room alone, so, bearing the cooking in mind, it is easy to picture the quantity of washing-up and the time taken in preparation required.

Factory hours averaged fifty-five a week, though in 1902 it was becoming more customary for employers to let off their men an hour early on Saturday afternoons so that they "could attend to football matches". The miners asked for an eight-hour shift, which was refused because the coal-owners said it would bankrupt them. In 1909 the duty on tobacco was raised to eightpence a pound, causing tobacconists to complain that the fivepenny packet of twenty-five Woodbines was doomed. A quarter-pound tin of Embassy mixture tobacco cost two shillings; seven Rajah cigars cost one shilling. Men in those days smoked pipes or cigars almost exclusively: cigarettes were still thought rather effeminate by many, a notion killed stone dead by the First World War when men speedily found that the length of time it took to light a pipe, or even a cigar, was more than ample for the soldier doing it to be observed and precisely fired-upon from the enemy trenches. (It is, of course, from this that the superstition of three-on-a-match evolved.) In 1901–1910 most cigarette smokers were women and they were certainly smoking more than before, but still hardly ever in public.

Drink, quite as important as tobacco in popular esteem, was also cheap by today's standards, though it could make a great dent in the weekly budget, whisky costing three shillings and sixpence a bottle. Licensing hours everywhere were from six in the morning to eleven at night, and in 1900 the number of public houses in London was thirty per cent higher than today's figure. Restaurant meals were not exorbitant, even in the fashionable eating-houses: Edgar Wallace, still in his early impecunious days, found a friend to buy him a lunch at the Trocadero that included filleted Sole Borghese, "which knocked him for half a dollar", pheasant at four shillings and sixpence, a Melba pear costing two shillings and a thimbleful of "most glorious" 1830 cognac half a crown.

Sir Laurence Jones, when a poor barrister, said that he could dine "pretty well" in Soho for half a crown, "and at a pinch for a florin", comparing this favourably with the Union Club where luncheons seldom cost more than three or four shillings, though that, too, provided an excellent meal and often the bill was less. Prices had not changed all that much over the previous decade. Students of Sherlock Holmes will remember Francis H. Moulton's hotel bill in *The Noble Bachelor*, which led Holmes unerringly to the most expensive hotels, for it listed eight shillings for a bed and eightpence for a glass of sherry, two shillings and sixpence for breakfast and the same for lunch, and a shilling for a cocktail.

It is, of course, unrealistic and misleading to compare prices of 1900 with those of today, but a look back is full of interest. *The Times* of February 1901 advertised flats in Bedford Square with four to nine rooms plus kitchen and bathroom at rents from one hundred pounds a year "including rates, taxes, and water"; also a flat in Portman Square of "seven spacious and newly decorated rooms and kitchen" in "an unusual elegant house" to be let at £165 per annum "to lady or gentleman of position"; and on 25 February, it carried the following advertisement:

BROOK-STREET, Grosvenor-square. — Unique SUITE of CHAMBERS in modern house, decorated in tasteful manner, and fitted with electric light, to be LET, unfurnished, containing capital sitting room, bed room, and bath room. Fixtures will be left for use of tenant. Rent £280 per annum, including first class attendance and valeting.

The same issue, and that of the following day, quoted sea passages to Australia at sixteen pounds three shillings and six pence to fifty-five pounds, to Cape Town at nine guineas to thirty pounds, first class transatlantic fares from ten pounds, and a forty-five day voyage to the Far East at first-class fares of forty pounds to Singapore, forty-five to Hong Kong, and fifty to Japan. Second-class fares were twenty-eight pounds, thirty pounds ten shillings, and thirty-three pounds. There were special West Indies cruises, sixty-five days for sixty-five pounds, and eight weeks' travel to the Caribbean and Mexico for forty. Cook's were running Easter tours to Rome and back for fourteen guineas inclusive, and to Egypt and back for thirty-six guineas.

At the top of the social scale, it was possible to spend lavishly even then. City banquets cost six pounds a head. At one reception given by the Prime Minister, the flowers alone cost the Treasury nine hundred and eighty pounds. The King's wardrobe, including his imposing array of military uniforms, was insured for fifteen thousand pounds. The Duke of Meldrum, not the richest duke in Britain, had an income rated at a thousand pounds a day.

Amid shrieks of despair and growls of disapproval, the Budget of 1909, needing to raise an additional fifteen million pounds to reach the required total of one hundred and sixty-four million, raised the level of income tax, imposed a supertax on incomes of five thousand a year and over, introduced death duties, and increased the tax on drink, petrol, and tobacco, putting up the price of whisky to four shillings a bottle. In the 1906 election the Liberals had won 377 parliamentary seats, the Conservatives 157, the Independents 83, and Labour 53; in the first of the two elections of 1910 the Liberals dropped to 275 and the Conservatives rose to 273, the Independents held remarkably steady at 82, and Labour fell to 40. It was probably the emergence of the outlandish Labour Members with fifty-three seats that caused an aunt of the former Prime Minister, Arthur Balfour, to write furiously to him: "Damn! damn! damn!"

Against this kind of background the great houses stood, as firmly as possible, swarming with servants. The very greatest houses employed a groom of the chambers, who lived in comfortable married quarters with servants of his own, kept the accounts, and was responsible for the overall management including the hiring (and, if necessary, dismissal) of domestic staff. If there were no groom of the chambers, then the butler was the senior servant in the household. In his charge were the wine cellar, the serving of meals, the silver, and the general arrangements for the reception of guests. The housekeeper — senior female servant — supervised the women staff generally (though she knew far better than to meddle with either the cook or the nanny), was responsible for the cleaning and the laundry, and presented the menus daily to the mistress of the house for her approval.

Menservants included footmen, who assisted the butler, waited at table, answered the door, took messages and went on errands, and helped to clean the silver, of which there were vast quantities. On duty they wore livery; in very grand houses they appeared in powdered hair. While the butler was invariably called by his surname (with Mr in front of it from every other domestic employee), the footmen were called by their first names. There were the personal menservants, or valets, the Jeeveses to the master of the house and to his grown-up sons, who looked after the clothes of their employers, ran their baths, shaved them, and provided them with streams of gossip about everybody else in the house. Some houses employed pageboys, who with maturity would rise to the rank of footman; some had a knife-and-boot boy. The term "page", however, is misleading: the King, and the great dukes and marquesses, could, and did, have pages who were mature, well-bred, well-educated gentlemen. Certainly the present Queen still does.

On the female side, apart from the housekeeper, the governess, and the nanny with her attendant nursery-maid, there was the cook, a person of immense prestige and power. In a food-loving age, with the great Escoffier employed as chef in Cesar Ritz's new hotel in Piccadilly (where, incidentally, a poor student from the Far East called Ho Chi Minh took a part-time job for a few months), cooks mattered. Good cooks were greatly prized. Whatever her actual marital status, the cook was invariably addressed as Mrs. Working directly under her supervision were the kitchen-maids, who did all the duller things like cutting up and preparing ingredients, and the scullions, who did the washing-up and much of the rough cleaning and were possibly the hardest-worked servants in the house.

Much of the cleaning above stairs fell to the lot of the housemaids, whose day started with the clearing out of the many fire-places. Whether burning coal or wood, these had to be raked and swept, their iron frames brushed with black-lead, their metal edges burnished, their fire-dogs and fire-irons polished until they gleamed. The parlour-maids were the female counterpart of the footmen; the lady's maids, who were sometimes French, especially if the lady of the house aspired to high fashion, were the parallel of the valet. The family washing and the heaviest cleaning were done by daily washerwomen and charwomen.

All these operated within the house. Outside was the realm of three groups of employees: the stables, with the coachman, the grooms and the stable-boys, and a chauffeur if the family had a car or cars; the head gardener with his undergardeners and garden-boys; the head gamekeeper with his assistants. If the main gate had a lodge, there was of course a lodge-keeper, who dwelt with his wife and children in the lodge itself.

Various traditions clung to some of these many occupations. One obvious one was that each person aspired to the rank above his or her own, or, if already at the top of the heap, to move in time to a still grander house or (not always the same thing) to a still grander family. It was believed that governesses were always unhappy; that house-maids pined for the butler; that parlour-maids favoured policemen and kitchen-maids soldiers; that a state of warfare or, at best, an armed truce, existed between the nanny and the cook; that every valet hoped one day to set up his own outfitter's shop; and that head gardeners all came from Scotland. Certainly the prospects of promotion, the security and stability of living, the frequent kindness or even affection of the families they served, the beautiful objects they handled and the splendid settings in which they spent their time, made many people choose domestic service in preference to work in shops or factories, where conditions were often far harsher and prospects of eventual marriage less attractive.

Into the leading feminine role in houses like this — often a matter only of weeks out of the schoolroom — came the newly married lady. Perhaps her husband owned several houses — each with its retinue of servants, its grounds, its estate with its tenantry — and she must step smoothly into her appointed place as if she knew all the answers. This is where her own upbringing showed. If she had grown up in such a setting herself, she did at least know what to expect, and what ought to happen. If she came new to it, she needed character. Most of the Edwardian married ladies had some of both: a few had character in plenty.

Not that such ladies actually had to be able to *do* anything themselves: they simply had to know, or at least to learn, what had to be done by other people. As they grew older, they showed not the slightest reluctance in laying down the law to every younger woman they met, although they had never posted a letter, sewn on a button, made a pot of tea, gone out alone in the dark, or left the house without a maid in attendance even to visit the dentist.

The very young married ladies were sometimes naïve to the point of screaming boredom but some of them had an enchanting innocence that was refreshing. The nineteen-year-old Lady Fingall on her first shopping trip in London hailed a hansom and found that the driver was a very good-looking young man. He drove her to four places — to Busvine to have her habit altered, to Hodgkinson's to buy silk handkerchiefs and hunting ties, to her dressmaker in Dover Street for a fitting, and to the Berkeley where she had an appointment for lunch. He knew, she noticed, exactly where all these places were, and what services and goods they all supplied, and displayed not the least impatience at having to wait for her outside the first three addresses. Anxious that she might be running up too heavy a bill, the pretty young lady smiled up at him as he let her out at the Berkeley, saying that she would have liked very much to keep him, but was afraid that she could not afford it. The driver took off his hat and bowed to her, saying cheerfully: "That's just what I was thinking about you, miss."

But most girls knew, when they married, that they were just starting on a kind of endless London season that would last for the rest of their lives. With the way the marriage market was arranged, it was too much to expect that many couples would truly love one another. Of course, it is by no means certain that most couples truly love one another any way: in time with the less exacting a kind of genuine quiet devotion arises which does very well. The Edwardian aristocracy, however, understood that intrigues and affairs went on, and this was perfectly acceptable, provided — the all-important point — that it was never openly acknowledged. The consequences of admitting the facts, or of having them brought inescapably to the attention of one's spouse, were harsh indeed, for the code was then seen to have been violated.

Perhaps the most notorious example was that of Lady Londonderry, who was born Theresa Chetwynd-Talbot. She had a love affair with the Honourable Henry Cust, a tremendous lady-killer whose conquests were, by all accounts, numerous and easy. Lady Londonderry wrote stacks of impassioned love letters to Mr Cust, a rash action, seeing that he kept them. They were found — no one seems to know quite how — by her successor in Mr Cust's affections, Lady de Grey, who first read them (or bits of them) aloud to all her friends and then packaged them up and sent them to Lord Londonderry. His reaction was to send, by one of the footmen, a note to his wife that simply read: "Henceforth we do not speak." For over thirty years he never addressed a word to his wife except when absolutely necessary in public, a resolve maintained literally to the death, for when he was dying in 1915 and she sent a servant with a note imploring him to see her, he refused. Three years later when Lady Londonderry herself lay dying, Lady de Grey, now the Marchioness of Ripon, sent a telegram asking for forgiveness: again the answer was no, though perhaps the second refusal is less surprising than the first.

The extraordinary emphasis on never letting these things become openly known was probably caused by the unfortunate fact that, daily life among these people being what it was, it was impossible to keep a love affair really secret. Friends, relations, acquaintances, servants were everywhere; the social circle was small and one kept meeting the same faces in the same places. Also, as we have seen, time was essential, mainly because of the elaborate clothes of the period. How, one wonders, did any love affair ever mature? There were certain well-established conventions that helped.

Because great marriages involved great properties, it was absolutely essential for a woman to produce a legitimate heir first, and the sooner the better. Two or three genuinely legitimate children ensured the succession. But in the large families of the day, nobody minded all that much (or at any rate did not show it if they did), if the youngest two or three children came out with very different looks and temperaments compared with their elder brothers and sisters. Having done her duty, a woman was more or less free to look about for some amusement, if not for a real chance of experiencing deeper feelings.

If a love affair was going to happen, it seldom (if ever) was a matter of lightning speed. The social and political round, full and complex as it was, made many encounters fleeting — at least at first. Months might go by, filled — on the lady's part if not on the gentleman's — with glances, looks, blushes, hesitant fragmentary conversations, the exchange of little notes, before the first quivering assignations, which were usually "accidental" meetings in the Row in the morning, one dance in the course of a ball, a few words in the interval at the play or the opera when a good deal of visiting between the boxes was customary. Prolonged like this, plenty of potential fire could be banked up, before moving on to the next stage, which was, oddly enough, at tea-time.

Afternoon calls could be made without warning; a lady paying a call did not have to leave her carriage while her footman mounted the steps, rang the bell, and asked whether Lady X or Mrs Y was at home. If the answer was no, meaning either that she was absent from the house or that she did not choose to receive Mrs A or Lady B, the butler would walk up to the waiting carriage carrying a silver salver, on which the lady dropped her card, with one corner lightly turned up to show that she had called in person.

Afternoon tea was a delicately complicated ritual even when no love affair was in contemplation, and was a key event in the fashionable Edwardian day. It meant at least one servant on duty to admit callers and perhaps to bring the tea as well, (if no second servant appeared for that purpose), in charge of the whole apparatus of polished silver teapot, prettily flowered china, the little bell to tinkle for more hot water, and, of course, the food.

Men were expected to go out to tea frequently. One convention was that a man visiting a house at tea-time never handed his silk hat, gloves, and stick to the footman or maid opening the door to him, but carried them with him and placed them on the floor beside his chair in the drawing-room, keeping up the appearance of one who was merely "looking in for a few minutes". A hostess could have half a dozen men and women sitting in her drawing-room, like Mrs Higgins in *Pygmalion*: she makes it clear that she is "at home" on certain fixed days for this purpose, and the guests were never expected to stay long; indeed, Clara Eynsford Hill says that she and her mother have three at-homes to go to still that afternoon.

It follows that no one ever expected to eat much at tea, unless, of course, a mother brought with her one of her sons in his last half at Eton or down for the vacation from the university, when, like Algernon Moncrieff in *The Importance of Being Earnest*, he would devour all the tiny cucumber sandwiches, as well as much of the wafer-thin bread and butter (eaten rolled up if one felt compelled to keep one's gloves on), hot buttered muffins, and fingers of cake as he could manage to get hold of in fifteen minutes.

But it was simple to reduce afternoon tea to one guest and to instruct the servants that one was not at home to anyone else. For an hour or more one could be absolutely free from interruption: the children would not come down from the nursery until half-past five or six, the master of the house was out at tea-parties himself, or at his club, or even at the House of Lords, the servants never entered the room at tea-time unless rung for, and, free from prying eyes, the happy couple could carry the palpitating process of their affair a few steps further. Not much further: the clasp of hands, a kiss or two, and a good many breathless avowals, protests, and declarations were all that could be achieved at this stage. Not a bad thing, either, if one wants to extract the last drop of mileage from a fascinating situation: the Edwardians were, or quickly learnt how to be, sophisticated enough to know that appetites are destroyed as soon as they are gratified, if only for the time being.

If, however, a loving but illicit pair wanted to have an affair, only two ways of attaining this were normally possible. Either the lady must entertain the gentleman in her own home in her husband's absence, or both must be invited to the same house-party. The former course was difficult, if not impossible, if the servants were old retainers from the husband's family, for, though they would probably be discreet, the wife would feel guilty, a state of mind that destroys light-hearted pleasure. It would be difficult, too, if there were young children in the house, for they might — later if not at the moment — ask awkward questions, or make some comment that would be hard to explain.

The house-party was by far the best solution, even though it meant that others would be aware of the indiscretion: the hostess and her upper servants certainly, in order that the man could be invited and given a room reasonably close to that of the lady, whose husband, if at all possible, was staying with another house-party elsewhere or habitually slept in a separate room from that of his wife. Then the man must at all costs make certain that he visited the right room in the middle of the night. To be sure, every door bore its name-card, beautifully written with the visitor's title and slotted into its brass-framed holder. But in dark or dim passages in an unfamiliar house it was all too easy to make mistakes. Lord Charles Beresford once picked the wrong room and, dashing in with loud crowing noises, leaped into the bed where he found himself between the Bishop of Chester and the Bishopess. He got out rather faster than he had gone in and, because it was obviously impossible to explain, left the house before breakfast next day.

House-parties themselves encouraged the flowering of many a romantic liaison. One of the most popular games was (not surprisingly) hide and seek, especially before the installation of electric light. Ladies were expected to be frightened of going alone around the dimly lit corridors of a great house, so the hiders always went in pairs, and, as a matter of course, the seekers paired up too. This pastime afforded one of the very few chances for an unmarried girl to snatch a few minutes alone with a young man, though such a couple must on no account be among the first to vanish or the last to reappear.

Naturally the longer an affair persisted, the easier it became to maintain. Gossip died down after a while. Some affairs lasted so well that they were like second marriages, and, in due time, became so in fact. One of the most successful examples of this concerned the beautiful Louisa von Alten, who married the Duke of Manchester and then for thirty years was the mistress of Lord Hartington. Lord Hartington's father died and he became the Duke of Devonshire. The Duke of Manchester died and Louisa married her lover, so that she was then known among her friends as the "double Duchess".

The one person whose affairs could never be kept secret was Edward VII. Actually there is plenty of circumstantial evidence to support the view that, as King, his affairs were more matters of loving friendship than of technically physical liaisons. His age, his portliness, the long dissipations of his youth and his early middle-age, all indicate this, as well as the comments of the ladies themselves, revealed at a time when they had nothing to lose or gain either way. But all his life he had favourites. He needed the company of charming, appreciative women (obviously to compensate for the constant criticisms he had lived with as a boy) and, whether carried to fulfilment or not, he went on visiting them, writing letters, giving them presents, until the onset of the illness that put an end to his life in 1910.

Everyone knew when the King — or the Prince of Wales as he was before 1901 — called on a lady. His carriage was impossible to mistake or conceal. He wrote the ladies' names in his engagement book which lay openly on his desk for anyone to read. Being the Prince of Wales, certain things were permissible for him that would have been impossible for anyone else: he could entertain a lady to lunch or even to midnight supper after the theatre, something that no other man could expect to do, though in fairness the midnight suppers were usually for ladies of the *demi-monde* rather than for "real" ladies.

The Prince chose his lady friends and lovers from the ranks of mature women who were safely and correctly married. Nothing would have horrified him more, or shocked him more deeply, than the notion of an affair with a young girl. These were simply not fair game. The married ladies had a front to keep up, just as he had; they knew what it was all about; they would not make scenes or ask unreasonable favours; they would cause no trouble; they would behave with propriety (for the most part); and they would never, in any circumstances, do anything to embarrass Alix. He had various little forays after actresses and dancers but his escapades were invariably with ladies entrenched in society. Present-day analysts have reduced these to three genuinely important loves. Lillie Langtry and Alice Keppel have already appeared in these pages: the first and the last of the three. Now we must glance at the middle one, in many ways the most influential and remarkable, Frances Warwick.

The Countess of Warwick's life was crowded with incident, much of it scandalous — at least to somebody. Born Frances Maynard, her family descended on her father's side from the Tudor Maynard who had been granted lands in Essex by Elizabeth Tudor, and, on her mother's, from the Dukes of Grafton and St Albans, the latter springing from the illegitimate son of Charles II and Nell Gwynn. When Frances was fifteen she was invited to join a theatre-party by no less a personage than Benjamin Disraeli, Lord Beaconsfield. Frances, already a pretty girl, was clearly going to burgeon into radiant beauty, and Disraeli recommended her to the Queen as a possible bride for Prince Leopold — that same son who had scandalized his mother by hanging a picture of Lillie Langtry over his bed.

Queen Victoria approved. She knew that Frances was wealthy as well as well-known. Her father, dying at fifty, had left his three-year-old elder daughter heir to her grandfather's Maynard estates, valued at more than twenty-one thousand pounds. Prince Leopold was almost thirty and it was time he was settled. Delicate hints were dropped to Frances's mother and stepfather, the Earl of Rosslyn, and, when Frances was approaching her eighteenth birthday, all three were commanded to Windsor. After one of the Queen's rather terrifying cross-examinations Frances was judged to pass and Prince Leopold was ordered to pay a call of ceremony on Frances at home.

An insurmountable obstacle prevented the match: the Prince had fallen in love with a German cousin, Princess Helen of Waldeck-Pyrmont. When he dutifully visited Miss Maynard, he took with him an equerry, Lord Brooke, heir to the fourth Earl of Warwick. It was a fortunate choice of companion. Frances thought the Prince a pleasant, gentle person, but sparkled at the sight of Lord Brooke, whose glance answered hers. She and Francis Richard Charles Guy Greville (to give his full name), a powerfully built, handsome, lively fellow, came to a conclusion quickly. The pair were married in 1881, when Frances was twenty, in a brilliant ceremony in the Henry VII Chapel of Westminster Abbey, with Prince Leopold as best man. As a gesture of gratitude Frances called her eldest son Leopold.

Nine other members of the Royal Family attended the wedding, headed by the Prince and Princess of Wales, who signed the register. The cheers of the crowd outside startled the horses, who broke away from the decrepit old Warwick state coach and left the newly married couple marooned in front of the west door. By command of the Queen, Lord and Lady Brooke dined at Windsor the following day with Frances wearing her wedding dress. The Queen asked her to sign her birthday book, in which Frances, no doubt from force of habit, wrote her maiden name.

The Prince of Wales was then forty, twice the age of Frances. Certainly he admired her from that moment, for the Brookes were invited everywhere by the Prince, including invitations to what were then regarded as the peak of society life — the "small evenings" at Marlborough House. The main feature of these events was romping. Pieces of soap were put among pieces of cheese, frothed-up soap-suds spread on puddings instead of cream, medicines poured into wine-glasses, the young men slid down the stairs on tea-trays, the Princess turned cartwheels until her increasing rheumatic stiffness prevented this, people squirted soda syphons at each other, and the carpets were rolled back to make room for somewhat uninhibited dancing. Those who attended were automatically included in the biggest house-parties, before each of which the hostess had to work out who would wish to spend the night (or most of the night), with whom, and to ensure that everything used by the Prince, and by the Princess if she came, was new.

Lord Brooke belonged to that stratum of society who preferred out-door sports. His tastes lay in hunting, shooting, and fishing, though even he was not immune to feminine charm. He once took Elinor Glyn round the rose-garden at Warwick Castle, seized her in his arms and kissed her repeatedly. Elinor, less adventurous than her heroine, broke free, helped by the appearance of other guests in the distance, scampered upstairs, and, while dressing for dinner, told her husband what had happened. Her husband's response was simply: "Good old Brookie!"

But Lord Brooke was not a man to waste time pursuing other men's wives when there were field sports to be had, and Frances admitted years afterwards that from the beginning of her married life her husband assumed, or seemed to assume, that she would have admirers. It is difficult to fathom what he thought: clinging to the code of the day, he said nothing openly. Frances, of course, did the same at first.

Elinor Glyn invited her to read *Three Weeks* in manuscript, and Frances advised against publication, saying that Elinor would be ostracized; whatever one did, one should not write about it. Mrs Pat Campbell said much the same thing when she declared that it was immaterial what one did in the bedroom as long as one did not do it in the street and frighten the horses. (It was she who memorably remarked that wonderful was the peace of the double bed after the hurly-burly of the chaise-longue.) But Frances soon found herself talked about in scandalous terms.

In the third and fourth years of her marriage, Frances had a passionate love affair with Lord Charles Beresford, who was conspicuous for three things: his dashing naval career, his love affairs, and his astoundingly casual manner to the Prince. (He is reputed to have telegraphed the Prince declining an invitation (something unheard-of as royal invitations were akin to commands) writing blithely: "Can't possibly. Lie follows by post.") Be that as it may, he and Frances disported themselves for a long time, so long that everybody knew about it, and each developed jealously proprietary feelings towards the other. Frances suddenly heard that Beresford's wife was expecting a child. Although by then the temperature had cooled between them, she boiled into one of her famous rages and wrote him a furious letter. It was a highly compromising document and by a stroke of misfortune for Frances, or, in the light of subsequent events a fortunate stroke depending on how one views it, the letter arrived during Beresford's absence on an official visit to Germany and was opened by his wife.

This lady instantly took legal advice, approaching George Lewis, the solicitor who throughout a long career specialized in society scandals. He was skilful at guiding his clients through the courts, but even more adept at ensuring that matters could be settled out of court. Mr Lewis warned Frances not to harass Beresford or embarrass his wife. Still smarting, she went to the Prince of Wales, to appeal for his help in retrieving the letter.

The Prince saw Lewis, who, appreciating in which exalted quarter the wind was blowing, advised his client to give up the letter. The Prince added pressure by excluding the Beresfords from social gatherings to which he, and of course Frances, went. Lord Charles was abroad on naval duties for long stretches just then, but his wife wrote him endless plaintive letters about the way she was being treated. He therefore wrote angrily to the Prince that at the first opportunity he intended to state publicly that His Royal Highness had behaved like a blackguard and a coward.

From the time when she had appealed to the Prince, Frances had been his mistress, an association that lasted for nine years. Throughout that time he plainly adored her, wrote dozens of extremely indiscreet letters in which he gossiped about all sorts of people and addressed her, using her pet name, as "my own lovely little Daisy" and "my darling little Daisy wife". He revealed, too, his opinions concerning the affairs of the day, some of which could have been, and were, highly damaging when divulged to others. He claimed that it would do England no harm to be ruled for a while as Germany was ruled; that the Tsar of Russia was talking foolishly when he hoped for international disarmament; and that the Tsarina and her so-called religious advisers badly influenced Nicholas II who was too weak to resist them any way.

He signed his letters to Frances: "Your only love."

Before Beresford came home to carry out his threat, the Prince was involved in the Tranby Croft scandal. It was only because of Lord Rosslyn's death that the Brookes were not staying at Tranby Croft at the time. Perhaps, if they had been, the Prince would have spent less time playing baccarat with his specially made counters — a gift from Alfred de Rothschild — and the newspapers would have been deprived of the sight of the Prince of Wales in the witness-box and the fizzing revelations that the smart Marlborough House set were gamblers, if not worse. But the trial took place; the newspapers and their readers buzzed; Beresford came home, still threatening; and the Prince decided that it was time to retaliate. He asked the Prime Minister, Lord Salisbury, to intervene.

Salisbury took the line that, whatever happened, nothing must be made public. Gossip and rumour were doing quite enough damage already: Beresford's sister-in-law, Mrs Gerald Paget, had written, and was busily circulating, an explosive pamphlet called *Lady River*, readings of which packed the drawing-rooms of London with delightedly horrified ladies; the echoes of Tranby Croft still reverberated; and Alix, visiting her parents in Denmark, cancelled her journey home for the Prince's fiftieth birthday, and went on to stay with her sister, the Empress of Russia, in the Crimea, giving no date for her return.

Lord Salisbury and a stroke of chance saved the situation. Prince George, the future King George V, fell victim to an attack of typhoid fever, the illness that had killed the Prince Consort, and Alix came home at once. Salisbury persuaded the Prince of Wales that the Beresfords would be satisfied with a formal exchange of dignified letters — already prepared by Salisbury for signature — plus an undertaking to exclude Frances from Court functions for a while. Edward agreed, provided that the incriminating letter could be returned to Frances. This was done, and the letter burnt.

Frances was not too cast down by her temporary banishment: she was missing mainly official functions, attended by the Princess, and there was nothing to prevent her from meeting the Prince far more easily in her own house, or in other country houses. In order to make visits easier to Easton Lodge, her big house in Essex north of Dunmow, she asked for a local railway station to be built. This was done, and the Prince's special train, crowded with guests and servants, could stop within a short carriage drive of the estate.

The Prince's extravagant tastes, together with the knowledge that he was susceptible to attractive women, caused hostesses or would-be hostesses to rise to extravagance also. He sometimes arrived unannounced during a country Saturday to Monday (the term "week-end" was still thought vulgar), so, just in case he might, stacks of costly foods and wines, including his favourite ptarmigan pie, lobster salad, Chablis and extra dry champagne, were kept in the huge larders; if he were actually staying at a country house, his rooms were re-decorated and often entirely refurnished in lavish style; and enormously complicated arrangements were made to accommodate not only the guests he brought or asked to meet, but the retinue of servants without whom he never travelled. He brought his own footmen to stand behind his chair and serve his meals, two grooms with at least two horses, a pair of loaders to accompany him when shooting,* a gentleman-in-waiting, two or three equerries, and two of his four valets. One pair stayed at home to look after the vast array of clothes he was not bringing, the other pair found each day barely long enough to maintain in perfect condition the wardrobe that accompanied him. His servants filled one wing of a house. Coping with these and the extra horses, carriages and grooms in the stables, and the high level of entertainment expected by the Prince — to say nothing of the necessity for keeping up with other hostesses who might, like the Duchess of Devonshire, have more than four hundred and fifty people under her roof at Chatsworth at any one time — it is easy to appreciate how money poured out too liberally. Frances, lacking the resources of a Rothschild, began to mount up ruinous debts.

But she kept up the pressure none the less. Huge parties with elaborate fancy dress, culminating in a *bal poudré* for four hundred guests in eighteenth-century French costume, drained her finances, yet this particular ball had an unexpected sequel.

It was held in 1895, when the Brookes had become the Earl and Countess of Warwick and had moved from Easton Lodge to Warwick Castle. For some years Frances had been increasingly and uneasily aware of the condition of the poor. She had talked many times with the crusading journalist William Stead, and had in 1894 been elected one of the local Poor Law Guardians. Moreover, she had opened a needlework school at Easton Lodge for poor or handicapped girls. It was her practice to read about the very grand social occasions of the day that were fully reported in the papers, and now, to her indescribable fury, she saw a sharply critical comment on the Warwick Castle *bal poudré*. The writer condemned the waste of "thousands of pounds spent on a few hours' silly masquerade" and stressed the plight of "men and women and children the while huddling in their ragged hovels, their meagre shrunken flesh pierced by the winter's cruel sting". The paper was the *Clarion*, the author of those lines the celebrated author of the blazingly

---

* King Edward VII once noted that in two days his party had shot 5,817 rabbits and 1,973 pheasants.

ironical and influential *Merrie England*, Robert Blatchford.

A nettle grasper by temperament, Frances went straight up to London and marched into the *Clarion* offices in Fleet Street. Blatchford, naturally, was astounded to see this beautiful, furious creature confronting him, but he began, rather shyly and politely yet with growing warmth, to put his own point of view. A long, enjoyable discussion followed, and Frances, returning home with a good deal to think about, realized that she believed Blatchford was right. She became a convinced Socialist.

The uproars previously created by Frances were nothing compared with what she caused now. She was regarded as a traitor to her own order; if she meant it, that was shocking, and if she did not, it was insane. The people who went to political meetings and roared their approval of the great Socialist speakers of the day found it hard to take this new recruit seriously. What did a woman know of such subjects, especially a woman who went to Paris with the Prince of Wales, travelled to Epsom on the Royal Special, and gave and attended huge lavish parties? But she meant it. She campaigned for the Socialist cause with a fervour that left her only when the flood tide of the First World War washed away many of the obstacles against which she had battered in vain. This new interest weighed, however slightly, in the slackening of her relationship with the Prince.

Undoubtedly he genuinely adored her, and equally there is no doubt that her feelings for him were less deep than his for her. She was fond of him, she loved being at the centre of events, the importance given her by his regard; but a great passion, never. That was reserved for his successor, Captain Joseph Laycock, a powerfully built and attractive man five years younger than she; with him, for the only time in her many amorous escapades, she felt the more vulnerable, the more needing, of the two.

As Frances declined in the Prince's company over the closing years of the century, the star of Alice Keppel rose over his horizon. In any case, matters were bound to change as soon as he became King. The Prince of Wales's indiscretions are one thing: the monarch's, quite another. Edward VII was advised and supervised far more carefully by his elderly courtiers than he had ever been since his marriage. They thought, and made no secret of it, that if he must have a mistress or loving friend with whom to enjoy himself, it had better be someone discreet who knew how to behave. Mrs Keppel filled these requirements perfectly. It is a long way from lavish great country house balls to the bread-and-butter game played in Mrs Keppel's modest sitting-room; and the Court, and Alix, breathed more freely.

Alix, however, was never one to bear ill will, nor would it ever have occurred to her to fight for her husband. Frances made friendly overtures to Alix and these were warmly received. She remained on good terms, even affectionate terms, with both the King and Queen throughout Edward's reign.

As that reign opened, one newly married couple entered the social scene with a buzz of speculation. These were Mr and Mrs George Cornwallis-West. Married at St Paul's, Knightsbridge, on 28 July 1900, a darkly overcast morning so that the electric lights had to be switched on in the church for the fully choral service held amid a mass of white flowers, the bride wore a pale blue chiffon gown with lace elbow-length sleeves, lace and chiffon ruchings on her pale blue silk underskirt, a hat of tucked chiffon decorated with lace, white roses, and a pale blue osprey with a diamond clasp, and a pearl and diamond necklace. She carried a few white roses and a prayer book and was given away by the Duke of Marlborough. She was a black-haired, bright-eyed, beautiful creature of forty-six, twenty years older than her husband, and she had been Lady Randolph Churchill.

George Cornwallis-West was closely associated with some spectacular Edwardian ladies, indeed: his two wives, his two sisters, and his mother. His father, William Cornwallis West (the hyphen was not added until the eighteen-nineties), was born in Florence in 1835. Educated at Eton, he was called to the Bar, but soon abandoned that for a dilettante existence in Italy, living in Florence and Rome, copying old paintings, and acquiring an Italian mistress who presented him with three daughters.

When he was thirty-three his elder brother died unmarried, and William reluctantly tore himself away from Italy (the whole process took four years) to come back to the family estates, ten thousand acres around Ruthin Castle in Denbighshire. He knew it was now his duty to marry and provide Ruthin with an heir. He was appointed Lord Lieutenant of Denbigh and then, rather surprisingly, he fell in love with one of the daughters of the Marquess of Headfort, a seventeen-year-old Irish beauty with the incredible name of Mary Adelaide Virginia Thomasina Eupatoria FitzPatrick. He called her Patsy. They were married in October 1872 at St Patrick's Cathedral in Dublin.

Their first child was a girl, Mary Theresa Olivia, first known in the family as Dany but then nicknamed Daisy — another of the bunch of famous Edwardian Daisies. Blonde and exceedingly attractive, she had hardly emerged from the schoolroom and the tomboyish life among horses and ponies at Ruthin before she caught the eye of Prince Hans Heinrich of Pless, heir to the comparatively distinguished House of Hochberg.

German court protocol demanded that any Hochberg bride should be able to display sixteen armorial quarterings in her pedigree, so William applied to the College of Heralds, saying, truthfully, that he could trace the family back to Henry III. In due time an enormous document, compared by the Wests with a patchwork quilt, arrived; Prince Heinrich was satisfied; and Daisy's wedding was celebrated at St Margaret's, Westminster.

She was now the mistress of two large, rich, and beautiful German castles, where uniformed trumpeters received her carriage as it entered the grounds, and every time she moved from one room to another a bell was rung and a liveried footman walked in front of her. At the Castle of Pless there was, however, no bathroom, until Prince Heinrich had one installed for Daisy, decorated lavishly in gold mosaic.

Daisy kept a diary in which she recorded her feelings fairly freely. She was a happy character: she loved her new homes, grew fond of her somewhat crusty old father-in-law, whom she enjoyed gently teasing, appearing at dinner one night in a dress she had made out of two sacks; she remained devoted to Prince Heinrich and to their three sons; she never ceased to love her family, and, although she often felt homesick for beautiful Ruthin and the life there as part of what the family called the wild West show, she did not allow this to undermine her humour. Daisy of Pless derived her amusement from the social round of parties, balls, riding and driving, yacht parties and gossip, without apparently feeling the need for extra-marital affairs. The only cloud in her sky, and it was a big one, was the agonizing later division of feeling between her countries of origin and marriage that arose through war.

The Wests' second child, George Frederick Myddelton, was born at Ruthin on 14 November 1874, sixteen days before the birth at Blenheim of his future stepson, Winston Churchill. Two days before his birth, the lovely Patsy had chased the gardener round the grounds of Ruthin with a hosepipe full on. She was one of the "Professional Beauties" of the period, her photographs were displayed and sold everywhere, and it was the custom to put on invitation cards the alluring words, written in ink above the engraved printing: "Do came — the PBs will be there." It is interesting to note that the PBs included Lady Randolph Churchill and Mrs Langtry, though Patsy and Lillie were the acknowledged leaders in this field. Proof of this comes in a story told by the Duke of Portland years afterwards. When he was travelling in Egypt, he discovered that the Egyptian donkey-boys advertised their best animals by calling them, regardless of sex, "Mrs Langtry" and "Mrs West"; the "second-class donkeys" were "only Antony and Cleopatra".

Much has been written about George Cornwallis-West's fear of his mother, how Patsy locked him up in cupboards if he behaved in a way that displeased her, of the impossibility of his ever being able to confide in her, which would seem to explain why both his wives were many years older than he. Certainly as a boy he developed interests unlikely to attract Patsy's attention: one of these was his abiding love of railway locomotives, which he learnt to drive on a quarry-line near the Menai Straits. In time he persuaded friendly engine-drivers to let him get on the footplate of the Bournemouth Belle at Basingstoke and take the controls as far as Brockenhurst, a thing entirely against the rules. In the summer of 1898, when he was twenty-three, he was invited to a house-party at Warwick Castle, where Frances Warwick presented him to Lady Randolph Churchill, then a widow.

Lady Randolph was, at least subconsciously, ready to marry again. Her increasingly disillusioned marriage to Lord Randolph had been further damaged by her long love affair with an Austrian nobleman, Count Charles Kinsky, who, according to many observers, was the great love of her life. When, apparently mainly for family reasons, he married, she told friends that she had no intention ever to remarry herself, unless a perfect darling with forty thousand a year appeared. George Cornwallis-West was — in Lady Randolph's opinion — certainly a perfect darling, though he did not possess anything like forty thousand a year: she chose to disregard that and the marriage took place, none too well received by her two sons, Winston and Jack.

Lady Randolph was one of the considerable number of rich and beautiful Americans who were appearing on the English scene and marrying into the English aristocracy. Leonard Jerome, an American of Huguenot origin, brought his three lovely daughters to England, where the eldest, Clare, married Mr Moreton Frewen; the youngest, Leonie, married Sir Jack Leslie and had a life-long love affair with Prince Arthur of Connaught; and the middle girl, Jeanette, married Lord Randolph Churchill after a love-at-first-sight encounter on shipboard at Cowes. But sometimes there was no question of love involved. When William Kissam Vanderbilt came to Europe, his wife had already selected, for their tall and beautiful nineteen year old Consuelo, a future husband: no less a personage that the ninth Duke of Marlborough, then twenty-one, known in his family as "Sunny". There was absolutely no question of ever consulting Consuelo's own preference; years later her mother admitted that she had always ruled her daughter with a despot's firmness and that she had simply ordered Consuelo to do as she was told. It cost William Vanderbilt about six million pounds, a hundred thousand dollars a year for life to the Duke as well as a huge block of stock in the Battle Creek Railway Company. The Duke's mother reacted to the marriage with basic simplicity, telling Consuelo immediately after the honeymoon that her first duty was to have a son because it would be quite unbearable if "that little upstart Winston

ever became Duke" and going on to ask brusquely: "Are you in the
family way?"

Consuelo joined in the social parade of the time with zest, riding in
the Row twice a day (in perfectly cut habits on horseback in the
morning, in lace and silks in a barouche in the late afternoon), watching
polo at Hurlingham or Roehampton, driving to Ranelagh, going to
Court (where once on her way to a ball she startled her escort by com-
plaining that her stays were too tight and going on with many contor-
tions to pull and wrench them out through the top of her dress), giving
and attending dinners and parties and all the rest of it: but the marriage
was not happy. George Cornwallis-West once told Winston Churchill
that it reminded him of Hogarth's Marriage à la Mode; and indeed the
couple separated in 1906.

George Cornwallis-West's younger sister, Constance Edwina, nicknamed Shelagh, a brunette as lovely as her elder sister, grew up to
marry England's richest duke, the Duke of Westminster.

Rumour has it that the Prince of Wales included Jennie Churchill
among his love affairs. This seems unlikely. His loving attention was
concentrated on Lillie Langtry and Frances Warwick at the periods
when Jennie was most vulnerable and, once she had discovered George,
she was single-mindedly concentrated on him. But it is true that the
Prince delighted in Jennie's appearance, in her warm, lively personality,
her dark-haired glowing looks. (One must remember that his three
great loves were fair.) She was indeed remarkable: one Edwardian
gentleman noted for his complete indifference to women's beauty said
forty years later that anyone would turn round to look at her in the
street, a striking testimonial.

It is probable that the Prince's admiration for Jennie caused him to
relent towards Lord Randolph, with whom he had quarrelled during
the Mordaunt divorce, and permit the Churchills' return from "exile"
in Dublin, where the Duke of Marlborough went as Lord Lieutenant in
1876, taking with him his younger son as unpaid secretary. This had
been Disraeli's tactful suggestion, and Lord Randolph performed his
secretarial duties between spells of shooting, hunting, fishing, sailing,
catching lobsters, playing chess, and accompanying his wife to dinners
and balls at Dublin Castle, where her looks, compared by more than
one observer with those of a black panther, lent glamour to the scene.

Later their small son remembered warnings against heedless walks
in Phoenix Park because people sometimes got shot there, of a garden
the size of Trafalgar Square which mysteriously dwindled to something
more like a tennis court by the time he revisited it as a young man, and
his viceregal grandfather saying, as he unveiled a military monument,
the exciting words: "with a withering volley he shattered the enemy's

line". When Winston was five, the Churchills came home, and once more the black panther graced the drawing-rooms of London.

Winston was twenty when his father died and his mother at last became approachable to him. She had been a lovely but remote vision throughout his childhood, and his father had not been close to his sons either. Consequently the new relationship, more like that of brother and sister than of mother and son, gave great pleasure to both. But his early years had implanted in him two cardinal needs: the thrill of a fight and the essential of a stable happy marriage. He eventually achieved both in ideal circumstances. In the spring of 1908, when he was President of the Board of Trade and a member of the Cabinet, he went to a dinner party given by Lady St Helier at her London house in Portland Place. He arrived, as usual, slightly late, and was introduced to a tall, beautiful girl in a white satin dress; she had light brown hair, grey eyes, and sparkling conversation. Her name was Clementine Hozier.

Winston naturally admired good looks, but he was agreeably cynical about the marriage market. He and Edward Marsh used to amuse themselves at parties by assessing the ladies on the basis of "the face that launched a thousand ships" — one might be rated at two hundred, or two hundred and fifty, or, dispiritingly, only at a sampan or small gunboat. One lady who was emphatically in the thousand class for Winston was the beautiful actress Ethel Barrymore. Miss Hozier was a similar type, and, once he had seen her, Winston looked at nobody else. They were married in September.

It was an enormous wedding — Sir Edward Carson said that it had been advertised nearly as much as Eno's Fruit Salts — with sixteen hundred people packing St Margaret's, Westminster, and a huge crowd outside. The King sent Winston a gold-mounted walking-stick; the presents included twenty-five candlesticks, twenty-one inkstands, ten cigarette cases and a quantity of books. The bridesmaids wore amber satin with wide black hats wreathed with camellias, and carried cream roses. The bride, of course, looked exquisite, but the bridegroom's suit was unkindly described by the *Tailor and Cutter* as "making the wearer look like a glorified coachman". Winston would never have appeared in a "best-dressed" list, but, in the light of history, no one minds that: he always looked exactly like himself.

Clementine Hozier was ten years younger than her husband. Her family was socially irreproachable, but not wealthy. Colonel Sir Henry Hozier had married Lady Blanche Ogilvy, daughter of the Earl of Airlie, a girl twenty-five years his junior; they had four children, but the marriage was not a success. Much of Clementine's early life was spent in rented lodgings, in London, Seaford, Berkhamsted, and in

France. She contributed to the London rent by giving private French lessons and also spent a year or two at the Berkhamsted School for Girls. When she came "out" her dress allowance was meagre for a debutante: thirty pounds a year.

Her great-aunt, Lady St Helier, saw to it that the Hozier girls met eligible young men; Clementine was hard to please, but she seems not to have hesitated when she met young Mr Churchill. It was a lucky choice for both: blessed as she was with charm, intelligence, and good looks, Clementine was not interested in the least in extra-marital enterprises, instead becoming that pillar of the state, the perfect parliamentary wife. As for Winston, his opinion was perfectly summed up in the smiling sentence with which he closes his book, *My Early Life*: he wrote that in 1908 he married and lived happily ever after.

Two more Edwardian ladies need to be passed in review in order to complete the range of what is today called "life-style" among the highly placed. The first is so closely identified with the subsequent reign that it is not always easy to remember that she qualifies as Edwardian: but there is no doubt of it. This is Victoria Mary Augusta Louisa Olga Pauline Claudine Agnes, daughter of the Duke of Teck, born on 26 May 1867, and known as Princess May.

There seems no doubt that Queen Victoria picked Princess May to be the next-but-one Queen of England. Her choice of the shy but eminently sensible, fair, clear-eyed, steadfast young woman was prompted by the uncomfortable fact that the heir to the throne, the eldest son of Edward and Alix, was Prince Albert Victor, the Duke of Clarence and Avondale, a most unfortunate young man. His appearance caused him to be nicknamed "Collars and Cuffs"; his family called him Eddy. He was delicate in health, weak in intellect, irresponsible and unpredictable in behaviour, and incapable of either concentration or control. A suggestion that he might marry Queen Victoria's granddaughter Alexandra of Hesse was rejected by the girl herself, which bewildered the Queen ("she refuses the greatest position there is," she wrote indignantly to her elder daughter). A very different destiny awaited Alexandra, for she married the last Tsar of Russia, Nicholas II. Meanwhile, Prince Eddy lackadaisically drifted in and out of mild attractions for entirely unsuitable English ladies, or European princesses who were either Catholics, or daughters or pretenders, or even both, until pinned down to a formal betrothal with Princess May. By great good luck from her point of view, not to mention that of England, Prince Eddy fell ill and died six weeks before the wedding was to have taken place.

Now it was essential to make a gradual, tactful and unobtrusive switch of policy to bring Princess May, Parliament, and the nation round to the idea that she should marry the new heir apparent, Prince

George, Duke of York. It took two years and three months to accomplish. In April 1893 Princess May accepted the Duke of York's proposal. Eighteen years later he sent her a note, one of the very many so written during his life (writing, incidentally, as always, with Prince Eddy's pen), stating that they suited one another admirably. He thanked God every day for the blessing of her loving companionship, especially considering the tragic events that had made it possible, and the way in which people had gone about saying that he only married her out of pity, which just showed, he declared robustly, what rubbish could be talked and believed. In other notes he used uncharacteristically ardent phrases like "I adore you sweet May".

Starting off unpromisingly with two shy people who found it difficult to express their feelings in words, the marriage grew into the most successful of royal marriages — not, perhaps, that this is saying much. But successful, happy, confident, and utterly monogamous it was. Princess May resembled Queen Victoria in that both women failed to fall into raptures about babies, and, indeed, both had a shrewd suspicion that those who do are less capable of dealing with grown-up people. Yet Queen Victoria had nine children, and Princess May had six: David, who became King Edward VIII and Duke of Windsor; Bertie, who became King George VI; Mary, Princess Royal; Henry, Duke of Gloucester; George, Duke of Kent, killed on active service in 1942; and John, whose permanent ill health from epilepsy forced him to lead a secluded life at Sandringham until he died aged thirteen in 1919. She was no more an ideal mother than, in her different way, Queen Victoria had been: but the old Queen had been perfectly right in selecting Princess May as future Queen Mary of England.

Prince George and Princess May, Duke and Duchess of York, were present at the marriage of the other lady, who also became a queen, but, in this case, her actual marriage brought her that rank at once. She was another of Queen Victoria's granddaughters, Princess Victoria Eugènie, daughter of Princess Beatrice and Prince Henry of Battenberg. She was known in the family as Ena, and, having grown up with three brothers, she loved open-air pursuits such as riding, rowing and fishing. She had been brought up in the Queen's household, for, after the death of Prince Henry in 1896, when Princess Ena was eight, the Queen had demanded the company of her youngest daughter again, just as she had required it for years before Princess Beatrice's marriage. In the calm if stuffy circle of the Queen's life, the young Ena had grown up without the smallest presentiment of what the future would hold for her.

Alfonso XIII, King of Spain, was being pestered by his ministers to marry, not a surprising thing when one considers the chequered history of Spain throughout the nineteenth century. Various European princesses were suggested, but the young king refused to marry a photograph: he wanted to look around and make up his own mind. Soon after his nineteenth birthday he went on state visits to Paris and London. Someone mentioned that the King's niece, Princess Patricia, daughter of the Duke of Connaught, was a delightful young lady, but neither she nor Alfonso was particularly impressed with the other.

Alfonso did, however, find his attention straying more than once towards the fair-haired, blue-eyed Princess Ena. Encouraged by Ena's godmother, the former French Empress Eugènie, the two met more often than the tight schedule of a state visit might otherwise have allowed. Six months later Princess Ena visited San Sebastian, where the pair met again. Now Alfonso was sure of his feelings, but one great obstacle barred the way: Ena, of course, was a Protestant. In answer to alarmed twitterings in Court circles, King Edward said that she was a Battenberg and could therefore adopt any religion she liked. She must, of course, renounce her claim to the succession, if she became a Catholic. Princess Ena did both: and her uncle saw her off with the unnerving comment that whatever things were like in Spain she must not come whining back home.

The wedding was enough to make any girl return if not indignantly marching back demanding sanctuary. In May 1906 the Princess and her mother arrived in Spain: naturally a king regnant had to be married in his own capital. The Spaniards, charmed by her physical appearance, greeted her as *la reina hermosa*, the beautiful queen, and Madrid was brilliant with decorations and packed with visitors. The thirty-first of May was warm and fine, and the three-hour wedding service in the Church of San Jeronimo went smoothly. Soon after two in the afternoon, the procession set off slowly through the packed streets to the Palacio Real and by Spanish custom an empty carriage, the carriage of respect, preceded the carriage of the King and Queen. The King's carriage was drawn by eight horses and had a gold crown on the roof.

Two-thirds of the way along the old, narrow Calle Mayor, the procession halted, presumably because of a traffic jam ahead where the front of the cavalcade was arriving at the palace. A large bouquet of flowers was flung from an upstairs window; it fell in the road beside the horses, and exploded. For a moment a cloud of black smoke filled the carriage so densely that the King could not see the Queen. There was a pandemonium of screams from the crowd and from the horses, and officials came running up to see how the King and Queen were. Alfonso was cool and prompt in his reactions: he ordered the carriage of respect to take them on to the palace and told his aides to let his mother and Ena's know that they were unhurt. When he reached the carriage of respect after helping his wife across the intervening space and trying to shield her from seeing the dead and wounded men and horses in the road, he commanded loudly that they should go on "slowly, very slowly". The pair managed to retain some sort of outward composure for the rest of the way, but, once inside the palace, the new Queen of Spain, sitting in a collapsed attitude on a chair, kept repeating, over and over: "I saw a man without any legs! I saw a man without any legs!"

The bomb-thrower, a young anarchist named Mateo Morral, was arrested two days later, and, as he was being led away, he shot his guard and then himself.

The wedding-breakfast must inexorably go on, bomb or no bomb. The toast was proposed by Prince George, then Prince of Wales, who was shaken himself but manfully did his duty. The King visited the wounded in hospital that afternoon, and there was a state banquet that night: the whole day had lasted some seventeen hours.

It marked Queen Ena. In some way, deep inside, she was never quite the same again. But she was Queen of Spain: more complex than that, she was an *English* Queen of Spain. That meant that she had to live in the stiff atmosphere of the Spanish Court and not let her Englishness show, if possible, until everyone had accepted her, or appeared to have accepted her. In time she did introduce a touch of English fashion and manner. Lady Duff Gordon said that if she had been born a commoner she would have made a great fashion designer. She dressed in pastel colours, always with consummate elegance, though Alfonso had to stop her from wearing anything extreme in Spain (if one of her skirts had a slit in it the scandalous space had to be filled in with lace frills). She played golf, enjoyed dancing, drank tea with her ladies-in-waiting in a public café on the waterfront at San Sebastian, and was eventually one of the first women in Spain to wear a modern close-fitting bathing-dress, though whenever she swam she had to have two soldiers with her, fully dressed and armed. As the Queen went into the water, so did they, keeping rigidly at attention.

Alfonso and Ena had six children, and here was the other personal tragedy for the Queen of Spain: she was a carrier of haemophilia. One of Queen Victoria's sons, Prince Leopold, had it. Three of her daughters were transmitters of it: the Princess Royal, mother of the Kaiser; Princess Alice, mother of Alexandra of Russia; and Princess Beatrice. The first child of the Spanish marriage, Alfonso, Prince of the Asturias, was haemophilic; the second, Don Jaime, was a deaf mute. A stillborn baby came at one point. Their daughters, Beatrice and Maria Cristina, were healthy, or at least appeared to be; so was the third son, Don Juan, father of the subsequent King of Spain, Don Juan Carlos; but the fourth son, Don Gonzalo, was also haemophilic. Because the legitimist Spanish line had always produced few sons over the previous century, this disappointed many Spaniards; it gave encouragement to those who supported the Carlist line, the present claimant of which is Don Hugo Carlos of Bourbon-Parma.

Queen Ena's reign lasted twenty-five years. In 1931 Alfonso abdicated; he died in Rome in 1941. His wife was with him at his death, but the couple had been living separately for years. The youngest son had died in 1934, the eldest in 1937, both as a result of motor accidents. Queen Ena settled in Switzerland and lived on there for many years.

If one puts Princess May and Mrs Winston Churchill at one end of the scale and Frances Warwick at the other, it is not always easy to settle precisely where the rest of these Edwardian ladies can be placed. Princess May and Clementine Churchill were both single-mindedly devoted to husbands whose careers were all-important to them; husbands by nature monogamous, supporters of the established order, deeply absorbed in public life. Both ladies were potential intellectuals, both had perfect marriages and problems with their children.

But where are we to place the rest? Alix, Princess of Wales and later Queen, sweet, emotional, deaf and unpunctual, taking refuge from her husband's infidelities in her family and in the worshipping adoration of favourite courtiers, with never a breath of scandal? Princess Daisy of Pless, happily married, happy in her family, yet cruelly torn between two countries and still revelling in gossip? Leonie Leslie and Louisa, Duchess of Manchester, each cherishing one long love throughout years of being married to someone else? The unhappy Lady Londonderry, paying for her brief indiscretions with thirty years' silence from her injured, unforgiving husband? Queen Ena, shocked for life by the bomb on her wedding day that stained her white and silver dress and slippers with blood, mother of haemophilics, sent into exile? Alice Keppel, last and luckiest of the King's favourites, who made no mistakes? Jennie Churchill, seeking for love and thinking, for a while at least, that she had found it? Lillie Langtry, compensating with acting and celebrity for the lack of real warmth in her own life? Patsy West, with one daughter divorced and the other living abroad, herself barely older than either of her daughters-in-law? And Frances Warwick, with all her impulsive adventures, quick romantic essays with such surprising persons as — reputedly — Douglas Haig; the stormy, wilful Frances, so foolish and so beautiful, who won the King's love but so seldom knew love herself, who became a Socialist and sent her own children to the local elementary school, who went to the wedding of her daughter Marjorie when expecting her own fourth child (her daughter Mercy, so called because her first reaction on knowing she was pregnant was to exclaim "Oh, mercy!"), and who, in a forlorn attempt to recoup her

MISS LILY BRAYTON.

A photograph of a young beauty by Miss Kathleen Grant. Edwardian photography
was quite advanced and perhaps more conscious of painting than later photography.

(*above*) The theatre and the opera provided an outlet for remarkable displays of elegance and Edwardian good taste; (*below*) as did motoring: many ladies had their own cars. (*The Mansell Collection*)

Travel and adventure were a staple feature of most Edwardian ladies' lives. Reginald Cleaver's drawing of "The social process of 'breaking the ice' in a Nile steamer" (*The Mansell Collection*)

Lady Willoughby de Broke in her riding habit in November 1904. Her husband was
Master of the Warwickshire Hunt. (*Publishers' collection*)

A society drawing by **P. W. Gibbs. This** Edwardian beauty has put her hair up.

The stages of Edwardian girlhood. *(top)* young girls with their all-important nanny; *(bottom left)* schoolgirls (here, without their governess) as drawn by J. Young Hunter in 1909; *(bottom right)* young ladies in a neo-classical pose from a painting "A summer Shower" by C. E. Perugini, 1909.

The following captions appear within the illustration:

FIG. 2.
GRAND chapeau velours noir avec panache de trois plumes. Lien satin noir avec boucle jais.

FIG. 3.
PETIT chapeau en feutre rouge croqué par ruban velours. Grosse cocarde de ruban rouge avec pans.

FIG. 1.
CHAPEAU en feutre champagne clair avec biais mordoré. Couronne de roses ombrées mordoré. Nœuds de velours.

FIG. 4.
CHAPEAU en poiluchon bronze. Couronne de petites roses vieux rouge et orange avec brins de mousse. Grande amazone.

FIG. 5.
CHAPEAU en velours mordoré deux tons. Têtes de plumes tombant sur le côté. Couronne de raisin orange et violet dans feuillage de taffetas.

The lady's hat was an irremovable Edwardian institution, which never subsequently attained such panache and elegance. French *haute couture* set the English fashions, to which the French, in turn, were eager to cater. (*Mansell Collection*)

Royal Ascot was one of the annual peaks of the season. (*below*) The famous "Black Ascot" following Edward VII's death in 1910.

massive debts, planned to put pressure on George V by threatening to publish Edward VII's letters to her?

How much, one wonders, of the differences between the lives of all these women was due to fate? How much to character? How much to luck? The range of their opinions, attitudes, beliefs, and behaviour is so wide. How truly typical were they? Yet they set their stamp on the age: among them are the first figures, the first names that spring to mind when the phrase "the Edwardian lady" is spoken.

CHAPTER SIX

The Wider Stage

There are today lampshades in Scottish boarding-houses which owe their existence to Sheherazade.

— Richard Buckle

Stage-door Johnnies, champagne from a slipper, supper at Romano's, the Edwardian music-hall — these are images that cling to the period. Just how pervasive were they?

It is true that the Edwardians rated sport and the theatre as only a little lower than they rated food and sex, as Lord Northcliffe realized on taking over *The Times* for £320,000 in 1908 when its circulation was 38,000. (By 1913 it was over 150,000 and its price had been reduced from threepence to twopence.) Northcliffe lost no time in incorporating sporting comment and play reviews in his new acquisition. The music-halls did not, however, rise to the status of serious review: they were something apart.

The music-hall had started in the first place as a device to keep the drinking customers quietly, or more or less quietly, in their seats while their glasses were refilled, resembling in this respect the later cabaret. Entrance prices were low because the heavy sale of drinks helped to pay the rent of the buildings; the performers' fees were low because each could, and usually did, appear at several places in an evening. The practice had started in the provinces, where Victorian public-houses often had "singing rooms". As time went by, solo singers and comedians came along to perform in the singing rooms, and gradually the notion took hold that a mixture of tavern and theatre would catch on. It did, and it caught on in the provinces to the extent that for every music-hall in London there were at least fifty scattered about England, mostly in the industrial towns and cities.

This is the key: the music-hall was always urban, proletarian, and masculine. Its entertainers specialized in comedy acts and in excrutia-tingly sentimental ballads. Comedians would end their acts with comic songs, or perhaps lively songs with a topical flavour, like the famous one sung in 1901 and after by Pélissier's Follies:

> We'll have no woer
> Now we've got a king like good King Edward,
> We'll have no woer
> Cos he 'ates that kind of fing,
> Mothers needn't worry
> Now we've got a king like good King Edward,
> Peace wiv honour is 'is motter,
> Gawd sive the King!

And songs like "My old man said follow the van" and "Down at the old Bull and Bush" were popular too. The great comics of the day included Dan Leno, Harry Tate, Grock, Little Tich; there were male impersonators, a curious art, personified by Vesta Tilley; there was Marie Lloyd — her real name was Matilda (Tilly) Wood — who sang her famous numbers, "A Little of What You Fancy Does You Good", "The Boy I Love is Up in the Gallery", "Twiggy-Vous", "She's Never Had Her Ticket Punched Before", and "Oh, Mr Porter". The variety theatre developed so that singers and comedians were sharing the stage with jugglers, acrobats, and conjurers, and there were perform-ances twice nightly, the second a good deal more crowded and noisy than the first. Simultaneously the pantomime, in its variety-based form still known today, was evolving to include famous music-hall acts as part of the "story". Offshoots of the music-hall were the seaside pierrots, who performed on resort beaches in summer ("in the Floral Hall if wet"), and, a little later, the touring concert-party, both of which differed from the music-hall in providing one permanent group of players presenting a mixture of sketches, songs, dances, and comic turns.

All these, with their often famous theatres — the Canterbury, the Bedford, Gatti's, the Alhambra, all the Empires and Palaces in Holborn and Brixton and Victoria and Poplar and Kilburn — were quite outside the scope of the Edwardian lady: that is why we do not dwell on them. Some ladies could go to a West End theatre to see musical comedy, which was quite different. Of this art form, the undoubted king was George Edwardes, whose "young ladies" of the chorus were drilled to a manner absolutely opposed to that of the music-halls: delicate, languid, refined, no attempt to put over a number or to sweep the audience into singing along with them, twirling parasols and com-manding the devotion of the impressionable young men having a night out from Sandhurst or Eton.

Mr Edwardes expected some of his young ladies to marry into the peerage, and they did, one of the best known being Gertie Millar, who became the Countess of Dudley. Other stars were Lily Elsie and Camille Clifford; and one dazzling example was Gaby Deslys. She appeared (to her special signature tune, "The Gaby Glide") very fair, fragile, shimmering and sparkling from head to foot in gleaming fabrics sewn with jewels and frothing with feathers, to dance a little, sing a little, embody all the light in the theatre, the last of a line of entertainers who included Lola Montez and La Belle Otéro.

Again these were theatrical experiences geared to the tastes of men rather than of women, particularly of ladies. Ladies, of course, joyfully went to the Savoy, where Gilbert and Sullivan still happily reigned supreme; to musical comedies like *The Merry Widow* or *The Geisha Girl* or *The Country Girl* or *San Toy*; and to the straight theatre, though here the Feydeau-type farce was the most popular with very young ladies.

Next to a dance or ball, a little party to go to the play was the most elegant social occasion. The young people would make up a party for the theatre; their elders gave the preliminary dinner party, Best clothes, apart from best ball dresses, were worn. Hair was specially important because heads were more noticeable than clothes when sitting in the theatre. Plays never began before half-past eight or a quarter to nine; not for these lucky audiences the uneasy awareness of the last tube train out to the suburbs, and plenty of time had to be allowed for dinner. It was never the same if one went to a matinée: Miss Grosvenor commented disarmingly that one always felt faintly guilty at enjoying oneself in the afternoon.

Between 1895 and 1909 about eight thousand plays were submitted to the Lord Chamberlain for licence. Some thirty were refused, most of them by great writers such as Ibsen, Tolstoy, Maeterlinck, Shaw, Laurence Housman, and even Wilde, whose *Salome* had to wait a long time before being allowed on the stage. A few provincial theatres showed a progressive spirit, notably the Manchester Gaiety, whose Miss Horniman, smoking cigarettes openly in the lounge of the Midland Hotel, encouraged young playwrights like Harold Brighouse and Stanley Houghton, author of *Hindle Wakes*.

The great standbys of the London theatre were Arthur Wing Pinero and Henry Arthur Jones, along with Oscar Wilde in his brilliant comedies, and a few elderly legendary actors could fill a theatre whatever the piece was: Henry Irving, now nearing the end of his spectacular career, and even Sarah Bernhardt, who, despite age, lameness, and strong corsets, played the Duc de Reichstadt in Rostand's *L'Aiglon* to prove she could still work miracles.

But gradually the new revolutionary plays were breaking through: Ibsen, whose merciless revelations of the awful motives underlying surface respectability threw critics and audiences alike into a ferment yet made many traditional subsequent plays appear vaguely un-satisfactory; and Shaw. In 1905 *Man and Superman, You Never Can Tell, Major Barbara*; in 1906 *The Doctor's Dilemma* (during which, at Louis Dubedat's dying creed of believing in Michelangelo, Velasquez, and Rembrandt, one lady loudly protested and walked out) startled and delighted audiences.

There were revivals of popular plays of the nineties — *The Notorious Mrs Ebbsmith, The Prisoner of Zenda* (a dramatized version of the novel that put the word Ruritania into the dictionary) — and new plays like those of J. M. Barrie, *Quality Street* and *The Admirable Crichton* in 1902, and *Peter Pan* in 1904. *The Only Way*, wherein Martin Harvey played Sydney Carton, ran to packed houses; so did the excellent *Hamlet* of Forbes Robertson, after a performance of which Susan Grosvenor went home weeping bitterly to the astonishment of her two companions who were officers in the Brigade of Guards. There was *The Twelve-Pound Look*; there was *What Every Woman Knows*. There were Irene and Violet Vanbrugh, Charles Hawtrey, Cyril Maude, Oscar Asche, Gerald du Maurier, Lily Brayton, Marie Tempest (who was criticized as perhaps not being beautiful enough for a leading actress) and Hilda Trevelyan. Actresses were supposed to be beautiful and sinful and dowagers remarked disparagingly of particularly chic pretty young women: "Any one would take her for an actress!"

But in general the English theatre did tend to ignore much of the mainstream of European drama, principally because there was always Shakespeare if one wanted to be serious and because a night out, with a play between dinner and supper, in a festive spirit, did not really match the atmosphere of Ibsen or Strindberg or Chekhov. The Edwar-dian playgoers honestly preferred a musical at Daly's or a "naughty" farce or a Barrie whimsy or, of course, a smart, sophisticated piece by Frederick Lonsdale or Somerset Maugham. Maugham was particularly successful, at one time having four plays running simultaneously in London. For experimental, new and daring plays, or Greek drama, one had to go to the Court Theatre in Sloane Square, where Harley Granville-Barker put on thirty-two plays in three years, including eleven by Shaw.

The most famous Edwardian actress who was also an Edwardian lady was probably Mrs Patrick Campbell, later the second wife of George Cornwallis-West.

It was still possible in those days for an actress to appear in the playbills as Mrs Something, and Beatrice Stella Campbell, widowed in 1887 when she was twenty-four, invariably used the name "Mrs Patrick Campbell" in the theatre. (Ellen Terry, another great actress and contemporary, called her "Mrs Pat Cat".) There is no need to puzzle about the inner characters of either of these ladies, at least up to a point: Shaw said that Lady Cicely in his play *Captain Brassbound's Conversion* was a skin-tight portrait of Ellen, and he wrote the part of Eliza in *Pygmalion* for Mrs Pat.

It was over the preliminary reading of that play that he met her, having openly lavished praise upon her for years in his sparkling theatrical criticisms. He fell wildly in love with her, wrote a stream of enchanting letters which elicited typical replies — all dashes, under-linings, exclamation marks and a good deal of shrewd comment mixed up with genuine affection — but neither party to this emotion could allow the heart to stop the head from functioning. Shaw was fifty-six, Stella forty-eight, and she was at the peak of her fame, with a genera-tion of theatrical triumphs behind her. He reached full international celebrity with *Pygmalion*. It was clear to him from the first that Mrs Pat was irresistible in love but impossible to live with; some aspects of her personality were expressed years later when he put the character of Orinthia into his play *The Apple Cart*.

Other adorers were not as wise as Shaw. When George Cornwallis-West's marriage to Jennie Churchill began to crumble, he fell in love with Mrs Pat, and married her. Again his wife was almost as old as his mother, and again he discovered that marrying an enchantress was not at all the same thing as loving one. The marriage failed after a few years and the couple separated. One peculiar detail concerning George Cornwallis-West's two marriages deserves a mention. Neither of his wives has gone down to posterity as "Mrs Cornwallis-West". Both of them have continued to be known by the names of their *previous* marriages: Lady Randolph Churchill and Mrs Patrick Campbell.

Young girls who went to the theatre were infatuated by famous actors, a phenomenon quite as old as the stage itself, but now one or two manifestations that belong to the present century were creeping in: the photograph of the admired object, precursor of the pin-up, and inscribed buttons. The first actor to have a "fan club" of sorts was Lewis Waller, whose adherents wore buttons bearing the letters "K.O.W.", standing for "Keen on Waller". They did not, however, cluster at the stage-door to ask for autographs.

Those who wanted to listen to music had to do so in the concert hall. The gramophone was hardly to be taken seriously before the nineteen-twenties, for its wax cylinders produced such scratchy, blurred sounds that most people sensibly preferred to wait for the inevitable technical improvements before spending their money on musical reproduction. So England was a good place for live concerts in those days, and orchestras, military bands, string ensembles and soloists played up and down the land, in concert halls, bandstands in the parks, assembly rooms, even in buildings like the local corn exchange.

Choirs and choral societies flourished, notably in the north of England and Wales; and of course in that period, before radio, before television, the piano was a prized feature in many homes, and families and friends gathered round it in the evenings for many an impromptu concert, aided by someone with a violin, or a cello, or a flute, or any other moderately portable instrument. If the piano-playing was not up to standard, one employed the nice device of the pianola, or player-piano, with rolls of perforated paper fixed inside the front of the upright and switches below the keyboard operating the speed of the roll as it unwound. A good example of pianola music is a collector's item now.

The wealthy families believed that it was their duty to support the local orchestra and subscribed annual sums for seats in the concert halls, giving rise to the saying "Diamonds in the circle, scores in the gallery". In this period Richter with the Hallé Orchestra and Nikisch with the London Symphony had great reputations. The London Symphony was the first British orchestra to tour America, which happened in 1912. A last-minute change of arrangements caused the orchestra to transfer its ship booking to another vessel. This was as well, since the original booking had been made for the *Titanic*.

If the Edwardian period proved that England was not a land without music — and it did, with Elgar, Delius, Henry Wood and the emerging Thomas Beecham, not to mention Cecil Sharp who rediscovered the folk-song — it ran into two full-scale upheavals over the question of art. One of these focused around the Post-Impressionist Exhibition of 1910 at the Grafton Galleries, where Roger Fry and Desmond MacCarthy showed works by Cézanne, Matisse, Van Gogh, Seurat, Gauguin and Picasso. Roars of rage, squeaks of fury went up from the crowds who packed the galleries, exclaiming at the depravity, pornography, and general indecency of these canvases. Of course it was a large strong dose and the Edwardian picture-gazers and portrait-commissioners, accustomed to realistic treatment and liking "problem pictures" as they did (expecting every picture to tell a story), found themselves in terror that the foundations of life as they knew it were being undermined. (So they were.) The Edwardian lady remained faithful to painters like Sargent, perhaps the most truly Edwardian portraitist. Following in Sargent's tradition was Orpen, who was also much admired. It was generally accepted that a lady would have her portrait painted, usually upon her marriage.

But one art form that was new and startling, or at any rate now appeared in a new and startling guise, and thereby attracted the enraptured attention of many Edwardian ladies, was the Diaghilev Ballet.

Ballet has been called the most aristocratic of the arts, and in the opening years of the century the supreme expression of the ballet existed in Russia, above all in St Petersburg. The Maryinsky Theatre enshrined it; if Russian society wished to place before the Tsar its most exquisite gift, it would order a gala ballet performance. Ladies and gentlemen in brilliant evening dress, in glittering uniforms, packed the theatre to watch with attentive eyes that missed nothing the performances of Karsavina, Kschessinskaya, Pavlova and the rest of that incomparable school. Occasionally a dancer would perform in another country: if that country were England, she would find herself displaying her art in the proletarian surroundings of the music-hall, one "turn" among the ballad-singers, comedians, jugglers and all the rest of them. Then in 1909 Serge Diaghilev took his company to Paris and two years later, to celebrate the coronation season, brought them to London.

It was no less than a theatrical bombshell. Diaghilev was the archetype of the impresario. He looked the part to perfection and he had above all else an inborn flair for spectacle, colour, light, brilliance, and amazing full-blooded dramatic effect. His great stage designer was Leon Bakst and between them they hurled at the head of the English capital *Sheherazade*, *The Firebird*, *The Rite of Spring*, *Le Spectre de la Rose* and *L'Après-Midi d'un Faune*. It is impossible to overestimate the effect of this. Fashionable people suddenly felt an electric excitement after years of pretty but saccharine stage productions: the future was addressing them directly. They were looking at the essence of the nineteen-twenties and -thirties years in advance. The word "streamline" was not yet invented, but Diaghilev streamlined his ballet, condensing, for example, the original three acts of *Swan Lake* into one shapely piece. In presenting this fresh new blaze of splendour in his complete repertoire he and his company took London by storm. Not only London: years later Mr Richard Buckle shrewdly pointed out that to this very day there are lampshades in Scottish boarding-houses that owe their existence to *Sheherazade*.

Possibly the most sensational artist in the Diaghilev Ballet was the unbelievable Vaslov Nijinsky, but the overall effect was the most important thing as far as the Edwardian lady was concerned. Not only did Diaghilev present ballet, he also produced Russian opera, focusing upon the heroic figure of Chaliapin. After years of old-style opera in the Italian mode, as Lady Diana Cooper remarked in her memoirs, there suddenly came this blast that could wake the dead, a blinding golden sunburst, and that was *Boris Godunov*. Suddenly the character-istics of contemporary interior decoration changed from pastel tones to brilliant orange, red, purple, jade green. Oriental or pseudo-Oriental shawls draped piano tops, divans took the place of chaises-longues, Russian or pseudo-Russian dolls concealed the telephone beneath their skirts, Chinese or Japanese lanterns were the newest lampshades (and paper versions of these came into the garden for parties, and remained there, right through the twenties). Mandarin robes replaced tea-gowns.

Art, or one form of one of the arts, was once again fashionable, for society had on the whole disliked the aesthetic movement and the Post-Impressionist paintings, but now, with the Russian Ballet vogue sweeping through Mayfair, the doors opened to a wider acceptance of Art Nouveau. It was possible, here and there among the dragon and peacock fabrics, to find slender water-lily designs in the style of Charles Rennie Mackintosh wreathing along a cornice, narrow chairs with immensely high backs, tinted glass in watery shades.

Quite a number of Art Nouveau objects found their way into the most hidebound Edwardian homes in this period, chiefly through the delightful new scientific marvels that promised so much. First of these was the newfangled blessing of electric light. One of the first great houses of England to use it was Hatfield. Lord Salisbury, Prime Minister from 1895 to 1902, enjoyed science as a hobby — he had a private laboratory at Hatfield — and his enormous ancient pile was strung with wires that fizzed and crackled (whereupon the members of his family threw cushions at them). But now in many houses there depended, from the middle of the ceiling, brass stalks branching into three or four subsidiary stalks ending in tinted glass flowers each containing its light bulb. The benefits of gas came too, not only in gas-lighting — with its looped wire pulled to raise or lower the light, both indoors and out — but in the new gas fires, humming or hissing through pinkish asbestos pierced blocks like miniature skyscrapers fitted inside ornate black-leaded frames embossed with flower patterns. In the wider world of international scientific research, names were appearing that still sound modern and progressive — Einstein, Ruther-ford, Freud, Bohr, Gowland Hopkins, Brearly, Geiger. Here, in the opening years of the century, comes the present, with theories of relativity and space, the transmutation of elements, psycho-analysis, the study of the atom, vitamins and dietetics, stainless steel, radiation; isotopes and cellophane evolve. Science could (and obviously did) work miracles. The motion picture arrived, and instantaneously caught on, so that by 1914 every sizable town had its picture palace. The Bijou, the Gem, the Picturedrome — often created from converted music-halls

— heralded the great age of the cinema.

If a symbol of the scientific marvels of the age had to be chosen, perhaps a majority — before April 1912 — would have selected the new kind of ocean liner. Ships eleven storeys high and one-sixth of a mile long, slender, graceful, beautiful in controlled power, with four huge funnels, and decorated inside with every refinement of art and luxury in state rooms and lounges, flights of stairs, vast murals, vases of flowers and all the Edwardian lavishness of food and drink and dance-music, could effortlessly cross the Atlantic — that most bad-tempered of the world's seven seas — in a manner so superb that comparisons with the early voyages were ludicrous. What would Columbus have thought if he had seen such ships? How could one compare them with the sixty-seven days of the *Mayflower*, one hundred and eighty tons, ninety feet long? Or even with the emigrant ships of the nineteenth century, wallowing across the ocean, crammed with distressful passengers who cooked their own meals, ignorant of delights like the barber's shop, the Turkish bath, the squash court, the Café Parisien?

How, indeed? The answer, as it turned out, was grim. The *Santa Maria*, the *Pinta*, the *Nina*, the *Mayflower* and the rest all got there. The *Titanic* did not.

The *Titanic* was built, like her sister ship the *Olympic*, as the White Star Line's answer to the Cunard Line's *Mauretania* and *Lusitania*. These superlative ships were designed for the rich American trade, and all their publicity stressed this fact. The atmosphere surrounding them grew more and more spendthrift; to present-day readers it seems to be tempting providence to an incredible degree. When the disaster came, it was so classic that *Titanic* is *the* ship disaster, millions of people without the smallest interest in the sea know the details, just as do millions of people without the smallest interest in railways know the name of the Tay Bridge.

Indeed, the story of the *Titanic* is so well known that it need not be recapitulated here. It is the Edwardian lady with whom we are concerned, and one or two points about her on board the ship may be mentioned. In this period, as Mr Walter Lord has pointed out in his fascinating account, *A Night to Remember*, it was the custom for gentlemen at the start of a voyage to offer their services to ladies travelling "unprotected" — without a male companion. While women were being advised to get into the lifeboats, a number of the men searched out those who, in their opinion, required escort up the stairs and across the deck.

One lady on the *Titanic* was Lady Cosmo Duff Gordon, who, travelling with her husband, was awakened by the collision: to her it seemed like a giant finger drawn along the side of the ship. She and her husband got up and dressed, and, joined by her secretary, Miss Francatelli, went up to the boat deck where they asked First Officer William Murdoch if they could get into life-boat number one. He said they could. Two Americans, Abraham Soloman and C. E. H. Stengel, who arrived at the same time, got in too. Murdoch looked around, saw no other passengers, called six stokers along and ordered them in, told Lookout George Symons to take charge, and lowered the boat — a boat with a capacity for forty, now holding twelve people. They pulled clear, and waited.

At twenty minutes past two, two hours and forty minutes after the crash, the ship disappeared below the surface of the sea. Just before she sank, she tilted up higher and higher, until she looked to Lady Duff Gordon like a black finger pointing at the sky: that comment gives an idea of how far away the life-boat was by then. As the flagstaff at the stern vanished from sight, Lady Duff Gordon said to Miss Francatelli: "There is your beautiful nightdress gone." As cries for help came to their ears, one crew member, Fireman Charles Hendrickson, said they ought to row back and pick up survivors. No one else spoke. A little later the suggestion came again, presumably from Hendrickson, whereupon Sir Cosmo replied that he did not think they should, as it would be too dangerous, the life-boat might be swamped. It is only fair to say that the people in the other boats reacted in the same way: only one boat went back, and only thirteen people were picked up altogether by the eighteen boats. Presently the cries died out.

Lady Duff Gordon spent most of the night being seasick. Miss Francatelli tried as best she could to help her. Sir Cosmo gave Hendrickson a cigar. He also squabbled with Mr Stengel, who had all sorts of ideas about what they should do. There was a diversion when a stoker named Pusey remarked that they had all lost their kit, and that, while the Duff Gordons and the two American passengers could replace theirs, it was not so easy for members of the crew. Sir Cosmo said he would give each of them five pounds towards replacements, but although he kept his word he regretted it later, for the payment looked dubious taken in conjunction with a life-boat not one-third full that had failed to row back to the rescue. This was not made any better by Lady Duff Gordon's photograph, taken of the life-boat's complement as a souvenir, when the party reached New York after being taken aboard the *Carpathia* with the rest of the survivors.

The Countess of Rothes was on board the *Titanic*, travelling with her cousin, Gladys Cherry, and her maid. They had difficulty in putting on their life-belts, and a courteous gentleman helped them; after that, he gave them some raisins to eat. The ship's purser, Herbert McElroy, called out as the Countess came towards him: "Hurry, little lady, there isn't much time." He added that he was glad she had not asked him for her jewels as some ladies had.

The Countess got into life-boat number eight, which was one of the first loaded and therefore fairly full. It was a job to load it at all: at first, as each lady was persuaded in, she got out again, preferring to go back inside where it was warm. Eventually it did fill up and was lowered. Several women manned the oars and the Countess held the tiller. The sailor in charge was reported as saying that he gave her the job because she was quiet, determined and strong-minded. Later he told the American enquiry that he "put her to steering the boat" because she had a lot to say. After the rescue, however, he detached the figure eight from the boat, had it framed, and sent it to her. When Mr Lord wrote his book she was still writing to Jones every Christmas. It was Jones who saw a light on the horizon soon after half-past three, and he whispered to the Countess to look next time they topped a wave, but not to say anything in case he was wrong. She obeyed, and glimpsed a faint gleam; after a few minutes there could be no doubt. The light grew brighter, another appeared, then a mass of lights: it could only mean a big ship. It was the *Carpathia*.

So it would seem that the miracles of science were not so miraculous after all. This beautiful ship, equipped with every luxury that man could command in 1912, had gone to the bottom. What use was science in the face of that? But one scientific wonder did emerge with credit. That was the radio. Radio messages had enabled six hundred and fifty-one people to be saved. From that time on, ships carried radio, and, what was more, radio operators kept a rota round the clock.

Because communication of all kinds was speeding up, and the quality of photographs and films improving, the beginning of great interest in spectator sports naturally developed. In 1908 on a single Saturday thirty-two football cup ties were watched by 450,000 people. At the foremost, the match in which Wolverhampton Wanderers of the Second Division beat Newcastle United of the First by three goals to two, the audience numbered 75,000. Transfer fees had been increasing for some time: in 1904 Middlesbrough sold a player to Sunderland for a thousand pounds. The boat race between Oxford and Cambridge had an enthusiastic following each spring. Every child, it seemed, wore a favour, and every cab driver in London tied a dark or light blue ribbon to his whip. The 1908 Olympics attracted vast crowds: at the White City a thousand athletes paraded before the King at the opening ceremony, 226 of them British. Denmark sent 126, including a group of girl gymnasts who, because they were girls, could win no medals or points; but they were admired none the less. Britain won that year, with thirty-eight medals as against the United States' twenty-two.

The incident everyone remembers about that Olympics is the Italian leader in the Marathon being helped over the finishing-line (where among others present was Conan Doyle). The only thing is that people always get his name wrong: it was Durando Pietri, not Dorando.

Films of sporting events interested and pleased the crowds who packed the picture palaces. Along with these and the serials went various short films, for the full-length feature had yet to come. It was noted that these early cinema audiences showed a marked taste for violence.

The Edwardian lady saw little of all this. To her — and perhaps to a number of her male companions, too — Edwardian England, sportingly speaking, remained one long golden cricketing afternoon. Feminine film addicts did not show in full force until the twenties, and the stage stars underrated the film as well: they thought the newfangled phonograph was the enemy whereas in fact it was the bioscope.

Medical science was improving, though here it ran up against rooted prejudice and even superstition: before the King had his appendix removed, many persons in high places believed that appendicitis was contagious. Shaw's Mrs Tarleton in *Misalliance* stated how shocked she was the first time she heard a marchioness talking quite openly about drains. Not only did she talk as if it was the most natural of subjects, but a duchess then asked Mrs Tarleton what her system was, and, when she tried to change the subject, a countess on the same committee told her that she had better learn something about it before her children died of diptheria. That was two months after she had lost a baby for that precise reason. She walked out of the meeting when one of the duchesses started talking about her inside.

H. G. Wells's Kipps was similarly shocked by the idea of people's insides, which he called chubes, and only came to his senses when faced with the master thing in life, birth. His first sight of his baby son somehow tilted him back into a sensible, modern frame of mind. Eliza Doolittle thought that baths were indecent, until Higgins brusquely ordered her to behave like a duchess. It is noticeable that two of England's most revolutionary Edwardian writers saw that high rank was less mealy-mouthed and prudish and genteel than the bourgeoisie; and it was then, too, that Suburbia found the first of its multitude of attackers. In an article on *The Suburbans*, published in 1905, T. W. H. Crossley wrote:

If you walk down the Clapham Road, from the end of the Common to Clapham Road Station with your eyes open you will have seen the best part of all Suburbia has to show you. You will understand, as it were, intuitively and without further ado, the cheapness and out-of-jointness of the times; you will comprehend the why and wherefore and raison d'être of halfpenny journalism. You will perceive that whizzers, penny buses, gramophones, bamboo furniture, pleasant Sunday afternoons, Glory Songs, modern language teas, golf, tennis, high school education, dubious fiction, shillingsworth of comic writing, picture postcards, miraculous hair-restorers, prize competitions, and all other sorts of twentieth century clap-trap, have got a market and a use, and black masses of supporters.

To George Augustus Sala in the *Daily Telegraph*, however, the world still wagged in its accustomed way. He enjoyed himself observing the fashionable demi-mondaines in Rotten Row. In the afternoon in the full season, he said, the sylphides floated by in "ravishing habits and intoxicatingly delightful hats", some of which were wickedly cocked cavalier hats with green plumes, some the orthodox cylindrical beaver with its veil, some "roguish little wideawakes", while the breeze fluttered skirts to reveal "the tiny, coquettish, brilliant little boot, with its military heel" — kept so brilliant by applications of new varnish-like polishes.

Refrigeration was coming in, with freezing-machines containing ice and salt, and, in the country, ice-stacks or ice-pits, prepared during the winter and covered with thatch. This undoubtedly helped with the ice-puddings that were deservedly so popular, though the basis of Edwardian meals remained hot dishes. Breakfasts, to be sure, had a cold table with ham and grouse, but these were mere trimmings to the main spread of eggs, poached, boiled, and scrambled, bacon, kidneys, haddock, and hot rolls as well as toast. In a well-appointed house there would be three kinds of marmalade. This, of course, followed the early tea in bed. The writer Marie Belloc Lowndes, sister of Hilaire Belloc and author of gruesome stories in which she revelled, startled her own and other people's maids by getting up at six-thirty, making her own tea, and writing before breakfast. A little round woman who still wore Victorian bonnets, she lived in a small dark house in Westminster with her husband, who worked for *The Times*, and her two daughters; like her brother, she firmly believed that everything French was good.

The rest of England was slightly readier to follow her lead after the King made his preference for French things known, but in general Edwardian England disliked foreigners. Such criticisms of the King as did arise centred rather on his preference for his foreign friends than perhaps on anything else. The German-Jewish Baron Hirsch, Sir Ernest Cassel, the Rothschilds, the Sassoons, and the Portuguese Marquis de Soveral, were lifelong friends that he kept unfailingly. Of course, society was more cosmopolitan in outlook than the bourgeoisie, though society still contained plenty of xenophobic landed gentry to whom all aliens were anathema.

As in all periods, people were uneasy about the way society was changing, or appeared to be changing. The elderly Lady Dorothy Nevill, born in 1826 in the reign of George IV, wrote in 1906 that the question now was: Is X rich? It was not : Is X clever? She referred to Samuel Warren's *Ten Thousand A Year*, published in 1839, saying that such a sum was paid now for a single painting, that present-day entertaining on such an income was hardly possible, and commented:

> What is the life of a rich man of today? A sort of firework! Paris, Monte Carlo, big-game shooting in Africa, fishing in Norway, dashes to Egypt, trips to Japan.

It was observed that the aristocracy were penetrating business houses: by 1896 a quarter of the peerage were company directors. The open display of wealth came into a music-hall song:

> The Church Parade beats everything,
> The Church Parade when in full swing
> Is a thing to see and wonder at,
> For, oh, the wealth displayed,
> Of the millinery art,
> And costumes smart,
> In the Church Parade.

a viewpoint re-echoed in Edmund Yates's verse:

> In a church which is furnished with mullion and gable,
> With altar and reredos, with gargoyle and groin,
> The penitents' dresses are sealskin and sable,
> The odour of sanctity's eau-de-Cologne.
> But only could Lucifer, flying from Hades,
> Gaze down on this crowd with its panniers and paints.
> He would say, as he looked at the lords and the ladies,
> "Oh, where is *All Sinners'*, if this is *All Saints'*?"

This was written of an earlier period, but it reveals a timeless pre-occupation. Of course it was a time of almost film-like glitter and brilliance from the upper stratum, frank privilege, perhaps the last age of which it could be said that the wealthy believed that a display of affluence could give pleasure to the poor. The well-known pillars of society, in an epoch without films, radio, television, and long-playing records, occupied a position comparable only to that of the film stars of the thirties and the pop stars of today. (Does not *their* display of affluence give pleasure to the poorer people now? But this is not openly said.)

The Edwardian rich attended the three-month London season as if it were one long village fair, and the parvenu wealthy knew that the quick route into society lay through the purchase of a house in the country and participation in hunting, shooting, and lavish entertaining.

If the Edwardian period saw several distinguished ladies in their thirties (Nellie Melba, Marie Lloyd, Marie Tempest, Baroness Orczy, Beatrix Potter, Gertrude Bell, Clara Butt, Lilian Baylis, Laura Knight), it observed the deaths of other famous women. Kate Greenaway, Charlotte M. Yonge, Dorothy Beale and Louise de la Ramée who wrote as Ouida. Most astonishing of all, that colossal Victorian survival Florence Nightingale, who after half a century as a terrifying legend became the first woman recipient of the Order of Merit, died, ironically, a senile old darling in 1910.

But were all these real ladies in terms of 1900? Undoubtedly yes — most of them. If Shaw's Eliza Doolittle was right (and *Pygmalion* is an Edwardian play), the difference between a lady and a flower-girl is not how she behaves, but how she is treated. All these eminent women were given courtesy and distinguished consideration for most of their working lives at the very least. The only one of them who insisted frankly that she was *not* a lady in the accepted sense, but a Cockney child of the stage with no society pretensions, Marie Lloyd, was not only able to command all the luxuries available to a woman of her time, but was positively adored by the crowds who flocked to see her. Her funeral drew more spectators than the monarch's when she died in 1922.

As we have seen, the Edwardian lady did not usually go to the music-halls, but she could not escape a new kind of entertainment that blasted its way on to the London stage in 1912 with as loud an effect as that of the Russian opera: a revue called *Hullo Rag-time!* which came from America. Rupert Brooke, associated in many minds now with a somewhat finicking aestheticism, saw it ten times. The fashionable young responded to it at once and whole-heartedly.

The word "ragtime" was not new, it had been used for some years to describe this particular kind of music — exuberant, loud, cheerful, uninhibited — but this revue marked its full impact upon the audiences of the day. The song *Alexander's Ragtime Band* crossed the Atlantic (and is still around); *Waiting for the Robert E. Lee* and *Everybody's Doing It* (Doing what? The Turkey Trot — and so they were) followed. Then in 1913 came the revue *Hullo Tango!* and the furore redoubled. The tango, described by one shocked spectator as an assault rather than a dance, swept fashionable London. Ladies gave tango teas and tango parties. The sight of modish young men and women swooping and slinking across the dance floors, bringing a whiff of raffish South American exoticism into ballrooms hitherto sacred to the waltz, the Lancers, and the galop, shook the very foundations of the Establishment.

Thunders from the pulpit, alarmed protests in letters to the editor, resounded on all sides. There were to be many more such thunders and protests during the next sixty years. If a conventional older person could keep silent about the tango, he or she had perforce to burst out over the Hitchy Koo and the Bunny Hug. What was the country coming to? What, indeed?

Sometimes the words of the ragtime songs made sense of a sort (like those of *Alexander's Ragtime Band*), but usually the words were a high-spirited uprush of happy nonsense: why, for example, suddenly "It's a bear! Where?" in *Everybody's Doing It?* But occasionally comes a word that surprises. "Flapper" belongs, in most people's minds, to the twenties: yet in the summer of 1914 we find a music hall song with the lines:

Florrie was a flapper, she was dainty, she was dapper,
And her dancing was the limit, or the lid.

In 1913 another Florrie, Florrie Forde, then thirty-nine (she was Winston Churchill's age), stepped on to the stage and sang a new song. It was typical in that it rather wistfully proclaimed the singer's thought that in London it was far from the place where her (properly his) heart was, but, none the less, he was going. "It's a long way to Tipperary," sang Miss Forde, and the audience began to tap its feet in time to the music. That song was sung, says Mr James Cameron, as no song has ever been sung before or since. The two songs that edge the period have the fact of travelling in common, but in the song of 1900 the singer is frankly off to war:

Goodbye, Dolly, I must leave you,
Though it breaks my heart to go.
Something tells me I am needed
At the front to fight the foe.
See! the soldier-boys are marching,
And I can no longer stay —
Hark! I hear the bugles calling!
Goodbye, Dolly Grey.

Whereas the song of 1914 simply announces the singer's intention to return to Tipperary "to the sweetest girl I know", so goodbye, Piccadilly, farewell, Leicester Square.

Other details that seem to belong to the twenties and thirties, if not even later, were beginning to creep in. In July 1914 *Punch* printed a joke about the briefer bathing-dresses women were wearing: "She" says she can't find her bathing-dress anywhere; "He" remarks drily: "See if you've got it on". Virginia Woolf recalled that the Victorian cook lived in the kitchen depths like a leviathan, silent, formidable and withdrawn; the pre-War cook, in contrast, was sunny and quick, for ever in and out of the drawing-room to borrow the newspaper or ask advice about a hat. And we know that many an Edwardian motorist had the idyllic reaction to cars of Mr Toad — bliss, rapture, poop-poop in full measure.

Yet Mr Toad smashed his rapture to pieces.

CHAPTER SEVEN

Overture: Beginners

It was the best of times, it was the worst of times, it was the age of wisdom, it was the age of foolishness, it was the epoch of belief, it was the epoch of incredulity, it was the season of Light, it was the season of Darkness, it was the spring of hope, it was the winter of despair, we had everything before us, we had nothing before us, we were all going direct to Heaven, we were all going direct the other way — in short, the period was so far like the present ...

— Charles Dickens

Every age has its modern movement. Sometimes this is hard to discern, but the signs are there. One of the surest ways of finding it is to look at improvements, or suggestions for improvements, in domestic architecture. During the Edwardian period a groundswell of complaints about house design could be heard below the apparently unruffled surface of servant-filled households. H. G. Wells brought some of the thornier points into the open in *Kipps*, in that part of the book where Kipps and Ann are looking for a house. Because Ann has been a servant, she knows what it is like to work in the typical situation of 1910:

> ... a basement, no service lift, blackleading to do everywhere, no water upstairs, no bathroom, vast sash windows to be cleaned from the sill, stone steps with a twist and open to the rain into the coal-cellar, insufficient cupboards, unpaved path to the dustbin, no fire-place to the servant's bedroom, no end of splintery wood to scrub ... The Kippses, you see, thought they were looking for a reasonably simple little contemporary house; but indeed they were looking either for dreamland or A.D. 1975, or thereabouts, and it hadn't come.

And Ann bitterly comments that it was, she thought, having houses built by men that made all the work and trouble. Some poor girl had to tire herself out going up and down stairs, up which every drop of water had to be carried, because no one had the sense to leave enough space to give the steps a proper rise. The architect consulted by Kipps paid no attention to this jeremiad but produced plans for a modest villa with eleven bedrooms, a Tudor stained-glass window, a Moorish gallery, and pretence battlements over the portico, and admitted that it was almost too good for Hythe.

Even when a progressive architect got to work on a scheme it was in the Tudor style with half-timbering. Mr M. H. Baillie Scott designed The Haven for a site in Surrey in this style. It was to be constructed round a courtyard, and it incorporated a drawing-room, a dining-room, a boudoir and a studio, a billiard-room, eight bedrooms (two of which were for servants), a kitchen with a pantry, larder, and, close by, a servants' WC. It had a coach house, harness room, and stables, a coal-shed, a wash-house, and a cycle-shed, but it also had two bathrooms, one upstairs and one down, with heating-chambers underneath them. All the floors of the house were of oak or maple, and all the structural work in oak. The whole cost £2,300 to build.

A house such as this would reveal the new style of interior decoration and furnishing, a good deal more open, clean, and simple than the over-stuffed fashions that had gone before. In 1893 Mr Ambrose Heal went into his family's upholstering business and began to design machine-made furniture at a moderate price on new and appealing lines that worked out much less expensive than William Morris's hand-made pieces. It was also far more comfortable. One could have a Morris-like settle in an inglenook, but it had cushions on it; and Mr Heal's gateleg tables, plain bookcases and shelves, Windsor chairs and rush-matting helped to provide not only a sharp contrast in appearance and ease of maintenance but the tone of moral awareness and protest that lay beneath the choice of such a style.

Of course there was, to modern eyes, still a lot of clutter. Bedrooms still had wash-stands: a kind of table with two or three drawers, a marble (or pretence marble) top and tiled back splashboard, a towel-rail at either end, and a load of objects making up the toilet-set; also basin and ewer, soap-dish and brush-jar, pail, sponge-bowl and chamber-pot. These could range in price from Wedgewood's willow pattern or plain cream ware at seven shillings and sixpence or the Old Staffordshire at nine and six to Spode at twenty-five to thirty-shillings; oddly enough, a set in plain glass cost a guinea. Heal's hand-thrown pottery ranged from fifteen to twenty-three shillings. There were dressing-table sets, too, with pin-trays of several different sizes and a ring-holder. Hot water was brought up in polished brass cans with a folded towel laid across the top.

But the bathroom was gaining ground. By 1910, cast-iron baths were produced in large quantities; the more expensive baths were made in one piece out of porcelain crockery (which had to be carefully treated not to chip), with fancy decorated outsides and four elaborate legs to stand on. Sometimes such a bath had a flat mahogany surround. Sometimes there were several taps labelled "sitz" and "plunge". There were even complicated shower arrangements enclosed in glass or curtains at the tap end, or possibly a separate shower.

One of the few advantages of bathrooms at this time (especially if they had been added to a house originally built without one) was that they were *large*: an incredible sense of luxury and ease flows over the person who uses a big square bathroom the size of an ordinary bedroom when he has been used to the usual twentieth-century compartment in which it is possible to turn on the taps, brush one's teeth, open the window, change the light-bulb, pick up one's clothes and hang up the towels, all without moving one's feet. But equally the person accustomed to a daily bath that can be run quickly with reliable hot water from a tap knows the very real sense of deprivation when this is not available.

The Edwardian period brought in various extras that seem to the modern reader to have developed surprisingly early: heated towel-rails; metal holders fixed to the wall for tooth-glasses and tooth brushes; looking-glasses above pedestal wash-basins; tiled or half-tiled white floors covered in cork or linoleum; wndows of frosted glass (or screened with opaque paper). Some *nouveaux-riches* had marble walls and stained-glass windows. A honeycomb sponge of good quality cost thirty shillings; the soap might be plain coal-tar or Windsor, but it might also be a flower-scented Floris soap, like the Carnation, four shillings and sixpence, or the Royal Violet, six shillings.

Early morning tea, brought by a housemaid who lit the bedroom fire while the lady sipped her tea, was accompanied by paper-thin bread and butter, or plain biscuits: these were home-made, or probably Digestives at ninepence a pound, Osborne at sevenpence, or Thin Arrowroot at eightpence. The ritual of early morning tea was strictly observed in even moderately wealthy houses, regardless of architecture, decoration, or ideas.

Much extra toil was added to life by the undoubted fact that London was a very dirty city. Smoke-producing fuels gave a special thickness to autumn and winter mists, creating the archetypal London fog, the "London particular". Showers of grimy flakes fell on everything, the black fogs got into each house, clinging to fabrics, tarnishing metals, settling a velvety black film upon ceiling mouldings and quadrupling the already endless domestic tasks. Some of the new types of road transport increased the dirt. London photographs of the period show an amazing variety of vehicles: in 1901 there were 3,736 open-topped horse-drawn omnibuses in London but by 1908 there were 1,000 motor omnibuses in daily service, and though the hansom cab still jingled along, by 1910 over 6,300 taxi-cabs inspired the song:

> Oh, the car! the taximeter car!
> It's better than taking a trip to Spain,
> Or having your honeymoon over again,

The electric tram did not increase the dirt but it provided a fresh road hazard, taking as it did a predestined course and setting down passengers in the middle of the carriage-way. By 1905 tramlines had crept out as far as Richmond and Wimbledon. The growing tangle of traffic caused the Chelsea medical officer of 1903 to suggest (with a remarkable cast ahead to what his successors were worrying about seventy years later) a new main thoroughfare wide enough to provide a clearway for six or eight lanes with different speeds.

A horse-drawn cab took fifteen minutes to go from Piccadilly Circus to Baker Street Station and cost one shilling and sixpence. The two-penny bus journey took twenty minutes. The Bakerloo Line tube, opened in 1906, also charged twopence for the same journey, but accomplished it in seven minutes. In 1907 the Hampstead tube (later extended into the full stretch of the Northern Line and thereby creating the world's longest continuous vehicular tunnel) was opened, the last London Underground line to be constructed for sixty years, when work began on the Victoria Line.

Other forms of transport were receiving attention, notably aircraft. In 1910 the Women's Aerial League was formed with the somewhat startling aim "to stir up our country not to be left behind in this important branch of future warfare".

The enlargement of public and private transport facilities in London helped to swell the popularity of "a day's shopping in Town". Shopping, in the definition of the Edwardian lady, was fun, it meant going to buy something pretty, something not strictly necessary, and was regarded as important. Clothes in those days had to last — some ladies made a practice of keeping new dresses in their wardrobes for a year before appearing in them so as not to look vulgarly smart — and a vast amount of altering and fiddling went on. Miles of beaded trimming known as passementerie, cardboard boxes full of hand-made lace, yards of braid, lengths of tulle, were selected.

Susan Grosvenor's cousin Hilda Lyttleton objected that she wanted to do something better with her life than rush up and down Oxford

Street hunting for "beastly pieces of tulle". Miss Lyttleton, whose clear eye for clothes saw that all these renovations merely made the dresses look messy, reaped her reward in the end. When she married Mr Arthur Grenfell and was free to choose her own clothes she went to the revolutionary Italian designer Fortuny, who gave her a look of striking distinction by making her simple long pleated satin dresses held at the neck, wrists, and waist by strings of tiny iridescent shells.

Oxford Street, however, was burgeoning into a shopping centre of vast allure. The results showed in ladies' bedrooms and boudoirs: heavy cut-glass scent bottles with gilt stoppers, hairbrushes backed with tortoise-shell, dressing-jackets trimmed with swansdown, huge swansdown powder puffs, attractively littered rooms decorated with fresh pale chintz or spotted muslin flounces. Miss Grosvenor held dear in her memory the picture of such a room, with its small clear fire in the grate, the sun shining across a moss green carpet and gleaming on an old marquetry desk, and the breakfast tray with its pretty porcelain and shining silver, and a few violets in a slim glass, and the morning paper folded under a pile of letters.

There were plenty of splendid new shops in which to find attractive objects, or, indeed, to find romance itself. Marshall and Snelgrove's store was the scene of a celebrated episode, when Lady Florence Paget arrived there one day with her fiancé, Mr Henry Chaplin, to inspect part of her trousseau. She left Mr Chaplin waiting in the carriage at the Oxford Street entrance, walked into the shop, passed straight through, and came out into Henrietta Street where Lord Hastings was waiting in *his* carriage to meet her; they were married that day.

The majority of ladies, however, bought their clothes from tailors and dressmakers: each garment was made to measure for a particular customer. Some dressmakers sighed at the thought of a beautiful dress being worn over prosaic or even ugly underwear, but no one did anything positive about it until Lucy Christiana Sutherland, aged twenty-two, divorced James Stuart Wallace, then in his forties. The divorce left Mrs Wallace socially lowered and actually poor, with a small daughter to care for as well, and she began to make clothes for her friends. Her imaginative skill prospered, and created great interest when she made the wedding dresses for her younger sister Elinor's marriage to Clayton Glyn at the fashionable church of St George's, Hanover Square.

By the early eighteen-nineties Mrs Wallace, professional name Lucile, was doing well enough to set up her own shop in Old Burlington Street, where she created exquisite filmy lingerie, delicately coloured and expensive. Her clothes were delivered in green and white striped boxes, and she invented the mannequin parade, engaging lovely large girls called Phyllis, Dolores, Florence, Gamela and Hebe to show creations with equally sensational names. Until then dresses had merely been called "the black velvet" or "the white lace" or whatever, but Lucile's dresses, fittingly for Elinor Glyn's sister, had names like "The Sighing Sound of Lips Unsatisfied", "Give Me Your Heart", "Do You Love Me?", "A Frenzied Song of Amorous Things", and "When Passion's Thrall is O'er". It goes without saying that she succeeded brilliantly. Her enterprise became a company, and in 1900 she married one of the directors, Sir Cosmo Duff Gordon. In due time she set up branches in Paris, New York, and even Chicago.

The most celebrated dress designers of the period were Worth and Paul Poiret. Poiret's clothes were so much admired by Margot Asquith that she arranged a tea-party at which his dresses were shown, which caused a sensation — not just in the impressed ohs and ahs of the ladies present, but in the press, incensed that the Prime Minister's wife should promote foreign goods at the expense of British ones. It is easy to see why the mannequin parade caught on so quickly.

Before then, dresses were displayed either on wax dummies or on girls who had to wear long-sleeved black satin dresses and lace-up boots under the garments shown. It looked grotesque indeed if the outer dress were a low-cut evening gown. No wonder Gamela and Hebe and the rest of them, moving gracefully across the pale grey carpet, against the pale grey curtains, of Lucile's showroom, provoked gasps of pleasure and delight. Other shops were quick to follow, and soon the greatest stores were putting on fashion shows in their restaurants. By 1913 this practice had reached the provinces.

Lucile's lead was followed by Mrs Cyril Drummond, whose shop Mascotte, in Berkeley Street, advertised not only "Robes, Manteaux & Fourrures" but also "Trousseaux" and "Lingerie". Other fashionable houses included Reville & Rossiter, Russell & Allen, Redfern. If a lady wanted sports clothes or tailor-mades she went to Fred Bosworth; for riding habits, to Busvine, or, possibly, to Sears & Wells. If for under-clothes Lucile was too daring, there was George Givan of Belfast in New Bond Street from 1902, or, from 1906, the White House.

This feminine invasion of Bond Street was new: until the nineties it was a street for men's goods, consequently a centre for prostitutes, and young ladies never walked along it. But by 1911 there were a hundred shops catering for women: milliners, court dressmakers, glovers, shoe-makers, "complexion specialists" (that is, beauty and hairdressing establishments). But these were all in *New* Bond Street; Old Bond Street was still a masculine preserve. Buses in Bond Street were for-bidden, and the roadway was lined with waiting carriages, all of them gleaming, many of them with crests on the panels.

Debenham's presented what they called a "convent-made" trousseau which included fifteen chemises of different weights, twelve camisoles, eight pairs of combinations, seventeen pairs of knickers, seventeen petticoats, a dozen night-dresses, two dressing-gowns, dressing-jackets and boudoir caps, two dozen handkerchiefs, a nightdress case, and three dozen of something called "diaper towels". The whole lot cost one hundred pounds. They would, if that seemed too dear, provide a full trousseau for forty pounds, including two pairs of sports woollen knickers and a bathing costume. Both these were expensive trousseaux: Harrod's could furnish one for just over seven guineas.

In Harrod's, too, there were nineteen different types of stockings advertised in 1900, only two of them "coloured", the rest were black or white. Inside the main door of every big store was the complex haberdashery department, the sprat to catch, it was hoped, plenty of fat mackerel. In tiny price units invariably including farthings, one could take one's choice among dozens of articles, including the soft head-wraps called fascinators, garters, bullion fringe, cords or chains for eye-glasses, paste bandeaux, jet and sequin collars, stay laces, veils, feather trimmings, forty-six kinds of dress-shields, twenty-one kinds of pins, and ten sorts of elastic. Shops would give a paper of pins instead of the farthing change, a profitable exchange, for there were fifty-two pins on a farthing paper; for one penny the customer could buy two hundred and fifty pins.

Both Debenham's and Harrod's had suites of rooms known as the "Ladies' Club", delightfully decorated and furnished, spacious, quiet and supplied with writing-paper, telephones, newspapers, magazines and a poste restante. The Ladies' Cloak Rooms were superb. Harrod's had a Gentlemen's Club, too, and "Ladies' Hairdressing Courts" where manicure, pedicure and chiropody services were provided as well as those of the coiffeur. They advertised their restaurant in appealing terms:

THE GRAND RESTAURANT has prices of a strictly moderate tendency. Afternoon Tea is served to the strains of Harrod's Royal Red Orchestra.

In 1909 the shop celebrated its Diamond Jubilee, claiming, with justification, that the variety and quality of its goods in the thirty-six acres of its eighty departments had supplied the idea for its telegraphic address of "Everything, London". The musical comedy *Our Miss Gibbs* had a number of scenes set at "Garrod's".

In that same year, Gordon Selfridge completed the first department store ever purpose-built in the West End, after a long struggle to acquire the land for it. He had worked at the great American store of Marshall Field in Chicago, and he employed the head window-dresser from there to do spectacular things with the Selfridge windows. It will be remembered that Mr Polly's friend Parsons got the sack for trying to dramatize the window displays of the Port Burdock Drapery Bazaar; had he been employed at Selfridge's he would have won promotion. The Selfridge windows stayed lit until midnight. Colour mattered: the "Selfridge green" appeared in the house flag on the roof, in carpets, wrapping paper, bill-heads, and delivery vans. Other revolutionary ideas poured out: the first bargain basement in London, the first soda fountain, a huge order for silk stockings in five sizes and three hundred shades, fresh schemes of layout, advertising campaigns. By 1914 he almost had his complete island site.

The Edwardian lady could shop at a number of distinguished stores some of which are fortunately still there, though greatly changed in many ways. They include (in order of date from 1700) Fortnum & Mason, Dickins & Jones, John Harris Heal, Swan & Edgar, Debenham's, Harvey Nichols, Henry Heath, Lilley & Skinner, Peter Robinson's, Kendal Milne of Manchester, Marshall & Snelgrove, Daniel Neal, The Scotch House, Maple's, Harrod's, Burberry's, Gorringe's, William Whiteley, John Lewis, Bentalls of Kingston, Woollands, Barker's, Achille Serre, Peter Jones, The Army & Navy Stores, Liberty's, D. H. Evans, The Jaeger Company, Bobby's of Margate, Leamington, Folkestone, Eastbourne and Torquay, Fenwick's, Robinson & Cleaver, Bourne & Hollingsworth, John Barnes of Hampstead, and Selfridge's. John Barnes is worth a special mention: started in 1898 by six men including Barnes himself and Owen Owen of Liverpool, it was opened in 1900 on its present site. Barnes never saw it. In 1899 he was on board the *Stella* which ran on to the Guernsey rocks in a fog and sank in fifteen minutes.

Some of these shops still manage to retain faint drifting impressions of the opulent Edwardian atmosphere, but, if by magic any of them could look for a moment the way they looked then, the first thing every woman would notice would be the chairs aligned by the counters for the customers to sit. In most of the stores this feature persisted until the Second World War; but it is a collector's item now. Another difference is the enormous deference accorded to customers in that period: the lady not only had the door opened for her, but was bowed in by one of the shop-walkers, and, quite often, had goods she asked to inspect brought to her from other departments so that she need not get up and walk about unless she wished. And, of course, her carriage could stop outside the shop indefinitely, free from all thought of yellow lines or traffic wardens.

The purchasable object that carries with it undiminished the atmosphere of wealth and beauty of the Edwardian period is anything made by Peter Carl Fabergé. He was, of course, goldsmith to the Imperial Russian Court, having been appointed by Tsar Alexander III and maintained in his position by Tsar Nicholas II. His principal shop, opened in 1898, was at 24 Morskaya in St Petersburg, today's Leningrad, and there were branches in Moscow and Odessa. In 1903 examples of his wares were shown in London at the Berners Hotel, and then a shop was set up, first in Duke Street, then in Old Burlington Street, and in 1906 at 48 Dover Street, Piccadilly. This shop was jointly managed by Fabergé's fourth son Nicholas and by his biographer, Henry C. Bainbridge. After 1910 they transferred to 173 New Bond Street. Here they remained until the early part of the First World War.

The most celebrated objects ever made by Fabergé were the Easter eggs. The practice, started by Tsar Alexander III, was to produce one outstanding piece each year, with no limit set to either price or subject, apart from any other orders placed by the Tsar. Every year Fabergé created an Easter egg for the Tsar to give his wife, and, after the accession of Nicholas II, he made two annually, one for the Dowager Empress and the other for the new Empress. In all he made between fifty-four and fifty-seven of these. The first of them all, made probably in 1883, came from Fabergé's own idea: an egg with a surprise in it. What the Tsar received looked like an ordinary hen's egg, consequently it was presumably the same size. It was made of gold enamelled in opaque white. When opened, it revealed a gold yolk, which also opened, to show a chicken of gold in several colours, inside that was a minute model of the imperial crown, and inside *that* was a tiny ruby egg.

Naturally, the Tsar was enchanted by this exquisite object, and asked to have an egg every year. He always tried to find out what it was going to be, but Fabergé would never tell him, saying simply: "Your Majesty will be content."

He was, too. Reading the descriptions of these eggs, each one a marvel of craftsmanship and a charming object in itself, one is at a loss to know which was the most beautiful. Sometimes they were mounted in clocks, or on a base of rock crystal, or supported on a framework of gold. One of the prettiest was made in 1906 for the Empress, in mauve enamel (her favourite colour) with a delicate lattice-work of tiny diamonds all over it. Inside was a "lake" — a large aquamarine — trimmed with jewelled lilies on which rested a swan of gold covered in white enamel. A handle of water-lilies in four shades of gold enabled the "lake" to be lifted out of the egg, and a tiny device under one of the swan's wings caused the little bird to move: gold webbed feet moved, the head and neck were raised, the wings spread showing each feather separately. The egg was four inches high.

Another charming one was of rock crystal — also four inches high —

with frost patterns in rose diamonds all over, and more diamond frosting on the "ice" rock crystal base. The surprise inside was a tiny platinum and diamond basket filled with flowers — green jade leaves, gold stalks, tiny white cacholong blossoms with gold and olivine centres, the whole basket three and a quarter inches in height. It was presented to the Dowager Empress in 1913.

Perhaps the most spectacular egg, a bigger one this time, was the 1900 Great Siberian Railway egg, of enamels in blue, green, and yellow, with fine lines of silver showing the map of Siberia and the route of the railway line. The imperial double-headed eagle in gold surmounted the egg, and, when this was touched, the egg opened, revealing a scale model — twelve inches long and five-eighths of an inch wide — of the Siberian Express in gold, five carriages including one smoking-carriage, one with half the compartments reserved for ladies, one for children, one for luggage, and a church carriage with a Russian cross and gold bells on the roof. The engine was of gold and platinum with a ruby headlight. The whole thing was made with the most perfect precision so that a tiny gold key would set the miniature wheels in motion.

In addition to these masterpieces, Fabergé produced enormous quantities of cigarette boxes and cases, jewelled flowers, tiny animal figures and figures of Russian characters, brooches and pendants, clocks, vases, ornamental pieces of all kinds, all made from exquisite materials with matchless skill and art. Considering their quality they were not exorbitantly priced. The Tsar paid about thirty thousand roubles for each of the eggs, which are quite beyond price now.

It was inevitable that Edward VII would be attracted by the work of a craftsman as superb as this. He ordered presents for his wife, including a miniature set of animals carved in various stones, the animals being modelled on the real ones at Sandringham. Soon his friends realized how much he appreciated this kind of work and they would give him Fabergé presents. Mrs Keppel gave him a cigarette case in royal blue translucent enamel on guilloché gold with an encircling snake in diamonds and a diamond thumb-piece. After his death Alix gave it back to Mrs Keppel as a souvenir, then in 1936 Mrs Keppel gave it to Queen Mary for the Sandringham collection. The Duchess of Norfolk ordered a silver icon for the Duke. When it arrived there was a heated discussion as to whether it was all real silver, as parts of it had a mat surface. The Duchess asked the Duke, who said simply: "If Mr Fabergé says it is silver, then silver it must be."

Following the King's lead, all the great Edwardian ladies went to Fabergé for beautiful objects. (It would perhaps be more accurate to say that it was the gentlemen friends of the great ladies who went.) For Lady de Grey, Mr Poklewski-Koziell bought a Japanese tree in gold, small carved birds, and a Buddha in jadeite with ruby and diamond eyes, diamond ear-rings, a ruby tongue, and a white enamel belt studded with rubies and rose-diamonds; its head, tongue and hands were so delicately balanced that a touch set them in motion. This same Mr Poklewski-Koziell took two suitcases full of things from Fabergé when he went to house-parties, and once, after playing cards with the King and being a pound short at settling-up, he sent the pound along (a golden sovereign, of course) mounted in the lid of a Fabergé box.

Mrs Sackville-West, Mrs Leopold Rothschild, Lady Paget (who put Fabergé objects on public display for the first time at a charity bazaar in the Albert Hall in June 1904), Mrs Keppel, the Double Duchess (who inspired the saying that there were two sorts of society, those who went to Devonshire House and those who did not), Lady Londesborough, Lady Sarah Wilson, the Duchess of Westminster, Princess Daisy of Pless, Mrs Cornwallis-West, Lady Londonderry, such acknowledged beauties as Mrs Hwfa Williams and Mrs Willie James — all these ladies and more received Fabergé presents from the important men in their lives.

And, of course, the Queen herself had many such presents, most of them from the King. In a list of hundreds there were (for example) a painting, three inches by two and a quarter, of Sandringham Church in warm sepia enamel on a background of light pink opal enamel on gold, framed in Siberian jade and pearls; a sprig of raspberry, with four rhodonite and two green jade berries, nephrite leaves and a gold stalk, in a rock-crystal vase; a four-inch-high owl in variously coloured agate with gold feet and rose-diamond eyes; and a cigarette case in smoky rock crystal, the gold rim of its lid ornamented with translucent green enamel and rose-diamonds. Most of the items in the collection originally cost between fifteen and twenty pounds.

Fabergé's biographer, Mr H. C. Bainbridge, pointed out that the objects were the symbols of the spirit of the age. The closer one comes to Fabergé the more Edwardian one is. He also says that the criterion for judging a great goldsmith or jeweller is simple — it is perfection. Certainly Fabergé meets that test.

No wonder his flower-pieces were especially loved. Made to an astonishingly fine degree of detail — the leaf-veining is of course exact on both sides of each leaf — they appeared in a time when flowers were all-important. No social function, no private event, was complete without masses of glorious blooms, displayed with a whole-hearted lavishness impossible in epochs of "flower arrangements". Great gilded baskets crammed with carnations and sweet peas, drifts of orchids, stephanotis on flat trays, gardenias in bowls, and everywhere masses of roses and the malmaison carnations that almost ousted the violet as the Edwardian flower, filled the spacious rooms with their colour and scent. Head gardeners had to be tactfully treated in the matter of cut flowers. They detested — or according to contemporary accounts they detested — anyone's wanting to gather flowers for the house. There was no doubt, however, that gardeners, however tyrannical, did enable the Edwardian ladies to enjoy their gardens, for they took care of all the heavy work and dealt with the weeds and pests. No wonder an older lady advised young Miss Susan Grosvenor: "It is wiser to keep a garden as a plum for your middle age."

Miss Gertrude Jekyll was a notable adviser on gardens. She recommended colour-groupings in garden borders: in one, all blues and pinks, eighteenth-century French style; in another, orange and blue and lemon; in a long border, the colours should deepen as they came near the centre, so that at either end there might be blue, white, and pale yellow flowers with silver foliage, at the other pink, white, and mauve, also with silver, then the deeper yellows and peach and orange intensifying from both ends to the full reds in the middle.

Trees had to be severely pruned and set in carefully thought-out groups. Gardens should have seats at all points where a background might suit a mood, near a flight of stone steps with a cascade of aubretia and alyssum down either side and, possibly, tall foxgloves behind, by a small lily pond with spiky plants framing it and a gleam of goldfish in the water, or near a pleached alley or a pergola. In the gardens of a great house there would be fountains, and possibly a waterfall, so that the sound of water would refresh the ear on a hot day; and there were follies, left over from the age of the folly a century before, statues, a shell grotto, a miniature Greek pavilion, a Chinese bridge, all making places to walk to.

Sir Osbert Sitwell recalls in his entrancing book *Great Morning* how the last Edwardian summer was particularly perfect, how the flowers looked more velvety than ever, smelt more sweet, how the lawns spread rich and full and how the contrast of sun and shade and the distant glimpses of misty hills and little villages had a resemblance to Italy. Of course, there was always an Italian influence at work about Renishaw — particularly after Sir George Sitwell bought Montegufoni,the castle situated between Florence and Siena, and many of the guests at Renishaw had Italian connexions, notably the dread Miss Fingelstone, who lived in Venice on commissions from tradesmen and wrote a great many books with titles designed to attract the tourist, such as *Nights with the Doges, Tears from the Bridge of Sighs*, and *With Ruskin on the Rialto*. Sir Osbert escaped from the Miss Fingelstones when he went to London and joined the Brigade of Guards, for in London he could go to houses where the company was far more amusing, like Mrs Keppel's.

One distinctive feature of London life that Sir Osbert was able to enjoy — in common with dozens of his contemporaries — was the dinner party. It has already been observed that food was taken seriously by the Edwardians. Many recipes in cookery books of the day started with the forbidding words: "This dish takes two days to prepare." One recipe for orange jelly began: "Take eighteen oranges . . ." The 1907 catalogue of the Army & Navy Stores included a thirteen-course dinner, or at least its component parts. The comparatively modest dinner given at the Admiralty on 24 July 1912 read as follows:

Melon Glacé

———

Consomme de Volaille Froid
Potage Bisque

———

Truite Saumonée Norvègienne
Blanchailles

———

Soufflé de Cailles au riz

———

Boeuf Flamande à la Gélée

———

Jambon de Prague

———

Dindonneaux Froids
Salade

———

Glace d'Ananas
Pèches Bonne Femme

Another summer dinner, given at Hever Castle in Kent by William Waldorf Astor on 10 July 1909 from a menu compiled by himself also had eight courses:

Melon Glacé

———

Consommé Princesse

———

Bisque d'Écrevisses
Blanchailles

———

Suprème de Volaille à la Maréchale

———

Selle d'Agneau à la Chivry

———

Fois Gras à la Gélée
Salade Nantaise

———

Cailles rôtis sur canapés

———

Peches Rose de Mai
Caroline Glacé
Croutes de Merluche

The inclusion of quails was typical of the time: quail dishes were much liked, and the famous quail pudding of the Cavendish Hotel was remembered with tender affection by many famous people. The hotel itself was: after its renaissance in 1902, it was often patronized by the King and naturally his lead was followed by all sorts of fashionable people. A typical Cavendish dinner, served for no specific purpose, was (on 26 June 1908):

Consommé aux Ailerons

———

Truite froide à la Cavendish
Blanchailles

———

Soufflé de Cailles à la Valencienne

———

Pièce de Boeuf à la gélée en Bellevue

———

Jambon de Prague aux fèves

———

Poularde froide à la Parisienne

———

Salade
Asperges en branches

———

Pèches à la Marron
Bombe glacée Dame Blanche
Friandises
Laitances au diable

An interesting point here is that all these menus were worked out and the first two cooked by the same woman: Rosa Lewis, "The Duchess of Jermyn Street". She was born in 1867 and served her apprenticeship as a kitchen-maid — rising to various cooking jobs — in the London and Paris households of the Comte de Paris. By the time she was twenty and could replace a proper chef at a moment's notice, she left the Comte's employment and took a post as occasional cook to Lady Randolph Churchill. Her fame spread rapidly and she was in constant demand to cook for parties. She charged high fees for these services, and reaped her reward when it was said everywhere in London that Mrs Lewis's presence ensured the success of a dinner.

In 1902 she took over the moribund Cavendish, which, under her imaginative management, filled a need for a dining-out place in London as well as for an agreeable place to stay. Early clients known to be difficult to please so enjoyed the hotel that it was soon brilliantly fashionable, and remained so throughout the period between the two World Wars, when Mrs Lewis, an unashamed Cockney by birth, looked and was treated like the duchess of her nickname. One man who thoroughly approved of the hotel was Lord Ribblesdale, in whose honour Mrs Lewis had the double front doors painted Guardi green, his favourite colour. So much did he admire her splendid cooking and relish her uninhibited personality that he sometimes took her to the theatre, and once, when asked what the play had been like, she replied composedly that it was the sort you could take your cook to — and winked.

The Cavendish set a new tone in hotels: its broad chairs and sofas, upholstered in chintz and leather that did not look too new, its suites of rooms with private bath (one suite reserved always for the King, who paid at the standard rate), its wonderful food, its mellow lived-in atmosphere, enchanted people who had grumbled for years about there being so few places in London that were pleasant to dine at or stay in.

Of course, the Edwardian period was a great one for hotels: the Adlon in Berlin, the Crillon in Paris, set superlative standards, emulated in 1906 by the London Ritz. The Cavendish is gone, alas, but, if one wants to see an unspoiled Edwardian hotel interior, one can find it at the Ritz still. The entrance hall leads into the oblong space where the tea-tables are, under the glass roof trimmed with wrought iron and gilding, with cream-painted mirrored walls on three sides and marble pillars on the other, old-rose curtains matching the upholstery of the pretty chairs with their carved creamy-white frames, and its indescribable atmosphere, of sinking back into a calm, assured comfort that is unobtrusive yet unmistakable, unshaken (apparently) by seventy years' upheavals. It is revealing and highly therapeutic.

It was characteristic of Rosa Lewis that she named one of the main rooms at the Cavendish the "Elinor Glyn". According to Mrs Daphne Fielding, it was used for special parties and was a most beautiful room, with white panelling, an Adam chimney-piece, Sheraton and Hepple-white furniture, and the biggest sofa Mrs Fielding had ever seen — big enough for four people to have slept on in comfort; it was upholstered in glazed mauve chintz and strewn with cushions in mauve, pale green and pink.

Mrs Lewis always insisted on being present and drinking champagne at any party. As the years went by she appeared more and more the great lady in her black velvet or black or white satin evening dresses made by Worth or Jay's, her long amber necklace, her red rose scent and her beautifully dressed hair and manicured hands, but her vigorous manner and speech — straight from the shoulder — never altered. She died in 1952 and the Cavendish was pulled down ten years later.

Technically the Edwardian period ended on Friday, 6 May 1910 with the King's death. He had not been ill long. A week before he had got chilled through by the wind as he walked round the home farm at Sandringham. On the Monday he returned to London, coughing more than usual but able to dine with Miss Agnes Keyser. After that the next two days found him wheezing badly, showing an alarming colour and reduced physical strength. The Queen was sent for in Corfu where she was staying. She returned at once, and on Friday 6 May the King collapsed suddenly. He had eaten a light lunch in his room and was amusing himself watching and speaking to a pair of pet canaries in a cage by the open window, when he fell and suffered a series of heart attacks. Five doctors examined him, agreed that there was no hope, administered morphia, sent for the Archbishop of Canterbury, and prepared to wait for the end. The King had intervals of consciousness, during which various close friends came in by Alix's orders.

All this time, like Elizabeth Tudor, he refused to go to bed. Soon after five o'clock, when his son told him that his horse *Witch of the Air* had won the Spring Two-Year-Old Plate at Kempton Park, the King murmured: "I am very glad." Soon afterwards falling into a coma, he was lifted on to his bed, and lay there unconscious until he ceased to breathe at a quarter to midnight. His son wrote in his diary that in losing his best friend and the best of fathers, he felt heartbroken ("I never had a word with him in my life" — meaning, never an angry word).

The new King, George V, was proclaimed, the lying-in-state was visited by a quarter of a million people, and the state funeral took place with all its pomp in brilliant sunshine on Friday, 20 May. A servant in Highland dress walked behind the gun-carriage leading the King's dog Caesar. A sentimental pamphlet, entitled "Where's Master?" was published and wept over. So was a broadsheet verse, sold in the streets on the funeral day, which said in part:

Greatest sorrow England ever had
When death took away our dear Dad;
A king he was from head to sole,
Loved by his people one and all.

The funeral procession was heavy with portents of things to come if
anyone present had been able to read them. Nine kings — of Britain,
Germany, Spain, Portugal, Denmark, Norway, Belgium, Greece and
Bulgaria — and a host of princes (including one from China) and the
Archduke Franz Ferdinand of Austria followed the coffin. Among
other dignitaries walked a stout, burly figure in morning coat and silk
hat, the sun twinkling on his gold-rimmed eye-glasses: Theodore
Roosevelt, former President of the United States. He seemed a commonplace person among all those gorgeous uniforms, yet within less than a
decade America would have stepped reluctantly into the centre of the
world stage. Another figure who failed to attract much attention in
comparison with his brother monarchs was the tall young King Albert
of the Belgians. And walking behind his father, small in a naval
cadet uniform, was the fair-haired Prince David, the future Duke of
Windsor.

Of course, all the ladies went at once into unrelieved black, so that
the Ascot race-meeting a few weeks later was referred to in the papers
as "Black Ascot". The new King and Queen soon became known to
their people: this shy couple, far less flamboyant than their predecessors,
stood now in the full limelight, facing a fidgety future.

But for a while everything seemed to be going on just as before. The
militant suffragettes intensified their campaign; the great hostesses
brought out their daughters; the marriage market flourished as ever;
the little girls lived in the nursery and the schoolroom; the government
moved through its customary diplomatic gavotte. But it was not quite
the same: the King was a gruff, bluff, simple person, entirely uninterested in week-end parties, compulsive eating, pretty ladies, gossip and
intrigue. He disliked foreigners, travel, the great world of rank and
fashion. He was happiest spending his evenings reading aloud to his
wife while she embroidered, his days out shooting or pottering with his
stamp collection. Gradually the temperature lowered, the pace slack-
ened, so gradually that it hardly showed until it had happened. At first
the press, building up the personality of the new King, published photographs with rhyming captions, such as:

Prince of sportsmen, brilliant shot,
But happiest aboard his yacht.

But they soon found that the royal spotlight was focusing more and more upon the King's cousin, William II, Emperor of Germany, who, determined to make Europe hop, rattled his sabre with gusto, and, it is possible to see now with hindsight, a perfect lack of understanding of where it would lead him.

The Americans in 1912 elected a new President, Woodrow Wilson, who expressed the pious hope on entering office that his administration would not have to concern itself much with foreign affairs. Rumbles of unrest came out of Russia. The hair-trigger Balkan states fizzed and crackled with sporadic revolutionary movements. In Vienna the old Emperor, with more than sixty years' reign behind him, continued to move stiffly through the implacable Hapsburg etiquette, hating his heir, who had dared to marry a mere Countess. Only on military trips could the Archduke's wife receive proper, equal treatment with him; he liked to take her along whenever possible.

He took her on one such trip in June 1914, where they could celebrate their wedding anniversary by making an official visit of inspection in the town of Sarajevo. It was a national holiday there, the feast of the Vidovdan, and the Archduke's visit was the precise equivalent of an official tour of Belfast made by a leading figure in the Irish Republican Army on Orangeman's Day, or, conversely, a sight-seeing tour by an Ulster Unionist leader in a fervently IRA area.

A few people had premonitions of a sort. During Edward VII's reign there had been a quite remarkable vogue for "invasion scare" thrillers, in which the wicked invader was Germany, either hinted-at or specific. In 1903 Erskine Childers, born in 1870, published *The Riddle of the Sands*; in 1906 William le Queux, born in 1864, wrote *The Invasion of 1910*; in 1909 Guy du Maurier, born in 1865, brought out *An Englishman's Home*, which was in addition successfully dramatized. In 1908 H. G. Wells weighed in with *The War in the Air*. These were the most famous examples of a prolific school.

In the opening days of June 1914 the American Ambassador to the Court of St James's, Walter Hines Page, who had come to love England dearly during his term of office, and who was then in his sixtieth year, wrote in his diary: "The sunlight falls on our New World. Here we are very gay but — in the shadow."

In the early summer of 1914 many of Sir Osbert Sitwell's brother officers in the Brigade of Guards visited a fashionable fortune-teller. It became quite the thing to do. In practically every case, however, something mysterious happened. After a few moments of examining each palm, she paused, looked agitated, and muttered that she did not understand it, but there was the same thing again — after a few months, the line of life stopped short, and she could see nothing. The reaction among her clients was (outwardly at least) sceptical: they said robustly that she could indeed see nothing and chose that somewhat dramatic way of putting it. After four or five such incidents had reached Sir Osbert's ears he felt a faint unease, wondering what, if anything, it might portend.

But the sun shone, the sky was blue, the century was young, people went to the seaside and strolled on the pier and sat on the beach and looked at the sparkling water. The bands played and couples danced and hummed the tunes. Perhaps if one kept busy and cheerful and enjoyed everything, the danger — if danger there were — would go away.

The Edwardian lady was coming to an end. The Edwardian female in general might be thankful to have thought so, though there is no evidence that she expected any violent changes. But the lady, had she known, would almost certainly have shrunk from the prospect that the long, golden Edwardian garden-party was coming to a close. The little girls clustered round Nanny in the nursery and descended, frilled up, to the drawing-room each afternoon. The young girls fidgeted in the schoolroom until they could dash out to the stables. The young ladies put up their hair, put on their white dresses and their simple strings of pearls and came shyly down to dinner, wondering which stuffy old gentleman would be sitting next to them. The married ladies chattered, gossiped, exchanged glances with interesting married gentlemen across crowded rooms, told the servants they were not at home to anybody else that afternoon, juggled their guest lists, and listened for the soft footfall in the corridor at midnight. The older ladies did the same, and enjoyed their hobby of alarming the young whenever possible. The newly installed electric lights, often switched on a yard outside the door, crackled excitingly. In the city streets the lamplighters made their rounds, lifting their long poles to pull the loops of the gas-mantles, and the horses clip-clopped by, pulling the crested carriages home in the first light of the summer dawn.

Gabriel Princip fired his revolver, and the Austrian heir and his wife died. Austria issued her ultimatum and Russia bristled up to the defence. Germany sprang to the side of Austria. France leapt to the aid of Russia. The mobilization orders went out and the long troop-trains began to clank into motion. Germany demanded free passage through Belgium in order to attack France, but Belgium refused. And England came slowly to her feet with the moral issue clear to her at last. As all this happened in five weeks of that fine warm summer, so the Edwardian lady began to move away into history. The new conditions would produce the new woman: it was all going to be different.

There she goes in familiar silhouette — upright, rigidly corseted, swathed in rustling silks, moving out of sight, slowly, to be sure, but unmistakably. A particular kind of lady, not quite like any other, not to be seen again — there she goes. Assured, wide-eyed, much loved, greatly criticized — and dressed in black.

Appendix

Population of England, Scotland and Wales at census:
1901   37,000,000
1911   40,831,000

Number of working days lost through disputes:
1926   (year of the General Strike)   about 162,000,000
1921   about 86,000,000
1912   about 41,000,000
Between 1901 and 1914   total 115,300,000

Birth rate, Death rate, Infant mortality per thousand persons,
per thousand live births

England & Wales	b/r	d/r	i/m
1900	28·7	18·2	154
1901	28·5	16·9	151
1902	28·5	16·3	133
1903	28·5	15·5	132
1904	28·0	16·3	145
1905	27·3	15·3	128
1906	27·2	15·5	132
1907	26·5	15·1	118
1908	26·7	14·8	120
1909	25·8	14·6	109
1910	25·1	13·5	105
1911	24·3	14·6	130
1912	23·9	13·3	95
1913	24·1	13·8	108
1914	23·8	14·0	105

Women in Employment, 1901 and 1911

Occupation:	1901	1911
Public Administration	29,000	50,000
Professions and their subsidiary services	326,000	383,000
Domestic service	2,003,000	2,127,000
Commerce	76,000	157,000
Transport	27,000	38,000
Agriculture/Horticulture	86,000	117,000
Fishing	nil	nil
Mining/quarrying production	6,000	8,000
Metal manufacturing	84,000	128,000
Building and construction	3,000	5,000
Furniture, fittings, decoration	30,000	35,000
Bricks, pottery, glass, cement	37,000	42,000
Chemicals, oil, soap	31,000	46,000
Leatherwork, skins, feathers	27,000	32,000
Paper, printing, books	111,000	144,000
Textiles	795,000	870,000
Clothing	792,000	825,000
Food, drink, tobacco	216,000	308,000
Others	75,000	98,000
Not employed	10,229,000	11,375,000

Source for the above figures: B. R. Mitchell and P. Deane, *Abstract of British Historical Statistics* (Cambridge 1962)

Bibliography

ADBURGHAM, Alison: *Shops and Shopping* (George Allen & Unwin 1964)

ANGELOGLOU, Maggie: *A History of Make-Up* (Studio Vista 1970)

ARONSON, Theo: *Royal Vendetta* (Oldbourne, London, 1966)

ASHFORD, Daisy: *The Young Visiters* (Chatto & Windus 1919)

BAINBRIDGE, H. C.: *Peter Carl Fabergé* (Batsford 1966)

BELL, Lady, *At The Works* (Nelson 1911)

BENTLEY, Nicolas (editor): *Edwardian Album* (Cardinal Edition, Sphere Books 1974)

CARR, John Dickson: *The Life of Sir Arthur Conan Doyle* (John Murray 1949)

CECIL, Robert: *Life in Edwardian England* (Batsford 1969)

FIELDING, Daphne: *The Duchess of Jermyn Street* (Eyre & Spottiswoode 1964)

FISHMAN, Jack: *My Darling Clementine* (W. H. Allen 1963)

FURTH, Charles: *Life Since 1900* (George Allen & Unwin 1964)

GARNER, Philippe: *The World of Edwardiana* (Hamlyn, London 1974)

GATHORNE-HARDY, Jonathan: *The Rise and Fall of the British Nanny* (Hodder & Stoughton 1972)

GERSON, Noel B.: *Lillie Langtry* (Hale 1972)

GLYN, Anthony: *Elinor Glyn* (Hutchinson 1955)

GRAHAME, Kenneth: *Dream Days* (John Lane, The Bodley Head 1930)
         The Golden Age (John Lane, The Bodley Head 1928)
         The Wind in the Willows (Methuen 1930)

GUEDALLA, Philip: *Mr Churchill* (Hodder & Stoughton 1941)
         Palmerston (Hodder & Stoughton 1950)
         The Hundred Years (Hodder & Stoughton 1939)
         The Second Empire (Hodder & Stoughton 1946)

HYNES, Samuel: *The Edwardian Turn of Mind* (OUP London 1968)

KEPPEL, Sonia: *Edwardian Daughter* (Hamish Hamilton 1958)

LANG, Theo: *My Darling Daisy* (Michael Joseph 1965)

LESLIE, Anita: *Edwardians in Love* (Hutchinson 1972)

LORD, Walter: *A Night To Remember* (Longmans Green 1956)

MCLAUGHLIN, Terence: *The Gilded Lily* (Cassell 1972)

MAGNUS, Philip: *King Edward VII* (John Murray 1964)

MASSIE, Robert: *Nicholas and Alexandra* (Gollancz 1968)

MIDDLEMAS, Keith: *The Life and Times of Edward VII* (Weidenfeld & Nicholson 1972)

MUGGERIDGE, Kitty and ADAM, Ruth: *Beatrice Webb: A Life 1858–1943* (Secker & Warburg 1967)

NESBIT, Edith: *The Railway Children* (Benn 1957)
     The Treasure Seekers (Benn 1958)
     The Wouldbegoods (Benn 1958)

NOWELL-SMITH, Simon (editor): *Edwardian England 1901–1914* (OUP London 1964)

OUIDA: *Moths* (Chatto & Windus 1908)

PEARSON, Hesketh: *Bernard Shaw* (The Reprint Society 1942)

POPE-HENNESSY, James: *Queen Mary* (George Allen & Unwin 1959)

PRIESTLEY, J. B.: *The Edwardians* (Heinemann 1970)

QUELCH, Eileen: *Perfect Darling* (Cecil and Amelia Woolf 1972)

RAVERAT, Gwen: *Period Piece* (Faber 1952)

READ, Donald: *Edwardian England 1901–1915* (Harrap 1972)

SHAW, Bernard: *Collected Works*

SITWELL, Edith: *English Eccentrics* (Dobson Books 1958)
     Taken Care Of (Hutchinson 1965)

SITWELL, Osbert: *Great Morning* (Macmillan 1948)

TAYLOR, A. J. P.: *From Sarajevo to Potsdam* (Thames & Hudson 1966)
     A History of World War I (Hamish Hamilton 1963)

TAYLOR, Edmond: *The Fossil Monarchies* (Weidenfeld & Nicholson 1963)

THIRKELL, Angela: *Three Houses* (OUP reprint 1942)

TUCHMAN, Barbara W.: *The Guns of August* (Constable 1962)
     The Proud Tower (Constable 1967)
     The Zimmermann Telegram (Constable 1959)

TWEEDSMUIR, Susan: *The Edwardian Lady* (Gerald Duckworth & Company 1966)

WAKEFORD, Geoffrey: *Three Consort Queens* (Robert Hale 1971)

WELLS, H. G.: *Collected Works*

WESTMINSTER, Loelia Duchess of: *Grace and Favour* (Weidenfeld & Nicholson 1961)

WINDSOR, Duke of: *A King's Story* (Cassell 1951)

YATES, Dornford: *Collected Works*

Index

Accommodation, prices for, 105
Actors of the day, 132–3
Affairs, attitude towards, 108–12
Afternoon calls, 110
Afternoon tea:
    with the children, 44, 47
    as a social habit, 110
Aircraft, early days of, 150
Alexandra, Queen (*formerly* Princess of Wales), 16, 22, 26–31, 54, 113–19, 128, 156
Alfonso XIII, King (of Spain), 125–8
Architecture, 147–8
Art:
    and letters, 88
    galleries, 135
    Nouveau, 137
Ashford, Daisy, 20
Ashley, Edwina and Mary, 37
Astor, William Waldorf, 159
At-home, convention of being, 110
At the Works (Bell), 87
Austin, Alfred, 26
Authors of the day, 60–2, 164

Baden-Powell, Lady Olave St Clair, 94–5
Baden-Powell (Lord) Robert, 94–5
Baldwin, Monica, 70
Baldwin, Mrs Stanley, 39
Balfour, Arthur, 106
Ballet, 136
Balls, 65
Barabbas (Corelli), 85
Barnett, Henrietta, 93
Barrie, J. M., 133
Barrymore, Ethel, 123
Bathing machines, 15, 43
Baths, introduction of, 149
Battersea Park, bicycling in, 79
Beaconsfield, Lord (Disraeli), 113

Beale, Dorothea, 58, 144
Beaton, Cecil, 16
Bell, Lady Florence, 87–8
Bell, Gertrude, 87
Belloc Lowndes, Marie, 142
Beresford, Lord Charles, 29, 111, 115–16
Bernhardt, Sarah, 132
Biarritz, 37
Bibliography, 169–70
Bicycles, 78, 79
Birth rate, 167
"Black Ascot", 163
Black Beauty (Sewell), 39
Bland, Mr and Mrs Hubert, 95–7
Blatchford, Robert, 117–18
Blouses, 69
Bond Street, London, 152
Books of the day, 60–2, 84–5, 87, 97
Bournemouth, 35
Bowers, 48
Boy Scouts, 94
Breakfasts, Edwardian, 142
Brighton, 35–6
Bright Young Things, 41
Brooke, Lord (*later* Earl of Warwick), 113–14, 117
Brooke, Rupert, 144
Brooklands race-track, 80
Buildings:
    erection of famous, 13–14
    costs of, 148
Burberry, Thomas, 81
Burne-Jones, Edward, 47
Buses, 150
Business, women break into, 87, 168
Buss, Frances Mary, 58
Butler's duties, 106

Calling, social duty of, 110
Camisoles, 69

Campbell, Mrs Patrick (*later* Mrs George Cornwallis-West), 114, 133
Campbell de Laurentz, Baroness, 81
Card calling, 110
Carpathia, SS, 139–40
Cars, growing significance of, 10–11, 79–81
Chamberlain, Joseph, 88, 93
Chaperones, 56–7, 65, 67–8
Chaplin, Henry, 151
Chauffeurs, 80
Cheltenham Ladies' College, 58
Childers, Erskine, 164
Children:
   at afternoon tea, 44
   bringing up, 32–44 *passim*, 50, 54–5
   parties for, 46
Choral Societies, 135
Christmas shopping, 50
Churchill, Clementine (Mrs Winston Churchill), 123–4, 128
Churchill, Lord Randolph, 17–18, 119, 121, 122
Churchill, Lady Randolph (Jennie), 119–23, 128, 134, 161
Churchill (Sir) Winston S., 120–4
Cigarettes, price of, 104–6
Cinema, 137, 141
Clandestine affairs, 108–12
Clarence, Prince Albert Victor, Duke of, 124
Clothes, 69–70, 86, 151–3
   when motoring, 80–1
Cocktail parties, 92
Combinations, 69
Comedians of the day, 131
Comedy plays, 131–2
Coming-out, 64–5, 76–7
Composers of the day, 135
Conan Doyle, Lady, 95
Concert-going, 135
Conrad, Joseph, 61
Cooks, 106–7, 146
Corelli, Marie, 78–9, 84–5
Cornwallis-West, Mr and Mrs George, 119–21, 134
Cornwallis West, William, 119–20
Coronation of King Edward, 31
Corsetry, 42, 69
Cosmetics, 15–17
Country house routine, when owners away from, 62–3

Court, presentation at, 64–5, 76–7
Cowes Regatta, 22, 29, 121
Cruises, costs of, 105
   see also Ships
Crush parties, 92
Cubitt, Mrs, 47, 50–1, 53
Cust, Hon. Henry, 108–9

Dance programmes, 65
Davison, Emily Wilding, 89–90
Death rate, 167
de Grey, Lady, 109, 156–7
Demography, 167–8
Derby, The (1913), 89
Devonshire, Duke of, 112
Diaghilev, Serge, 136
Diamond Jubilee (1897), 30
Dining out, cost of, 104–5
Dinner party menus, 159–60
Dislikes of Marie Corelli (of period behaviour), 78–9
Disraeli, Benjamin (Lord Beaconsfield), 113
Divorce, 29, 98, 151
Domestic service, 12, 106
   staff maintained, 106–7
   wage rates of, 103–4
Dowagers, 60
Dresses, 69, 151–2
Drink, prices for, 104–6
Duff Gordon, Lady (Cosmo), 138–9, 152
Dunlop, John Boyd, 79
Duntreath, 36

Early morning tea, 149
Easter "eggs", 37, 155–7
Education for girls, 58, 59, 63
Edward VII, King (*formerly* Prince of Wales), 9, 17–23, 27–31, 37, 39, 51, 54, 112–18, 122, 142, 156
   death and funeral of, 162–3
Edwardes, George, 131–2
Electric light, emergence of, 137
Elgar, Sir Edward, 14, 135
Elopement with the lower class, 41
Eminent ladies of the time, 144
Employment of women, 168
Eton, 82, 119, 132

Fabergé Easter eggs, 37, 155–7
Fabian Society, 95–7

Fashion shows, 152
Female household staff, 106–7
Finglestone, Miss, 158
Finishing schools, 63
Flappers, 145
Flowers, 157–8
Fog, 149–50
Football, 140
Footmen, 106
Forde, Florrie, 145
Fortune-telling, 164–5
French Without Tears (Bell), 87
Freud, Sigmund, 66, 137
Furniture, 148

Gamekeepers, 107
Gardeners, 107
Garden parties, 24
Gardens, 158
George V, King (*formerly* Prince George, Duke of York; *later* Prince of Wales), 13–14, 22, 28, 116, 124–5, 129, 162–3
George VI, King, 23
Gilbert and Sullivan, 132
Girl Guides, 94
Gloves, arm length, 64–5
Glyn, Elinor (née Sutherland), 19, 25, 60, 82–3, 114, 151
Gossip columns, 14
Governesses, 40–4, 57–9, 62
Grahame, Kenneth, 33
Gramophones, 134
Grooms of the Chamber, 106
Grosvenor, Norman (*later* Lord Ebury), 61
Grosvenor, Susan, *see* Tweedsmuir, Lady Susan

Haemophilia, 127
Hair styles:
    dressing of, 19, 64
    false ringlets, 49
Hans Heinrich of Pless, Prince, 119–20
Hardy, Thomas, 61
Harrod's Limited, 10, 153
Hats, 69, 80
Hawtrey, Charles, 87, 133
Heal, Ambrose, 148
Heirs, the need to bear, 109
Hereditary weakness, custom of probing, 75–6
Hill, Octavia, 93

Hip-baths, 42
    see also Baths, introduction of
Hit tunes, 144
Holidays abroad, 37
Home, running away from, 51–2
Horses, love for, 10, 56–7
Hotels, names of some famous, 161
House design, 147–8
Household staff, 106–7
Housemaids, 107
House-parties, 111, 114
Hozier, Clementine (*later* Mrs Winston Churchill *and then* Lady Spencer-Churchill) q.v.
Hume, Colonel, 46
Hunting to hounds, 56

Ibsen, Henrik, 132–3
Income tax, 105–6
Infant mortality rate, 167
Irving, Henry, 132
"It", coining of, 83

Jerome, Jennie, *see* Churchill, Lady Randolph
Jewellery, 69–70
Jones, Sir Laurence, 104
Just-so Stories (Kipling), 38

Keppel, Alice, 36–8, 50–4, 112, 118, 128, 156
Keppel, Sonia, 36–7, 50, 53–4
Kinsky, Count Charles, 121
Kipling, Josephine, 38
Kipling, Rudyard, 25, 38–9, 88, 103
Kitchener of Khartoum, Lord, 13
Klickmann, Flora, 85–6
Knickers, 69, 81

Ladies' Club, Harrod's, 153
Ladies' Realm (magazine), 78
Lady, definition of, 11, 59, 107–8
Langtry, Lillie, 17–18, 112, 120, 122, 128
Languages, learning modern, 58–9, 63
Laycock, Captain Joseph, 118
Leopold, Prince, 18, 113
Levitt, Dorothy, 80–1
Lewis, George (a solicitor), 115
Lewis, Rosa, 160–2
Libraries, private, 60

Literary view of early 1900s, 25–6
　see also Books of the day
Literature for young ladies, 60–2
Livery for footmen, 106
Lloyd, Marie, 131, 144
Lodge-keepers, 107
Londesborough, Lord and Lady, 45, 49
Londonderry, Lady (Theresa), 108–9, 128
London Needlework Guild, 59
Lord Chamberlain's licence, 132
Love affairs, attitude towards, 108–12
Lovelace, Ralph, 62
Lower than Vermin (Yates), 76
Lucile's, 151–2
Lyttleton, Hilda, 150–1

Make-up, *see* Cosmetics
Male household staff, 106–7
Manchester, Duke and Duchess of, 112, 128
Mannequin Parades, 151–2
Marcel hair style, 19
Marlborough, Duchess (Consuelo), of, 121–2
Marlborough, Duke of (Sunny), 121
Marlborough House, London, 22–3, 114
Marriage market, 64, 67, 70, 75–7, 108
　see also Weddings
Mary, Queen (*formerly* Princess May of Teck, *then* Princess of Wales), 59, 124–5, 128, 156
Maugham, Somerset, 133
Mechanical propulsion, effects of introduction of, 79
Melba, Nellie, 16, 144
Menus, 159–60
Millar, Gertie, 132
Mistress of the Household, qualities of, 107–8
Mitford, Nancy, 68
Montagu, Oliver, 30
Mordaunt divorce case, 29
Moths (Ouida), 70–5
Motor cars, *see* Cars
Mourning in Queen Victoria's time, 9–10
Music-halls, 130–1
Myddelton, George Frederick, 120

Nannies, power and influence of, 39–44, 57
　see also Governesses
Nesbit, Edith, *see* Bland, Mr and Mrs Hubert

Nevill, Lady Dorothy, 143
Newspapers for women, 14–15
Nightingale, Florence, 144
Nijinsky, Vaslov, 136
Northcliffe, Lord, 130
North End House, Rottingdean, 47–8
Nursemaids, *see* Nannies; Governesses
Nursery Governesses, 40–4, 57–9, 62

Oliver, Sydney, 96
Olympic Games (1908), 140–1
Opera, 136–7
Orchestras, 135
Orczy, Emmuska Baroness, 83, 144
Order of Merit, 13
Order of the Garter, 31
Ostrich feathers, 64
Ouida (Louise Ramé), 70–5, 144
Oxford Street, London, 150–1

Pages (at Court), 106
Paget, Lady Florence (*later* Lady Hastings), 151
Paget, Mrs Gerald, 116
Pankhurst, Emmeline, 91
Pankhurst, Violet, 99
Pantomime, 131
Papier Poudré, 19
Pay of wage-earners, 103
Permissiveness discussed, 67
　see also Affairs, attitude towards
Peter Pan (Barrie), 133
Pethick-Lawrence, Mr and Mrs, 90, 99
Picnics with King Edward, 37–8
Picture palaces, 137, 141
Play-going, 132–5
Plays of:
　Florence Bell, 87
　G. B. Shaw, *see* Shaw, George B.
Playwrights of the day, 132–3
Pocket-money, 40, 50
Poetry, 25–6
Poiret dresses, 152
Poklewski-Koziell, Mr, 156–7
Ponsonby, Loelia, 39–40, 44–6, 49
　marriages of, 45
Population statistics, 167
Portraits, 135
Posture improvements, 40–1
Potter, Beatrice, *see* Webb, Beatrice
Potter, Beatrix, 144

Pottery, 148
Presentation at Court, 64–5, 76–7
Press Cuttings (Shaw), 99–101
Prices prevailing, 104–5, 148–9
Prince of Wales, *see* (1) Edward VII, King;
　　(2) George V, King
Probyn, Sir Dighton (VC), 30
Professions, girls taking up, 59, 168
Promenade concerts, 12
Prostitution discussed, 67
　　see also Affairs, attitude towards
Punch, 83, 146

Radio, advent of, 140
Rag-time, 144–5
Red Flag Act, 79
Refrigeration, start of, 142
Renishaw, 158
Resorts, seaside, 35–6
Richardson, Mary, 89
Roedean School, 58
Roosevelt, Theodore, 163
Rothes, Countess of, 139–40
Rottingdean, 36, 38, 47–8
Rubinstein, Helena, 16

St James's Palace, London, 39
Salisbury, Lord, 116
Sandringham, 23, 31
Sarajevo, effects of, 164–5
Scarlet Pimpernel, The (Orczy), 83–4
School-rooms in big houses, 58
Science, developments in, 137
Séances, 29
Seaside holidays, 34–5, 42–4
"Season", The, 64–5, 66, 144
Selfridges, Limited, 13, 17, 87, 153–4
Servants, *see* Domestic service
Sex, encouragement of ignorance about,
　　66–7
Shaw, George Bernard, 18, 56, 91, 93,
　　96–7, 99–101, 132, 134
　　some of his plays, 133–4, 141
Ships (ocean liners), 138–40
　　cruises, costs of, 105
Shopping:
　　by hansom cab, 108
　　for Christmas, 50
　　in London's Oxford St, 150–1
　　at the great stores, 154
Side-saddles, 68

Sitwell, Dame Edith, 40, 45–51, 52
Sitwell, Lady Ida, 45–7
Sitwell, Sir Osbert, 52–3, 158–9
Sitwell, Sacheverell, 52
Skirts, 69
"Slaveys", 12
　　see also Domestic service
Smyth, Ethel, 88
Soames, Olave St Clair, *see* Baden-Powell
Songs of the day, 131, 145
Sorrows of Satan, The (Corelli), 84–5
Spencer, Herbert, 92
Spencer-Churchill, Lady (Clementine)
　　(*formerly* Mrs Winston Churchill *and*
　　née Hozier), 123–4, 128
Sport:
　　increasing interest in, 140
　　women and, 81
Stores, names of London's greatest, 154
Strikes, days lost through, 167
Suffragists, 14, 79–80, 88–91, 99, 163
Sundays, 35, 42
Sutherland, Lucy Christiana (Mrs Wal-
　　lace), 151

Tango teas and parties, 144–5
Tatler, The (magazine), 44
Taxation, 105–6
Taxi-cabs, 150
Telephones, 87
Terry, Ellen, 18, 134
Theatres of the day, 131–5
Thirkell, Angela, 36, 38, 47
Three Weeks (Glyn), 82–3, 114
Tilley, Vesta, 131
Titanic SS, 138–40
Tobacco duty, 104
Train rides to the seaside, 36
Trams, 150
Tranby Croft, scandal at, 116
Tubes (trains), 150
Tweedsmuir, Lady Susan (née Grosvenor),
　　60–2, 132, 133, 151
Twopenny tube, 13
Tyres, advent of pneumatic, 79–80

Underground system, 150

Vanburgh, Irene, 133
Vanderbilt Family, 121
Variety theatre, 131

Victoria, Queen, 9–10, 18, 21, 24–5, 27–30,
    64, 113–14, 124
Victoria Eugènie, Princess (Ena) (*later*
    Queen of Spain), 125–8
Virginity, defence of, 66–8
Visiting cards, how used, 110
Voice, importance of a pleasant, 59

Wages, 103–4
Wallace, Edgar, 104
Wallas, Graham, 96
Ward, Mrs Humphrey, 88
Warwick, Countess (Frances) of, 113–22,
    128
  campaigns for socialism, 118
Wash-stands, 148
Watering-places, 35
Webb, Beatrice, 91–2, 93–4, 97
Webb, Sidney, 93, 96
Weddings:
  Princess Alexandra of Denmark, 28
  Beatrice Webb, 93
  Olave Baden-Powell, 95
  Jean Conan-Doyle, 95
  Frances Brooke (Countess of Warwick),
    113
  Cornwallis-West, Mrs George, 119
  Cornwallis-West, Daisy, 120

Jeanette Churchill, 121
Clementine Hozier, 123
Princess May, 125
Princess Victoria Eugène, 126–7
Florence Paget, 151
Elinor Sutherland, 151
Westminster, Duchess (Constance Ed-
    wina) of, 122
Westminster, Loelia, Duchess of, *see*
    Ponsonby, Loelia
Whistler, James McNeil, 18
Wilde, Oscar, 18, 68, 132
Wilhelm II, Kaiser, 13, 22, 164
Wind in the Willows, The (Grahame), 33–4
Women's:
  Aerial League (flying club), 150
  Anti-Suffrage Committee, 88
  employment, figures of, 168
  Social and Political Union, 91
Working hours, 104
Worth (the Paris dressmaker), 38, 152
Wortley, Caroline Stuart (*later* Lady
    Ebury), 61

Yachting parties, 81
  see also Cowes
Yates, Dornford, 76
Yates, Edmund, 143